USER INTERFACES IN C

PROGRAMMER'S GUIDE TO
STATE-OF-THE-ART INTERFACES

MARK GOODWIN

MIS:
PRESS

MANAGEMENT INFORMATION SOURCE, INC.

COPYRIGHT

DEDICATION

To Denise, Ryan, and Matthew: the most wonderful family in the whole world.

ACKNOWLEDGMENTS

I would like to express my most sincere thanks to the following companies:

- C Ware Corporation, Paso Robles, CA
- Computer Innovations, Inc., Titon Falls, NJ
- Borland International, Inc., Scotts Valley, CA
- Ecosoft, Inc., Indianapolis, IN
- Lattice, Inc., Lombard, IL
- MetaWare, Inc., Santa Cruz, CA
- Microsoft Corporation, Redmond, WA
- Mix Software, Inc., Richardson, TX
- The Stepstone Corporation, Sandy Hook, CT
- WATCOM Products, Inc., Waterloo, Ontario, Canada
- Zortech, Inc., Arlington, MA

Because of their generous contributions, the programs in this book are portable across a wide range of C compilers.

TABLE OF CONTENTS

ii

DISK ORDER FORM
ON LAST PAGE
OF BOOK

Since the dawn of the personal computer age, a staggering number of advances have occurred in computer technology. Perhaps the most noticeable advances have occurred in the computer hardware itself. Today's personal computers offer such a wide variety of sophisticated hardware features that their resemblance to their more anemic ancestors is practically nil. The modern features of these technological marvels include more powerful microprocessors; larger and faster memories, floppy disk drives, and hard disk drives; better monitors that offer beautiful high-resolution color graphics; high-speed printers (whether they are today's faster and more versatile dot matrix printers or the wonderfully innovative laser printers); pointing devices (mice, joysticks, trackballs, and more); not to mention CD-ROM drives and WORM drives. Personal computer hardware technology has certainly advanced in many areas.

While the personal computer hardware advances have captured a great deal of the spotlight, an equally impressive number of advances have occurred in computer software technology. After all, back when personal computers were first introduced, such necessities as a reliable operating system were almost totally unheard of. Not only do today's personal computers have a number of reliable operating systems, but today's modern programming languages are a far cry from yesterday's extremely rudimentary BASIC interpreters. Perhaps the most subtle, but important, advance in software technology has occurred in the area known as the user interface.

Essentially, a **user interface** is the method used by either an operating system or an application program to interact with the operator. A user interface that uses today's state-of-the-art techniques such as windows, pull-down menus, pop-up menus, dialog boxes, and on-line help is light-years ahead of the crude user interfaces used by programmers in the early days of the personal computer. In fact, a well-constructed user interface can almost totally eliminate the need for an external manual. Typically, operators will have to consult accompanying reference manuals only when they use unfamiliar program features.

Because the user interface is such an important part of an application program, many companies have started selling programming toolboxes that offer ready-made functions for implementing today's user interface features. Although purchasing a user-interface toolbox will certainly relieve programmers from writing their own user-interface routines, the generic functions supplied in the commercially available toolboxes aren't always the best choice for all programs. On the other hand, a self-written user interface toolbox will provide programmers with routines that are easily customized to fulfill an application program's specific needs.

Perhaps the biggest stumbling block in writing a user interface toolbox is the programmer's lack of knowledge in the area of low-level display programming. To remedy this knowledge gap, this book provides the C programmer with the necessary knowledge for quick and easy implementation of today's user interface techniques on the IBM PC and compatibles. Furthermore, this book presents a C user interface toolbox called WINDOWS.LIB (hereinafter referred to as WIN-DOWS). WINDOWS includes user interface functions for opening and closing text windows, pop-up menus, dialog box menus, pull-down menus, and more. When used properly in an application program, the WINDOWS functions will produce a user interface that is truly state of the art in appearance. Additionally, the WINDOWS functions can be easily customized to satisfy an application program's special needs.

USER REQUIREMENTS

To make the best use of information provided in this book, you should be an intermediate-level programmer and must have a working knowledge of C. This book was written using Microsoft QuickC 1.0. Software and hardware requirements include an IBM PC or compatible and one of the C compilers supported in this book (listed in Appendix C).

CHAPTER OVERVIEWS

- **Chapter 1** explains how the MS-DOS video functions, how the IBM PC ROM BIOS video functions, and how direct memory access techniques are used to perform display input/output.

- **Chapter 2** presents the low-level assembly language routines for filling portions of the display with a specific character, setting the attributes for a portion of the display screen, saving a portion of the display screen in a memory buffer, redisplaying a previously buffered screen display, drawing a single-lined or a double-lined border around a portion of the display screen, and retrieving keyboard input.

- **Chapter 3** presents the low-level C routines for turning the cursor on and off, positioning the cursor, displaying single characters, and setting individual character attributes.

- **Chapter 4** presents routines for dynamically opening and closing display windows, drawing windows, and scrolling windows and displaying horizontal and vertical scroll bars.

- **Chapter 5** presents routines for implementing pop-up menus, dialog box menus, and pull-down menus.

- **Chapter 6** presents routines for displaying error messages and trapping hardware errors and [Ctrl/C] interruptions.

- **Chapter 7** presents SIMPLE LEDGER, a complete general ledger accounting system that illustrates how the WINDOWS toolbox is used to build an actual application program.

APPENDIX OVERVIEWS

- **Appendix A** presents a complete reference guide for the WINDOWS toolbox. A summary of the syntax, a description of its purpose, and a coding example are given for each of the WINDOWS toolbox functions.

- **Appendix B** presents a reference guide for the IBM PC ROM BIOS video functions.

- **Appendix C** explains how the WINDOWS toolbox is compiled by a variety of IBM PC C compilers.

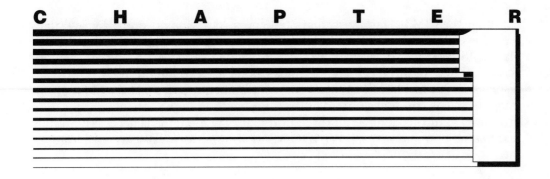

C H A P T E R

1

THE IBM PC DISPLAY

Although the IBM PC family of computers supports a wide variety of display adapters, there are only three basic methods for reading from and writing to the display: MS-DOS video services, ROM BIOS video services, and direct memory access. While all three display methods can be used to build effective program displays, such considerations as program portability, speed, and ease of programming should be considered before selecting a method for a particular application program. A further look at all three of the display methods is necessary to fully understand how and why the WINDOWS toolbox performs display input/output the way it does.

MS-DOS VIDEO SERVICES

Without a doubt, the MS-DOS video services offer the highest degree of program portability. Not only do they offer portability across all IBM PC and compatibles, they provide compatibility for any computer that is capable of running MS-DOS. Because MS-DOS video services are called as MS-DOS function calls (calls to INT 21H), their ease of use is quite high. Indeed, most high-level languages use MS-DOS video services to implement their generic display output commands (i.e., C's printf function and BASIC's PRINT statement).

Although the MS-DOS video services' high degree of compatibility makes them an excellent choice for writing highly portable programs, their lack of speed and versatility makes them unsuitable for windows environments such as WINDOWS. In fact, the MS-DOS video services' lack of such essentials as display reading functions and cursor control functions would make them entirely unsuitable for implementing the WINDOWS operating environment. With the exception of their use by a C compiler's run-time library, the MS-DOS video services are not used by the WINDOWS toolbox.

ROM BIOS VIDEO SERVICES

Because of the MS-DOS video services' shortcomings, many programmers have
had to go elsewhere to find video routines that offer the speed and versatility required by today's application programs. Fortunately, the ROM BIOS video services offer a wide variety of routines that are quite capable of meeting almost any
application program's demands. However, use of the ROM BIOS video services
does limit a program's portability to IBM PCs and true compatibles. Because of
a strong commitment by IBM and other manufacturers to maintain ROM BIOS
compatibility, all of today's PC compatibles have ROM BIOSes that are upward-
ly compatible with the original IBM PC's ROM BIOS. Therefore, use of the ROM
BIOS video services does not impose any real problems in porting a program from
one member of the PC family to another.

Function Name	Function Code
Set Video Mode	00H
Set Cursor Type	01H
Set Cursor Position	02H
Read Cursor Values	03H
Read Light Pen Position	04H
Select Display Page	05H
Scroll Window Up	06H
Scroll Window Down	07H
Read Character/Attribute Pair	08H
Write Character/Attribute Pairs	09H
Write Characters	0AH
Set Color Palette	0BH
Write Graphics Pixel	0CH
Read Graphics Pixel	0DH
Write Character in Teletype Mode	0EH
Get Video Mode	0FH

Figure 1.1   The IBM PC ROM BIOS video functions

Using the ROM BIOS video services is as simple as loading a few parameters into
the CPU's registers and making a call to INT 10H. Figure 1.1 outlines the ROM
BIOS video services. Furthermore, Appendix B provides a complete description
of all the ROM BIOS video services. The following code fragment shows how the
ROM BIOS **Set Cursor Position** function could be used to move the cursor to the
upper left corner of the display:

Example 1.1

```
        .
        .
        .
mov     ah,2            ;AH=Set cursor position function code
mov     bh,0            ;BH=Page 0
mov     dh,0            ;DH=Top row of the display
mov     dl,0            ;DL=Left column of the display
int     10h             ;Set the new cursor position
        .
        .
        .
```

Perhaps the most important point to make about the above program fragment is that the ROM BIOS video services' function code is always passed in register AH. Furthermore, when the video page number is required, it is usually passed in register BH. Instead of the two separate statements used in the above example, a **mov dx,0** statement could have been used to pass the new cursor position. For that matter, an **xor dx,dx** statement would be an even more efficient way to pass the Row 0, Column 0 cursor position. Remember, any number **xor**ed with itself will always produce a result of zero. Thus, **xor**ing the DX register with itself will result in the correct coordinates being passed to the ROM BIOS video services.

DIRECT MEMORY ACCESS

Although the WINDOWS toolbox could be completely implemented using the ROM BIOS video services, the ROM BIOS video services do not offer the speed required by certain time-critical functions (i.e., reading and writing to large portions of the display screen). Therefore, all of WINDOWS's time-critical functions will use direct memory access techniques to provide the necessary lightning-fast response times.

To understand how display memory is directly accessed, consider a detailed look at the IBM PC display adapters. The three major display adapters used by the IBM PC are the Monochrome Display Adapter (MDA), the Color Graphics Adapter (CGA), and the Enhanced Graphics Adapter (EGA). Although these three display adapters have a wide variety of differences, they share the important feature of all being memory-mapped devices. When a display adapter is a memory-mapped device, programs, with a few restrictions, can directly read from and write to that display adapter's memory by simply reading from and writing to a specific area of the computer's memory. Figure 1.2 presents a simple memory map for the IBM PC and the three display adapters just mentioned.

```
Memory Offset
                        +-----------------------------------+
                        |            ROM BIOS               |
         FE000H         +-----------------------------------+
                        |           System ROM              |
         F4000H         +-----------------------------------+
                        |     Reserved For BIOS Extensions  |
         C0000H         +-----------------------------------+
                        |   CGA Display Memory (16 Kbytes)  |
         B8000H         +-----------------------------------+
                        |   MDA Display Memory (4 Kbytes)   |
         B0000H         +-----------------------------------+
                        |   EGA Display Memory (256 Kbytes) |
         A0000H         +-----------------------------------+
                        |   Transient Part of COMMAND.COM   |
                        +-----------------------------------+
                        |      Transient Program Area       |
                        +-----------------------------------+
                        |             MS-DOS                |
                        +-----------------------------------+
                        |        Interrupt Vectors          |
         00000H         +-----------------------------------+
```

Figure 1.2   The IBM PC memory map

The Monochrome Display Adapter

The MDA is the most basic of the three display adapters. It only offers an 80-column by 25-row black-and-white text mode. The memory map in Figure 1.2 shows that the MDA uses 4K of memory, starting at 0B0000H (B000:0000H).

The Color Graphics and Enhanced Graphics Adapters

The CGA offers four text modes (40-column by 25-row black-and-white, 40-column by 25-row color, 80-column by 25-row black-and-white, and 80-column by 25-row color) and three graphics modes (320-horizontal-pixel by 200-vertical-pixel four-color graphics, 320 by 200 four-color graphics (without color burst), and 640 by 200 two-color graphics). The EGA offers all seven CGA modes and more. This book deals with the 80-column by 25-row text modes, so only the CGA compatible modes will be discussed in detail.

As the memory map in Figure 1.2 illustrates, the CGA and the EGA while in the CGA compatible modes, use 16K of memory starting at 0B8000H (B800:0000H). Unfortunately, this area of memory is different from the one used by the MDA. Although this may seem to be a serious drawback in implementing the WINDOWS operating environment, the WINDOWS initialization function is able to correctly determine the display adapter type and make the necessary adjustments to the WINDOWS operating environment.

DISPLAY COORDINATES

Figure 1.3 illustrates the display coordinates for an 80-column by 25-row display screen. While the ROM BIOS video services use the coordinates 0,0 for the upper left corner and 24,79 for the lower right corner, the WINDOWS operating environment uses the more standard coordinates of 1,1 for the upper left corner and 25,80 for the lower right corner. Because the coordinate numbering system the WINDOWS operating environment uses is the one most commonly used by high-level languages, most programmers should feel right at home using it.

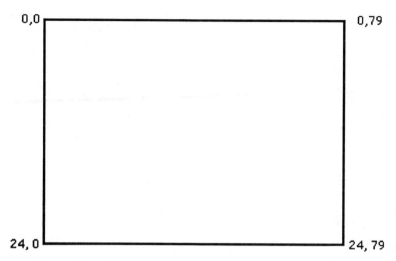

Figure 1.3   80-column by 25-row display screen coordinates

CHARACTER/ATTRIBUTE PAIRS

As shown in Figure 1.3, an 80-column by 25-row display screen is composed of 2000 individual display characters (80 columns × 25 rows = 2000); therefore, it would seem logical to assume that an 80-column by 25-row display screen would require 2000 bytes of display memory. Unfortunately, this assumption would be incorrect. The IBM PC display adapters use a system of character/attribute pairs to display each of the individual characters. The character portion of each character's character/attribute pair is simply its ASCII value. Accordingly, the first byte of screen memory would hold 4DH if an **M** is displayed in the upper left corner of the display screen. Figures 1.4 and 1.5 illustrate how the attribute byte for each display character's character/attribute pair is constructed. If the character in the upper left corner of the display screen has a normal (white-on-black) attribute (07H), the second byte of screen memory holds the value 07H.

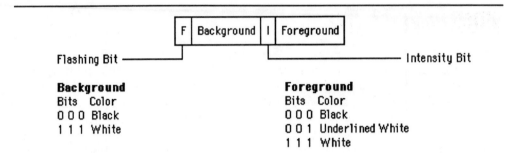

Flashing Bit – When set (1) the character will flash on and off.

Intensity Bit – With a normal attribute (white character on a black background), the character's intensity will be doubled if this bit is set. With a reverse attribute (black character on a white background), the character's intensity will be halved if this bit is set.

Figure 1.4   The monochrome display attributes

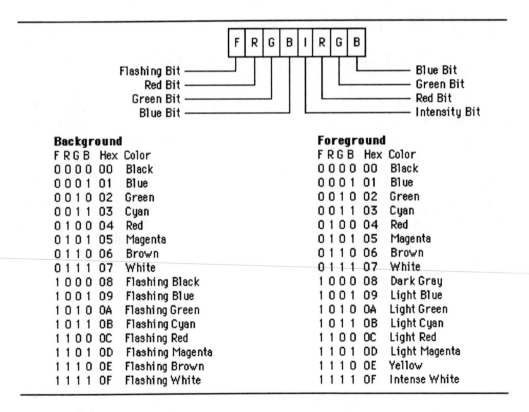

Figure 1.5   CGA and EGA attribute bytes

VIDEO MEMORY OFFSETS

To access a character's position in video memory, you must devise a method for figuring the character's video memory offset. A display character's video memory offset is figured by multiplying the character's row position by 160 (remember there are two bytes per character, so there are 160 bytes for each display screen row) and adding the character's column position to the result (row × 160 + column). For this method to work correctly, the ROM BIOS video services' coordinate system must be used for the row and column values. However, you can use the WINDOWS coordinate system just as easily by subtracting one from both the row and column numbers before applying them in the above formula. A display character's attribute offset is figured by using the above formula and adding one to the result (row × 160 + column + 1).

Although the MDA only provides enough memory for one display page, the CGA and EGA have sufficient memory for multiple display pages. To adjust the above formulas for multiple display pages, the page number is multiplied by 4096 (each display page is allocated 4K and not the minimum 4000 bytes) and added to the character or attribute offset. The WINDOWS operating environment is set to page zero by its initialization routine, thus eliminating the additional complexity of having to take display pages into account.

AVOIDING INTERFERENCE

Even though displaying or reading a display character can be accomplished by simply reading from or writing directly to display memory, directly reading from and writing to an IBM CGA's memory can cause snow to appear on the display. This snow is a result of the computer and the video controller accessing display memory at the same time. Fortunately, this is not a problem with the MDA and EGA display adapters. Furthermore, most non-IBM CGA adapters will not have this problem either. While this snowy effect is a problem, it can be easily overcome by performing direct memory access during the video controller's horizontal and vertical retrace intervals.

The Horizontal Retrace Interval

Whenever the video controller is in the horizontal retrace interval, one byte of display memory can be safely accessed without unwanted snow appearing on the display screen. Figure 1.6 shows that bit 0 of the video controller's status register (port 03DAH) is set to 1 whenever the video controller is in the horizontal retrace interval. The following code fragment illustrates how this bit is used to successfully display a byte in AH to the display memory address in ES:DI:

Example 1.2

```
              .
              .
              .
              mov    dx,03dah         ;DX=Status port address
              cli                     ;Disable the interrupts
horizontal1:  in     al,dx            ;Get the controller's status
              and    al,1             ;Loop if already
              jnz    horizontal1      ; in horizontal retrace
horizontal2:  in     al,dx            ;Get the controller's status
              and    al,1             ;Loop till start
              jz     horizontal2      ; of horizontal retrace
              mov    es:[di],ah       ;Display the byte
              sti                     ;Enable the interrupts
              .
              .
              .
```

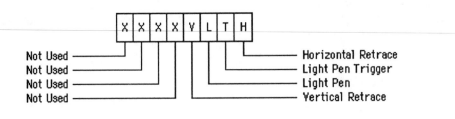

Figure 1.6   Video controller status register (Port 03DAH)

Because the horizontal retrace occurs in such a short period of time, the previous program fragment disables the interrupts before attempting to access display memory. If the interrupts weren't disabled, an interrupting routine (such as the system clock) could steal valuable execution speed from the previous algorithm. Thus, an ill-timed interrupt would defeat the algorithm's purpose by causing snow to appear on the display. Additionally, the above code does not interrupt any horizontal retrace intervals that are already in progress. Attempting to access display memory during a partial horizontal retrace interval would almost certainly result in unwanted display interference.

The Vertical Retrace Interval

Although the horizontal retrace interval is useful for reading and writing a limited number of display characters, the inherent overhead in the previously mentioned algorithm makes it too slow to use for reading and writing an extensive amount of display characters. Fortunately, the vertical retrace interval is very well-suited for displaying or reading a large number of characters in one operation. Figure 1.6 shows that bit 3 of the video controller's status register is set to 1 whenever the video controller is in its vertical retrace interval. Whenever the video controller goes into the vertical retrace interval, large areas of display memory can be accessed by disabling the video controller, performing the necessary display memory accesses, and re-enabling the video controller. Because the video controller's vertical retrace interval only lasts 1.25 milliseconds, the video memory accesses must be completed as fast as possible, or a flickering screen could result. When the low-level video functions are coded in assembly language, the WINDOWS operating environment totally eradicates screen flickering. The following code demonstrates how to move an entire screen display from the memory buffer pointed to by DS:SI to the display memory pointed to by ES:DI:

Example 1.3

```
                        .
                        .
                        .
                mov     dx,3dah          ;DX=Controller status port
disable_cga1:   in      al,dx            ;Get controller status
                and     al,8             ;Loop if not
                jz      disable_cga1     ; in vertical retrace
                mov     dl,0d8h          ;DX=Control select register
                mov     al,25h           ;Disable
                out     dx,al            ; the CGA
        rep     movsw                    ;Move buffer contents
                push    ds               ;Save DS
                mov     ax,40h           ;Set DS to
                mov     ds,ax            ; ROM BIOS data segment
                mov     bx,65H           ;BX=Ctr mode select value pointer
                mov     al,[bx]          ;AL=Ctr mode select value
                out     dx,al            ;Reenable the CGA
                pop     ds               ;Restore DS
                        .
                        .
                        .
```

A few points of interest in the above code fragment are the methods used to disable and re-enable the CGA. After determining that the video controller is in the vertical retrace interval, the CGA is disabled by simply sending a value of 25H to the video controller's select register (port 03D8H). As soon as the desired operation has been fully carried out, the video controller is re-enabled by sending the previous controller select value. Fortunately, the ROM BIOS video driver stores the last value sent to the video controller select register at memory location 0040:0065H; therefore, the above code retrieves the previously saved select value and sends it to the video controller to restore the controller's previous state.

After examining the three basic text display methods, you can see that the MS-DOS video services do not provide sufficient speed and versatility for the WINDOWS operating environment. Although the ROM-BIOS video services have sufficient versatility, their lack of speed in certain areas limits their usefulness when implementing certain time-critical functions. Therefore, the WINDOWS operating environment uses a mixture of the ROM BIOS video services and direct memory access techniques. Such functions as display initialization, cursor positioning, and turning the cursor on and off will use the ROM BIOS video services. Other operations, such as reading and writing large segments of the display screen, filling large segments of the display screen with one particular character, and displaying strings, will be handled by direct memory access techniques. The WINDOWS operating environment uses a mixture of these tools for the best possible blend of speed and programming ease.

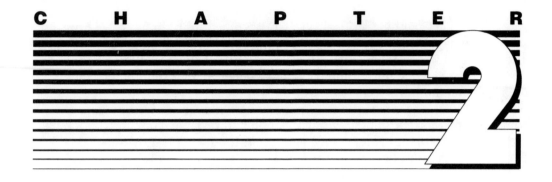

LOW-LEVEL ASSEMBLY LANGUAGE FUNCTIONS

As explained in Chapter 1, critical WINDOWS functions must be coded using assembly language. Furthermore, a general-purpose keyboard input function must also be coded in assembly language. Although the low-level WINDOWS functions are coded using fairly simple assembly language programming techniques, their implementation is complicated by the way C calls an assembly language function. The C calling conventions require strict syntactic conformity with the C compiler's method for implementing function and variable names. Additionally, the C compiler's method for passing parameters to a function and returning values from a function must be strictly observed.

FUNCTION AND VARIABLE NAMES

Selecting a C function or variable name is a fairly straightforward task. For example, a C function that adds two integers and returns the result could be named **addints**. It would be logical to assume that the name addints could also be used for a similar assembly language function's name. Although addints would work correctly with some C compilers, most C compilers would not recognize addints as a legitimate function name. Indeed, the most commonly used naming convention requires all function and variable names to begin with an _ (underscore) character. To further complicate matters, a few C compilers use a naming convention that requires all function and variable names to end with an _ character. Therefore, depending upon the C compiler, an assembly language addints function could be named **addints**, **_addints**, or even **addints_**. Fortunately, it is quite simple to handle the different C compiler naming conventions by using conditional assembly directives.

In addition to adhering to the C compiler's naming convention, an assembly language function or variable name must be made global before a C program can either call the function or reference the variable; therefore, all global assembly language function and variable names are declared public. By using a **public** declaration, the linker will be able to correctly link the assembly language functions and variables to any C functions that use them.

PARAMETER PASSING

To pass parameters to an assembly language function, C builds a **stack frame**. Upon entry to the assembly language function, the stack frame consists of a return address (two bytes for **near** calls or four bytes for **far** calls) followed by the first parameter and the last parameter. An example stack frame for the addints function is presented in Figure 2.1. This stack frame assumes that addints uses a function prototype of **int far addints(int firstint, int secondint);**. Because addints is declared to be far, the C compiler puts a four-byte return address on the bottom of the stack. To reference the passed parameters, the assembly language function first saves and then points register BP to the bottom of the stack as follows:

Example 2.1

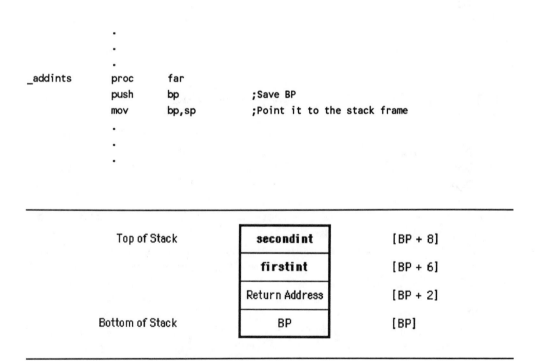

```
              .
              .
              .
_addints    proc    far
            push    bp          ;Save BP
            mov     bp,sp       ;Point it to the stack frame
              .
              .
              .
```

Top of Stack		
	secondint	[BP + 8]
	firstint	[BP + 6]
	Return Address	[BP + 2]
Bottom of Stack	BP	[BP]

Figure 2.1 **addints** *stack frame*

With BP pointing to the bottom of the stack frame, **firstint** can be referenced by using the offset 6[bp]. Remember, BP was pushed onto the stack below the four-byte return address; therefore, the first parameter is located six — not four — bytes from the bottom of the stack. Additionally, **secondint** can be referenced by using an offset of 8[bp]. By accessing the parameters through the register BP offsets, the coding of addints can be continued as follows:

Example 2.2

```
    .
    .
    .
mov     ax,6[bp]        ;Get the first integer into AX
add     ax,8[bp]        ;Figure the result
    .
    .
    .
```

RETURNING TO THE CALLING PROGRAM

Now that addints has performed its function, it must return to the calling program with the calculated result. With most C compilers, a value is returned to the calling program by placing the return value in a CPU register or combination of CPU registers. With all of the C compilers supported in this book, integer values are returned in the AX register. Because the addints function's result is already in the AX register, no further steps are necessary to pass the value back to the calling program. However, suppose the result ended up in the BX register instead of the AX register. To return the value to the calling program, the addints function would be required to execute a **mov bx,ax** instruction before returning control back to the calling program.

In addition to preparing the return value, the addints function must clean up the stack before returning to the calling program. Because register BP was pushed onto the stack, it must be retrieved with a **pop bp** instruction. After retrieving register BP from the stack, the stack has been restored to its entry condition. Therefore, the addints function returns to the calling program by executing a **ret** instruction. The following is the remainder of the addints function's code:

Example 2.3

```
                .
                .
                .
            pop   bp              ;Restore BP and the stack
            ret                   ;Return to the calling program
_addints    endp
                .
                .
                .
```

OTHER CONSIDERATIONS

Although not required by the addints function, many assembly language functions will require stack space for local variables. Local variable space is allocated by subtracting the required number of bytes from the stack pointer. Suppose the addints function had required local variable space for two integers (*row* and *col*). The following revision to the addints function would allocate the necessary space:

Example 2.4

```
                .
                .
                .
_addints    proc  far
            push  bp              ;Save BP
            mov   bp,sp           ;Point BP to the stack frame
            sub   sp,4            ;Adjust stack for local variables
                .
                .
                .
```

With the necessary local variable space allocated, the local variables can be referenced as negative offsets to the BP register. Thus, *row* and *col* could be referenced by the offsets -2[bp] and -4[bp]. It doesn't matter which location is selected for a variable; however, a variable's location must remain constant once it has been assigned.

Because the stack pointer is moved by the local variable space allocation, the assembly language function must deallocate the local variable space before attempting to restore register BP. Deallocation of the local variable space is accomplished by a **mov sp,bp** instruction. Recall that before the local variable space was allocated, registers BP and SP were pointing to the same memory location. Therefore, loading register SP with the pointer in register BP effectively removes the local variable space from the stack. The following code fragment shows how the addints function deallocates its local variable space before returning to the calling program:

Example 2.5

```
                .
                .
                .
            mov  sp,bp        ;Restore the stack pointer
            pop  bp           ;Restore BP
            ret               ;Return to the calling program
_addints    endp
                .
                .
                .
```

One last consideration must be taken into account by an assembly language function. Most C compilers require that certain CPU registers cannot be altered by an assembly language function; therefore, any unalterable registers used in an assembly language function must be saved on the stack at the start of the function and retrieved from the stack before returning to the calling program. Functions that do not require local variable space allocation should save the necessary registers just after the stack frame pointer has been set by the mov bp,sp instruction. Retrieving the saved registers must occur before register BP is restored during the function's exiting routine. Functions that do require local variable space allocation shouldn't save the required registers until after the local variable space allocation has occurred. Accordingly, all of the saved registers must be retrieved before the assembly language function deallocates the local variable space. If the local variable space is deallocated first, the registers' contents will be lost and erratic program execution is almost certain to result.

THE 80286 AND OTHERS

The 80286, 80386, V20, and V30 microprocessors all have additional assembly language instructions for handling stack frames. These instructions are the enter and leave instructions. The **enter** instruction automatically sets up register BP as the stack frame pointer and will allocate any necessary local variable space. The **leave** instruction will deallocate any previously allocated local variable space and restore register BP to its original value. Because the enter and leave instructions use less memory and are faster than their equivalents, they should be used whenever the computer is known to have a supporting microprocessor; furthermore, using enter and leave greatly simplifies the implementation of the stack frame coding requirements. The following program fragment illustrates how the addints function could be rewritten to take advantage of the enter and leave instructions:

Example 2.6

```
                    .
                    .
                    .
_addints    proc    far
            enter   0,0             ;Set up the stack frame
            mov     ax,6[bp]        ;AX=First integer value
            add     ax,8[bp]        ;Figure the result
            leave                   ;Restore the stack
            ret                     ;Return
_addints    endp
                    .
                    .
                    .
```

Note that the code in Example 2.6 does not allocate any local variable space. To allocate local variable space with the enter instruction, you need to indicate the required number of bytes with the first value in enter's operand field. Thus, four bytes of local variable space could be allocated with an **enter 4,0** instruction.

SOURCE LISTING: video.asm

Listing 2.1, **video.asm**, contains all of the low-level assembly language functions. This version of video.asm is compatible with most of the C compilers supported by the WINDOWS toolbox. Because not all of the C compilers support mixed memory models, other compiler-specific versions of video.asm are presented in Appendix C. To comply with the various naming conventions and to provide support for an 80286 version, video.asm makes extensive use of conditional assembly directives.

Listing 2.1: video.asm

```
;
; VIDEO.ASM - For the WINDOWS Toolbox
;              Low-Level Input/Output Routines
;

        ifdef    cpu286
        .286
        endif

        ifndef  POWERC
non_ibm          equ     <__nonibm>
set_text_80      equ     <_settext80>
fill_screen      equ     <_fillscreen>
set_attrib       equ     <_setattrib>
save_screen      equ     <_savescreen>
restore_screen   equ     <_restorescreen>
draw_box         equ     <_drawbox>
print_string     equ     <_printstring>
wait_key         equ     <_waitkey>
        else
non_ibm          equ     <_nonibm>
set_text_80      equ     <settext80>
fill_screen      equ     <fillscreen>
set_attrib       equ     <setattrib>
save_screen      equ     <savescreen>
restore_screen   equ     <restorescreen>
draw_box         equ     <drawbox>
print_string     equ     <printstring>
wait_key         equ     <waitkey>
        endif


;
; ROM BIOS Locations
;
bios_data        equ     40h
crt_mode_set     equ     65h
```

continued...

...from previous page

```
DGROUP          group   _DATA
_DATA           segment word public 'DATA'
                assume  ds:DGROUP

                ifdef   @VERSION
%               public  non_ibm
                else
                public  non_ibm
                endif


non_ibm         dw      1
displayseg      dw      0b800h


_DATA           ends


VIDEO_TEXT      segment para public 'CODE'
                assume  cs:VIDEO_TEXT

                ifdef   @VERSION
%               public  set_text_80,fill_screen,set_attrib
%               public  save_screen,restore_screen,draw_box
%               public  print_string,wait_key
                else
                public  set_text_80,fill_screen,set_attrib
                public  save_screen,restore_screen,draw_box
                public  print_string,wait_key
                endif


;
; Set to 80 x 25 text mode
;
set_text_80     proc    far
                mov     ah,15           ;Get the
                int     10h             ; video mode
                cmp     al,2            ;Jump
                je      settext801      ; if
                cmp     al,3            ;   it's
                je      settext801      ;     already
                cmp     al,7            ;       a 80 x 25
```

continued...

...from previous page

```
                je      settext801      ;    video mode
                mov     ax,3            ;Set it to
                int     10h             ; 80 x 25 color
settext801:     mov     ax,0500h        ;Set the
                int     10h             ; page to 0
                mov     ah,12h          ;Check
                mov     bl,10h          ; for
                int     10h             ;   EGA
                cmp     bl,10h          ;Jump
                jne     settext803      ; if EGA
                mov     ah,15           ;Get the
                int     10h             ; video mode
                cmp     al,7            ;Jump
                je      settext802      ; if MDA
                mov     non_ibm,0       ;Flag IBM CGA
                jmp     short settext803 ;Jump
settext802:     mov     displayseg,0b000h ;Set the display segment address
settext803:     ret                     ;Return
set_text_80     endp


;
; Fill text window
;
fill_screen     proc    far
row1            equ     <6[bp]>
col1           equ     <8[bp]>
row2           equ     <10[bp]>
col2           equ     <12[bp]>
char           equ     <14[bp]>
att            equ     <16[bp]>
rows           equ     <-2[bp]>
cols           equ     <-4[bp]>
               ifdef   cpu286
               enter   4,0             ;Set up the stack frame
               else
               push    bp              ;Save BP registers
               mov     bp,sp           ;Point it to the stack
               sub     sp,4            ;Reserve local space
```

continued...

...from previous page

```
            endif
            push    di              ;Save DI
            mov     ax,row1         ;Figure
            mov     bx,col1         ; the
            call    fig_vid_off     ;  video offset
            mov     di,ax           ;DI=Video offset
            mov     es,displayseg   ;ES=Video segment
            mov     ax,row2         ;Figure
            sub     ax,row1         ; the number
            inc     ax              ;  of rows
            mov     rows,ax         ;Save it
            mov     ax,col2         ;Figure
            sub     ax,col1         ; the number
            inc     ax              ;  of columns
            mov     cols,ax         ;Save it
            cld                     ;Flag increment
            mov     al,byte ptr char ;AL=Display character
            mov     ah,byte ptr att ;AH=Display attribute
            call    disable_cga     ;Disable the CGA if necessary
fillscreen1: push   di              ;Save the video offset
            mov     cx,cols         ;CX=Number of columns
      rep   stosw                   ;Display the row
            pop     di              ;Restore the video offset
            add     di,160          ;Point it to the next row
            dec     word ptr rows   ;Loop
            jnz     fillscreen1     ; till done
            call    enable_cga      ;Enable the CGA if necessary
            pop     di              ;Restore DI
            ifdef   cpu286
            leave                   ;Restore the stack
            else
            mov     sp,bp           ;Reset the stack pointer
            pop     bp              ;Restore BP
            endif
            ret                     ;Return
fill_screen endp
```

continued...

...from previous page

```
;
; Set attributes
;
set_attrib      proc    far
row1            equ     <6[bp]>
col1            equ     <8[bp]>
row2            equ     <10[bp]>
col2            equ     <12[bp]>
att             equ     <14[bp]>
rows            equ     <-2[bp]>
cols            equ     <-4[bp]>
                ifdef   cpu286
                enter   4,0             ;Set up the stack frame
                else
                push    bp              ;Save BP
                mov     bp,sp           ;Point it to the stack
                sub     sp,4            ;Save space for local data
                endif
                push    di              ;Save DI
                mov     ax,row1         ;Figure
                mov     bx,col1         ; the
                call    fig_vid_off     ;  video offset
                mov     di,ax           ;DI=Video offset
                inc     di              ;Bump it to the first attribute
                mov     es,displayseg   ;ES=Video segment
                mov     ax,row2         ;Figure
                sub     ax,row1         ; the number
                inc     ax              ;  of rows
                mov     rows,ax         ;Save it
                mov     ax,col2         ;Figure
                sub     ax,col1         ; the number
                inc     ax              ;  columns
                mov     cols,ax         ;Save it
                cld                     ;Flag increment
                mov     al,byte ptr att ;AL=Display attribute
                call    disable_cga     ;Disable the CGA if necessary
setattrib1:     push    di              ;Save the video offset
                mov     cx,cols         ;CX=Number of columns
```

continued...

...from previous page

```
setattrib2:     stosb                       ;Set the attribute byte
                inc      di                 ;Bump the video pointer
                loop     setattrib2         ;Loop till done
                pop      di                 ;Restore the video offset
                add      di,160             ;Point it to the next row
                dec      word ptr rows      ;Loop
                jnz      setattrib1         ; till done
                call     enable_cga         ;Enable the CGA if necessary
                pop      di                 ;Restore DI
                ifdef    cpu286
                leave                       ;Restore the stack
                else
                mov      sp,bp              ;Reset the stack pointer
                pop      bp                 ;Restore BP
                endif
                ret                         ;Return
set_attrib      endp


;
; Save screen
;
save_screen     proc     far
row1            equ      <6[bp]>
col1            equ      <8[bp]>
row2            equ      <10[bp]>
col2            equ      <12[bp]>
array           equ      <14[bp]>
rows            equ      <-2[bp]>
cols            equ      <-4[bp]>
                ifdef    cpu286
                enter    4,0                ;Set up the stack frame
                else
                push     bp                 ;Save BP
                mov      bp,sp              ;Point it to the stack
                sub      sp,4               ;Make room for local data
                endif
                push     di                 ;Save the
                push     si                 ; registers
```

continued...

...from previous page

```
                mov     ax,row1          ;Figure
                mov     bx,col1          ; the
                call    fig_vid_off      ;  video offset
                mov     si,ax            ;SI=Video offset
                mov     ax,row2          ;Figure
                sub     ax,row1          ; the number
                inc     ax               ;  of rows
                mov     rows,ax          ;Save it
                mov     ax,col2          ;Figure
                sub     ax,col1          ; the number
                inc     ax               ;  of columns
                mov     cols,ax          ;Save it
                cld                      ;Flag increment
                call    disable_cga      ;Disable the CGA if necessary
                push    ds               ;Save DS
                les     di,array         ;ES:DI=Array pointer
                mov     ds,displayseg    ;DS:SI=Video pointer
savescreen1:    push    si               ;Save the video offset
                mov     cx,cols          ;CX=Number of columns
        rep     movsw                    ;Save the row
                pop     si               ;Restore the video offset
                add     si,160           ;Point it to the next row
                dec     word ptr rows    ;Loop
                jnz     savescreen1      ; till done
                pop     ds               ;Restore DS
                call    enable_cga       ;Enable the CGA if necessary
                pop     si               ;Restore
                pop     di               ; the registers
                ifdef   cpu286
                leave                    ;Restore the stack
                else
                mov     sp,bp            ;Reset the stack pointer
                pop     bp               ;Restore BP
                endif
                ret                      ;Return
save_screen     endp
```

continued...

...from previous page

```
;
; Restore screen
;
restore_screen  proc    far
row1            equ     <6[bp]>
col1            equ     <8[bp]>
row2            equ     <10[bp]>
col2            equ     <12[bp]>
array           equ     <14[bp]>
rows            equ     <-2[bp]>
cols            equ     <-4[bp]>
                ifdef   cpu286
                enter   4,0             ;Set up the stack frame
                else
                push    bp              ;Save BP
                mov     bp,sp           ;Point it to the stack
                sub     sp,4            ;Make room for local data
                endif
                push    di              ;Save the
                push    si              ; registers
                mov     ax,row1         ;Figure
                mov     bx,col1         ; the
                call    fig_vid_off     ;  video offset
                mov     di,ax           ;DI=Video offset
                mov     es,displayseg   ;ES=Video segment
                mov     ax,row2         ;Figure
                sub     ax,row1         ; the number
                inc     ax              ;  of rows
                mov     rows,ax         ;Save it
                mov     ax,col2         ;Figure
                sub     ax,col1         ; the number
                inc     ax              ;  of columns
                mov     cols,ax         ;Save it
                cld                     ;Flag increment
                call    disable_cga     ;Disable the CGA if necessary
                push    ds              ;Save DS
                lds     si,array        ;DS:SI=Array pointer
```

continued...

...from previous page

```
restorescreen1: push    di              ;Save the video offset
                mov     cx,cols         ;CX=Number of columns
        rep     movsw                   ;Save the row
                pop     di              ;Restore the video offset
                add     di,160          ;Point it to the next row
                dec     word ptr rows   ;Loop
                jnz     restorescreen1  ; till done
                pop     ds              ;Restore DS
                call    enable_cga      ;Enable the CGA if necessary
                pop     si              ;Restore
                pop     di              ; the registers
                ifdef   cpu286
                leave                   ;Restore the stack
                else
                mov     sp,bp           ;Reset the stack pointer
                pop     bp              ;Restore BP
                endif
                ret                     ;Return
restore_screen  endp

;
; Draw box
;
draw_box        proc    far
row1            equ     <6[bp]>
col1           equ     <8[bp]>
row2           equ     <10[bp]>
col2           equ     <12[bp]>
flag           equ     <14[bp]>
att            equ     <16[bp]>
rows           equ     <-2[bp]>
cols           equ     <-4[bp]>
                ifdef   cpu286
                enter   4,0             ;Set up the stack
                else
                push    bp              ;Save BP
                mov     bp,sp           ;Point it to the stack
                sub     sp,4            ;Save space for local data
                endif
```

continued...

...from previous page

```
            push    di                      ;Save DI
            mov     ax,row1                 ;Figure
            mov     bx,col1                 ; the
            call    fig_vid_off             ;  video offset
            mov     di,ax                   ;DI=Video offset
            mov     es,displayseg           ;ES=Video segment
            mov     ax,row2                 ;Figure
            sub     ax,row1                 ; the number
            dec     ax                      ;  of rows - 2
            mov     rows,ax                 ;Save it
            mov     ax,col2                 ;Figure
            sub     ax,col1                 ; the number
            dec     ax                      ;  of columns - 2
            mov     cols,ax                 ;Save it
            cld                             ;Flag increment
            mov     ah,att                  ;AH=Display attribute
            call    disable_cga             ;Disable the CGA if necessary
            push    di                      ;Save the video offset
            mov     al,201                  ;AL=Double line character
            cmp     word ptr flag,0         ;Jump if
            je      drawbox1                ; double line
            mov     al,218                  ;AL=Single line character
drawbox1:   stosw                           ;Save the character/attribute pair
            mov     al,205                  ;AL=Double line character
            cmp     word ptr flag,0         ;Jump if
            je      drawbox2                ; double line
            mov     al,196                  ;AL=Single line character
drawbox2:   mov     cx,cols                 ;CX=Line length
      rep   stosw                           ;Display the line
            mov     al,187                  ;AL=Double line character
            cmp     word ptr flag,0         ;Jump if
            je      drawbox3                ; double line
            mov     al,191                  ;AL=Single line character
drawbox3:   stosw                           ;Save the character/attribute pair
            pop     di                      ;Restore the video pointer
            add     di,160                  ;Point it to the next row
```

continued...

...from previous page

```
drawbox4:      push    di                        ;Save the video pointer
               mov     al,186                    ;AL=Double line character
               cmp     word ptr flag,0           ;Jump if
               je      drawbox5                  ; double line
               mov     al,179                    ;AL=Single line character
drawbox5:      stosw                             ;Save the character/attribute pair
               add     di,cols                   ;Point to
               add     di,cols                   ; the right side
               stosw                             ;Save the character/attribute pair
               pop     di                        ;Restore the video pointer
               add     di,160                    ;Point it to the next row
               dec     word ptr rows             ;Loop till the
               jnz     drawbox4                  ; sides are complete
               mov     al,200                    ;AL=Double line character
               cmp     word ptr flag,0           ;Jump if
               je      drawbox6                  ; double line
               mov     al,192                    ;AL=Single line character
drawbox6:      stosw                             ;Save the character/attribute pair
               mov     al,205                    ;AL=Double line character
               cmp     word ptr flag,0           ;Jump if
               je      drawbox7                  ; double line
               mov     al,196                    ;AL=Single line character
drawbox7:      mov     cx,cols                   ;CX=Line length
         rep   stosw                             ;Display the line
               mov     al,188                    ;AL=Double line character
               cmp     word ptr flag,0           ;Jump if
               je      drawbox8                  ; double line
               mov     al,217                    ;AL=Single line character
drawbox8:      stosw                             ;Save the character/attribute pair
               call    enable_cga                ;Enable the CGA if necessary
               pop     di                        ;Restore DI
               ifdef   cpu286
               leave                             ;Restore the stack
               else
               mov     sp,bp                     ;Reset the stack pointer
               pop     bp                        ;Restore BP
               endif
               ret                               ;Return
draw_box       endp
```

continued...

...from previous page

```
;
; Display string
;
print_string    proc    far
row             equ     <6[bp]>
col             equ     <8[bp]>
string          equ     <10[bp]>
                ifdef   cpu286
                enter   0,0             ;Set up the stack frame
                else
                push    bp              ;Save BP
                mov     bp,sp           ;Point it to the stack
                endif
                push    si              ;Save
                push    di              ; the registers
                mov     ax,row          ;Figure
                mov     bx,col          ; the
                call    fig_vid_off     ;  video offset
                mov     di,ax           ;DI=Video offset
                mov     es,displayseg   ;ES=Video segment
                cld                     ;Flag increment
                cmp     word ptr non_ibm,0 ;IBM CGA?
                push    ds              ;Save DS
                lds     si,string       ;DS:SI=String pointer
                je      print_string2  ;Jump if IBM CGA
print_string1:  lodsb                   ;Get the next character
                or      al,al           ;Jump
                jz      print_string6  ; if done
                stosb                   ;Display the character
                inc     di              ;Bump the video pointer
                jmp     print_string1  ;Loop till done
print_string2:  mov     dx,03dah        ;DX=Video status register
print_string3:  lodsb                   ;Get the next character
                or      al,al           ;Jump
                jz      print_string6  ; if done
                mov     ah,al           ;Put it in AH
                cli                     ;Disable the interrupts
print_string4:  in      al,dx           ;Loop
                and     al,1            ; if in
                jnz     print_string4  ;  horizontal retrace
```

continued...

...from previous page

```
print_string5:  in      al,dx              ;Loop
                and     al,1               ; if not in
                jz      print_string5      ;  horizontal retrace
                mov     es:[di],ah         ;Display the character
                sti                        ;Reenable the interrupts
                inc     di                 ;Bump the
                inc     di                 ; video pointer
                jmp     print_string3      ;Loop till done
print_string6:  pop     ds                 ;Restore
                pop     di                 ; the
                pop     si                 ;  registers
                ifdef   cpu286
                leave                      ;Restore the stack
                else
                pop     bp                 ;Restore BP
                endif
                ret                        ;Return
print_string    endp


;
; Get a Key
;
wait_key        proc    far
                mov     ah,01h             ;Has a key
                int     16h                ; been pressed?
                jz      wait_key           ;Loop if not
                mov     ah,0               ;Get
                int     16h                ; the key
                or      al,al              ;Jump if
                jz      wait_key1          ; extended key
                xor     ah,ah              ;Erase the scan code
                jmp     short wait_key2    ;Jump
wait_key1:      xchg    ah,al              ;AX=Scan code
                inc     ah                 ;AX=Scan code + 256
wait_key2:      ret                        ;Return
wait_key        endp
```

continued...

...from previous page

```
;
; Figure video offset
;
fig_vid_off     proc    near
                push    dx              ;Save DX
                push    bx              ;Save the column
                dec     ax              ;Decrement the row
                mov     bx,160          ;Figure the
                mul     bx              ; row offset
                pop     bx              ;Restore the column
                dec     bx              ;Decrement it
                sal     bx,1            ;Figure the column pair offset
                add     ax,bx           ;AX=Video offset
                pop     dx              ;Restore DX
                ret                     ;Return
fig_vid_off     endp


;
; Disable CGA
;
disable_cga     proc    near
                cmp     non_ibm,0       ;Jump if it
                jne     disable_cga2    ; isn't an IBM CGA
                push    ax              ;Save the
                push    dx              ; registers
                mov     dx,3dah         ;DX=Video status port
disable_cga1:   in      al,dx           ;Wait
                and     al,8            ; for
                jz      disable_cga1    ;  vertical retrace
                mov     dl,0d8h         ;DX=Video select register port
                mov     al,25h          ;Disable
                out     dx,al           ; the video
                pop     dx              ;Restore
                pop     ax              ; the registers
disable_cga2:   ret                     ;Return
disable_cga     endp
```

continued...

...from previous page

```
;
; Enable CGA
;
enable_cga      proc    near
                cmp     non_ibm,0       ;Jump if it
                jne     enable_cga1     ; isn't an IBM CGA
                push    ax              ;Save
                push    bx              ; the
                push    dx              ;  registers
                push    ds              ;
                mov     ax,bios_data    ;Set the
                mov     ds,ax           ; data segment
                mov     bx,crt_mode_set ;BX=Video mode set value pointer
                mov     al,[bx]         ;AL=Video mode set value
                mov     dx,03d8h        ;DX=Video select register port
                out     dx,al           ;Reenable the video mode
                pop     ds              ;Restore
                pop     dx              ; the
                pop     bx              ;  registers
                pop     ax              ;
enable_cga1:    ret                     ;Return
enable_cga      endp

VIDEO_TEXT      ends

                end
```

Function Description: settex80

The **settext80** function initializes the WINDOWS operating environment. Its implementation is illustrated by the following pseudocode:

```
if (current video mode ! = 80 x 25 text mode)
    set video mode to 80 x 25 color text mode
switch (display adapter) {
    case CGA:
        set _nonibm flag to indicate an IBM CGA
    case MDA:
        set display segment to 0xb000
}
```

As the pseudocode and the actual program code illustrate, the settext80 function could easily have been coded in C instead of assembly language; however, good programming practice dictates that related functions should be grouped into a single program module. This keeps the linking requirements to a minimum and makes the WINDOWS toolbox easier to maintain.

Function Description: fillscreen

The **fillscreen** function fills a text window with a specified character/attribute pair. Its implementation is illustrated by the following pseudocode:

```
figure the video offset
figure the number of rows
figure the number of columns
disable the display adapter if it's an IBM CGA
for (i = 0; i < number of rows; i+ +) {
    for (j = 0; j < number of columns; j+ +) {
        display the character/attribute pair
    }
}
re-enable the display adapter if it's an IBM CGA
```

Function Description: setattrib

The **setattrib** function sets an entire text window's attributes to a specified attribute value. Its implementation is illustrated by the following pseudocode:

```
figure the video offset
bump the video offset to point to the first attribute
figure the number of rows
figure the number of columns
disable the display adapter if it's an IBM CGA
for (i = 0; i < number of rows; i+ +) {
    for (j = 0; j < number of columns; j+ +) {
        set the position's attribute
    }
}
re-enable the display adapter if it's an IBM CGA
```

Function Description: savescreen

The **savescreen** function saves the entire contents of a text window to a specified buffer area. Its implementation is illustrated by the following pseudocode:

```
figure the video offset
figure the number of rows
figure the number of columns
disable the display adapter if it's an IBM CGA
for (i = 0; i < number of rows; i+ +) {
    for (j = 0; j < number of columns; j+ +) {
        save a character/attribute pair in the buffer
    }
}
re-enable the display adapter if it's an IBM CGA
```

Function Description: restorescreen

The **restorescreen** function redisplays a previously buffered text window. Its implementation is illustrated by the following pseudocode:

figure the video offset
figure the number of rows
figure the number of columns
disable the display adapter if it's an IBM CGA
for (i = 0; i < number of rows; i + +) {
    for (j = 0; j < number of columns; j + +) {
        display a character/attribute pair
    }
}
re-enable the display adapter if it's an IBM CGA

Function Description: drawbox

The **drawbox** function draws a border around a text window. Its implementation is illustrated by the following pseudocode:

figure the video offset
figure the number of interior rows
figure the number of interior columns
disable the display adapter if it's an IBM CGA
display the upper left corner
for (i = 0; i < number of interior columns; i + +) {
    display a horizontal line character
}
display the upper right corner
for (i = 0; i < number of interior rows; i + +) {
    display the left side character
    display the right side character
}
display the lower left corner
for (i = 0; i < number of interior columns; i + +) {
    display a horizontal line character
}
display the lower right corner
re-enable the display adapter if it's an IBM CGA

Function Description: printstring

The **printstring** function displays a string at a specified display screen position. Its implementation is illustrated by the following pseudocode:

```
figure the video offset
while (!(end of string)) {
    if (display adapter ! = IBM CGA) {
        display a character
    }
    else {
        while (in horizontal retrace) ;
        while (not in horizontal retrace) ;
        disable the interrupts
        display a character
        enable the interrupts
    }
}
```

Function Description: waitkey

The **waitkey** function waits for the operator to press a key. Once a key is pressed, the key's ASCII code is returned for nonextended keys, or the key's scan code + 256 is returned for extended keys. The waitkey function's implementation is illustrated by the following pseudocode:

```
while (key not pressed) ;
get the key's value
if (extended key)
    return(scan code  + 256)
else
    return(ASCII code)
```

Function Description: fig_vid_off

The **fig_vid_off** function is used internally by the other video functions to figure video offsets. Its implementation is illustrated by the following pseudocode:

```
decrement the row number
figure the row offset (row * 160)
decrement the column number
figure the column offset (column * 2)
figure the video offset (row offset + column offset)
```

Function Description: disable_cga

The **disable_cga** function is used internally by the other video functions to disable IBM CGA display adapters. Its implementation is illustrated by the following pseudocode:

```
if (display adapter = = IBM CGA) {
    while (not in vertical retrace) ;
    disable the CGA
}
```

Function Description: enable_cga

The **enable_cga** function is used internally by the other video functions to re-enable a previously disabled IBM CGA. Its implementation is illustrated by the following pseudocode:

```
if (display adapter = = IBM CGA) {
    enable the CGA
}
```

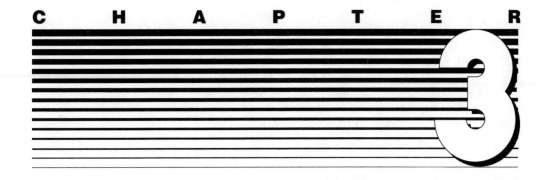

C INPUT/OUTPUT FUNCTIONS

Although Chapter 2 presented a diverse collection of low-level input/output functions, the WINDOWS toolbox implementation requires a number of other low-level input/output functions before it can support the higher-level window and menu functions. Unlike the assembly language code used in Chapter 2, the remainder of the low-level input/output functions can be completely coded using C. Thus, the remaining low-level input/output functions are easier to code and offer a much higher degree of portability.

HEADER FILE LISTING: windows.h

Listing 3.1, **windows.h,** is the WINDOWS toolbox header file. Like most other C header files, the chief purpose of windows.h is to define constants, global variables, macros, and function prototypes. To achieve correct program compilation, windows.h is included in all of the WINDOWS programs. Additionally, windows.h should be included in any application program that uses the WINDOWS toolbox.

In addition to performing the normal header file tasks, windows.h performs a very important secondary task of addressing a number of portability problems: undefining the **far** keyword for C compilers that don't support mixed memory models; defining the **max** macro for C compilers that don't include it in stdlib.h; defining the ANSI versions of **va_list, va_start, va_arg, va_end**, and **atexit**; and defining constants, macros, and function prototypes for C compilers that support hardware error trapping. Without the foundation windows.h provides, portability across all of the C compilers that WINDOWS supports would be an impossible task.

Listing 3.1: windows.h

```
/****************************************************************************
* windows.h - For the WINDOWS Toolbox
*             Definition File
****************************************************************************/
/* undefine far if necessary */
#ifdef DC88
#define far
#endif

#ifdef ECOC88
#define far
#endif

#ifdef LATTICEC
#define far
#endif

#ifdef ZORTECHC
#define far
#endif

/* logic constants */
#define TRUE 1
#define FALSE 0

/* display type constants */
#define _IBM_CGA 0
#define _NONIBM_CGA 1

/* border line constants */
#define _DOUBLE_LINE 0
#define _SINGLE_LINE 1
#define _NO_BORDER 2
```

continued...

...from previous page

```
/* window constants */
#define _DRAW 1
#define _NO_DRAW 0
#define _UP 0
#define _DOWN 1
#define _LEFT 2
#define _RIGHT 3
#define _UPA 4
#define _DOWNA 5
#define _LEFTA 6
#define _RIGHTA 7

/* boolean data type */
typedef int boolean;

/* menu structure definitions */
typedef struct {
    char *string;
    int hotkey;
    void (*function)();
    void (*help)();
} MENU;

typedef struct {
    char *heading;
    int hotkey, number;
    MENU *mptr;
} MENU_HEAD;

/* window structure definition */
typedef struct {
    int row1, col1, row2, col2;
    char *videoarray;
} WINDOW ;

/* external variable declarations */
extern int _nonibm;
extern int _menu_att, _menu_hotkey, _menu_highlight;
```

continued...

...from previous page

```
/* macro definitions */
#define clearone(row, col, att) fillone(row, col, ' ', att)
#define clearscreen(row1, col1, row2, col2, att)\
        fillscreen(row1, col1, row2, col2, ' ', att)

#ifndef max
#define max(a, b) (((a) > (b)) ? (a) : (b))
#endif

#ifdef ECOC88
typedef char *va_list;
#define va_start(ap,v) ap = (va_list)&v + sizeof(v)
#define va_arg(ap,t) ((t *)(ap += sizeof(t)))[-1]
#define va_end(ap) ap = NULL
#endif

#ifdef LATTICEC
typedef char *va_list;
#define va_start(ap,v) ap = (va_list)&v + sizeof(v)
#define va_arg(ap,t) ((t *)(ap += sizeof(t)))[-1]
#define va_end(ap) ap = NULL
#define atexit onexit
#endif

/* function prototypes */
WINDOW *close_window(WINDOW *);
void cursoroff(void);
void cursoron(void);
int dialog_menu(int, int, int, MENU *, int, ...);
void display_error(char *);
void far drawbox(int, int, int, int, int, int);
void draw_window(int, int, int, int, int, int, ...);
void fillone(int, int, int, int);
void far fillscreen(int, int, int, int, int, int);
void getcurpos(int *, int *, int *, int *);
void horizontal_bar(WINDOW *, int, int, int);
void hotstring(int, int, int, int, char *);
WINDOW *open_window(int, int, int, int, int, ...);
int popup(int, MENU *, int, int);
```

continued...

...from previous page

```
void printcenter(int, int, char *);
void printone(int, int, int);
void far printstring(int, int, char far *);
void pulldown_bar(int, MENU_HEAD *, int);
int pulldown(int, MENU_HEAD *, int, int, void (*)());
void far restorescreen(int, int, int, int, char far *);
void save_initial_video(void);
void far savescreen(int, int, int, int, char far *);
void scroll_window(WINDOW *, int, int, int);
void far setattrib(int, int, int, int, int);
void setone(int, int, int);
void setcurpos(int, int);
void setcursor(int, int);
void far settext80(void);
void vertical_bar(WINDOW *, int, int, int);
int far waitkey(void);

#ifdef MICROSOFTC
#define HARDERROR
void far error_handler(unsigned, unsigned, unsigned far *);
#endif

#ifdef POWERC
#define HARDERROR
void far error_handler(unsigned, unsigned, unsigned, unsigned);
#define _harderr harderr
#define _hardresume hardresume
#define _HARDERR_IGNORE 0
#define _HARDERR_RETRY 1
#define _HARDERR_ABORT 2
#endif

#ifdef TURBOC
#define HARDERROR
void far error_handler(unsigned, unsigned, unsigned, unsigned);
#define _harderr harderr
#define _hardresume hardresume
#define _HARDERR_IGNORE 0
```

continued...

...from previous page

```
#define _HARDERR_RETRY 1
#define _HARDERR_ABORT 2
#endif

/* redefine far if necessary */
#ifdef LATTICEC
#define far far
#endif

#ifdef ZORTECHC
#define far far
#endif
```

FUNCTION DEFINITIONS

Before the first WINDOWS C program is listed, the issue of function definition portability must be addressed. There are two basic types of C function definitions: the old-fashioned definition type and the newer ANSI definition type. If the old-fashioned definition type is used, function parameters are defined after the function declaration as follows:

Example 3.1

```
void oldstyle(a, b, c)
double a, b, c;
{
        /* function body goes here */
}
```

The ANSI definition type includes the parameter definitions right in the function declaration as follows:

Example 3.2

```
void newstyle(double a, double b, double c)
{
        /* function body goes here */
}
```

Although the ANSI definition type is today's preferred method for defining functions, the LATTICE C compiler only supports the old-fashioned definition type. Accordingly, the WINDOWS toolbox programs only use the old-fashioned definition type.

Another function definition problem can arise whenever a function that allows a variable number of parameters is defined. Although some C compilers allow ellipses (. . .) in function definitions, many of the C compilers the WINDOWS toolbox supports only allow ellipses in function prototypes; therefore, the WINDOWS toolbox programs only use ellipses in function prototypes and not in the actual function definitions. This allows the WINDOWS toolbox programs to be easily compiled with a minimum number of conditional compilation statements.

SOURCE LISTING: windio.c

Listing 3.2, **windio.c**, contains all of the low-level C input/output functions. These functions support such diverse operations as turning the cursor on and off; positioning the cursor; displaying single characters, attributes, and character/attribute pairs; and centering strings.

Listing 3.2: windio.c

```c
/*************************************************************************
* windio.c - For the WINDOWS Toolbox
*            Low-Level Input/Output Routines
*************************************************************************/
#include <stdio.h>
#include <dos.h>
#include <string.h>
#include "windows.h"

#ifdef DC88
struct WORDREGS {
     unsigned int ax;
     unsigned int bx;
     unsigned int cx;
     unsigned int dx;
     unsigned int si;
     unsigned int di;
     unsigned int cflag;
};

struct BYTEREGS {
     unsigned char al, ah;
     unsigned char bl, bh;
     unsigned char cl, ch;
     unsigned char dl, dh;
};

union REGS {
     struct WORDREGS x;
     struct BYTEREGS h;
};

extern unsigned int _rax, _rbx, _rcx, _rdx, _rsi, _rdi, _res, _rds;
extern unsigned char _carryf, _zerof;
void _doint(char inum);
```

continued...

...from previous page

```
int int86(int inum, union REGS *iregs, union REGS *oregs)
{
     _rax = iregs.x->ax;
     _rbx = iregs.x->bx;
     _rcx = iregs.x->cx;
     _rdx = iregs.x->dx;
     _rsi = iregs.x->si;
     _rdi = iregs.x->di;
     _doint(inum);
     oregs.x->di = _rdi;
     oregs.x->si = _rsi;
     oregs.x->dx = _rdx;
     oregs.x->cx = _rcx;
     oregs.x->bx = _rbx;
     oregs.x->ax = _rax;
     oregs.x->cflag = _carryf;
     return(_rax);
}

#endif

static void initcur(void);

static int cursorstart = -1, cursorend = -1;

void cursoroff()
{
     union REGS regs;

     initcur();
     regs.h.ah = 1;
     regs.x.cx = 0x2000;
     int86(0x10, &regs, &regs);
}
```

continued...

...from previous page

```c
void cursoron()
{
    union REGS regs;

    initcur();
    regs.h.ah = 1;
    regs.h.ch = cursorstart;
    regs.h.cl = cursorend;
    int86(0x10, &regs, &regs);
}

void setcurpos(row, col)
int row;
int col;
{
    union REGS regs;

    regs.h.ah = 2;
    regs.h.bh = 0;
    regs.h.dh = --row;
    regs.h.dl = --col;
    int86(0x10, &regs, &regs);
}

void setcursor(cstart, cend)
int cstart;
int cend;
{
    cursorstart = cstart;
    cursorend = cend;
    cursoron();
}

void getcurpos(row, col, cstart, cend)
int *row;
int *col;
int *cstart;
int *cend;
```

continued...

...from previous page

```
{
    union REGS regs;

    regs.h.ah = 3;
    regs.h.bh = 0;
    int86(0x10, &regs, &regs);
    *row = ++regs.h.dh;
    *col = ++regs.h.dl;
    *cstart = regs.h.ch;
    *cend = regs.h.cl;
}

void fillone(row, col, chr, att)
int row;
int col;
int chr;
int att;
{
    union REGS regs;

    setcurpos(row, col);
    regs.h.ah = 9;
    regs.h.al = chr;
    regs.h.bh = 0;
    regs.h.bl = att;
    regs.x.cx = 1;
    int86(0x10, &regs, &regs);
}

void printone(row, col, chr)
int row;
int col;
int chr;
{
    union REGS regs;
```

continued...

...from previous page

```
        setcurpos(row, col);
        regs.h.ah = 10;
        regs.h.al = chr;
        regs.h.bh = 0;
        regs.x.cx = 1;
        int86(0x10, &regs, &regs);
}

void setone(row, col, att)
int row;
int col;
int att;
{
        union REGS regs;

        setcurpos(row, col);
        regs.h.ah = 8;
        regs.h.bh = 0;
        int86(0x10, &regs, &regs);
        regs.h.ah = 9;
        regs.h.bl = att;
        regs.x.cx = 1;
        int86(0x10, &regs, &regs);
}

void printcenter(row, col, string)
int row;
int col;
char *string;
{
        printstring(row, col - (strlen(string) >> 1), string);
}

static void initcur()
{
        union REGS regs;
```

continued...

...from previous page

```
    if (cursorstart == -1 && cursorend == -1) {
        regs.h.ah = 3;
        regs.h.bh = 0;
        int86(0x10, &regs, &regs);
        cursorstart = regs.h.ch;
        cursorend = regs.h.cl;
    }
}
```

Function Definition: int86

The **int86** function calls 8086 INTs. Because the DeSmet DC88 C compiler is the only C compiler that doesn't include an int86 function in its run-time library, int86 is conditionally compiled only for the DeSmet DC88 C compiler. Its implementation is illustrated by the following pseudocode:

load all of the register variables with their int86 equivalents
call the _doint function
load all of the int86 equivalents with their register variable equivalents
load the carry flag
return the value in register AX

Function Definition: cursoroff

The **cursoroff** function turns the blinking cursor character off. Its implementation is illustrated by the following pseudocode:

if (called for the first time)
    save the cursor character's starting and ending lines
use the ROM BIOS to turn the cursor off

Function Definition: cursoron

The **cursoron** function turns the blinking cursor character on. Its implementation is illustrated by the following pseudocode:

if (called for the first time)
    save the cursor character's starting and ending lines
use the ROM BIOS to turn the cursor on

Function Definition: setcurpos

The **setcurpos** function sets the display screen's cursor position. Its implementation is illustrated by the following pseudocode:

decrement the row
decrement the column
use the ROM BIOS to position the cursor

Function Definition: setcursor

The **setcursor** function sets the cursor character's starting and ending lines. Its implementation is illustrated by the following pseudocode:

save the cursor character's new starting line
save the cursor character's new ending line
use the **cursoron** *function to perform the action*

Function Definition: getcurpos

The **getcurpos** function retrieves the cursor's row position, column position, starting line, and ending line. Its implementation is illustrated by the following pseudocode:

use the ROM BIOS to get the cursor values
bump the row position
bump the column position
return the cursor values

Function Definition: fillone

The **fillone** function displays a character/attribute pair at a specified display screen position. Its implementation is illustrated by the following pseudocode:

set the cursor position
use the ROM BIOS to display the character/attribute pair

Function Definition: printone

The **printone** function displays a character at a specified display screen position. Its implementation is illustrated by the following pseudocode:

set the cursor position
use the ROM BIOS to display the character

Function Definition: setone

The **setone** function sets the attribute for a specified display screen position. Its implementation is illustrated by the following pseudocode:

set the cursor position
use the ROM BIOS to get the position's character
use the ROM BIOS to display the character/attribute pair

Function Definition: printcenter

The **printcenter** function centers a string on a specified display screen position. Its implementation is illustrated by the following pseudocode:

*use the **printstring** function to display the string at the*
   position defined by (column - (length of the string/ 2))

Function Definition: initcur

The **initcur** function saves the initial cursor character's starting and ending lines. The initcur function is used internally only by the cursoroff and cursoron functions. Its implementation is illustrated by the following pseudocode:

```
if (the initial values haven't been saved) {
    use the ROM BIOS to get the cursor values
    save the cursor character's starting line
    save the cursor character's ending line
}
```

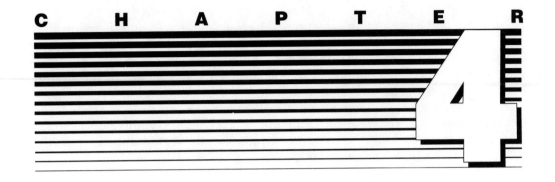

DYNAMIC WINDOW
FUNCTIONS

Chapters 2 and 3 present an assortment of low-level input/output functions. By using these low-level input/output functions as a set of basic building blocks, this chapter is able to present the C functions for dynamically opening and closing display screen windows. Additionally, this chapter features C functions for drawing windows, displaying horizontal and vertical scroll bars, moving blocks of memory, scrolling windows, and saving the initial display screen's contents. So you will better understand how these functions operate, a text window's components and the C dynamic memory management functions are discussed before the dynamic window function's source code is introduced.

A TEXT WINDOW'S COMPONENTS

Figure 4.1 illustrates the many components that are used to construct a text window. Because many of these components are optional features, a text window may only require a few key components to generate its desired appearance on the display screen. A more detailed explanation of these components is as follows:

- **Upper Left Coordinates and Lower Right Coordinates**: The upper left and lower right coordinates are used to define a text window's size and screen position. A text window can be as small as a single character or as large as the whole screen.

- **Border**: The WINDOWS toolbox supports both single-lined and double-lined window borders. **Note**: Borders are an optional text window component.

- **Horizontal Scroll Bar**: A horizontal scroll bar is used by the text window to indicate the cursor's current line position. Because a text window may not be wide enough to display an entire line, a horizontal scroll bar provides a very useful visual aide for indicating the displayed portion's relation to the whole line. **Note**: Horizontal scroll bars are an optional text window component.

- **Vertical Scroll Bar**: A vertical scroll bar is used by the text window to indicate the cursor's current file position. Because a text window may not be tall enough to display an entire file, a vertical scroll bar provides a useful visual aid for indicating the displayed portion's relation to the whole file. **Note**: Vertical scroll bars are an optional text window component.

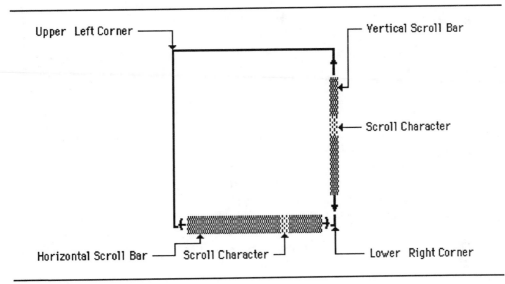

Figure 4.1   A text window

C DYNAMIC MEMORY MANAGEMENT FUNCTIONS

Before it actually displays a text window, the WINDOWS toolbox must first save the current text window's portion of the display screen. If the current contents of the text window are not saved, the WINDOWS toolbox would not be able to properly restore a closed text window's portion of the display screen. Because the WINDOWS operating environment can't possibly know in advance the number and size of an application program's windows, the WINDOWS toolbox makes extensive use of the C dynamic memory management functions to obtain and release text window buffer space.

The four most important C dynamic memory management functions are the malloc, calloc, realloc, and free functions. The **malloc** function is used to dynamically allocate a memory block. The following program demonstrates how malloc might be used to allocate space for a 100-element array of type int:

Example 4.1

```
#include <stdio.h>
#include <stdlib.h>

int *intarray;

main()
{
        /* Allocate space for a 100 element integer array */
        intarray = (int *)malloc(100 * sizeof(int));
        if (intarray == NULL)
                printf("Not enough memory to allocate the request array\n");
        else
                printf("A 100 element integer array has been allocated space\n");
        exit(0);
}
```

Example 4.1 illustrates that malloc returns a **NULL** pointer if it is unable to allocate an adequate amount of memory space; therefore, allocation errors can be easily trapped by performing a NULL pointer check.

The **calloc** function allocates a memory block for an array of n elements, each with a length of *size* bytes. Furthermore, each of the array elements is initialized with a value of zero. The program in Example 4.2 demonstrates how the calloc function might be used to allocate memory space for a 50-element array of type double:

Example 4.2

```
#include <stdio.h>
#include <stdlib.h>

double *dblarray;

main()
{
        /* Allocate memory space for 50 element double array */
        dblarray = (double *)calloc(50, sizeof(double));
        if (dblarray == NULL)
                printf("Insufficient memory space\n");
        else
                printf("Allocation was successfully completed\n");
        exit(0);
}
```

Like the malloc function, the calloc function returns a NULL pointer to indicate a memory space allocation error.

The **realloc** function changes the size of a previously allocated memory block. Furthermore, most C compilers will automatically call the malloc function if a NULL pointer is passed to the realloc function. Example 4.3 demonstrates how the realloc function might be used to change a previously allocated array's size:

Example 4.3

```
#include <stdio.h>
#include <stdlib.h>

int *intarray;

main()
{
        /* Allocate memory space for a 50 element integer array */
        intarray = (int *)malloc(50 * sizeof(int));
        if (intarray == NULL) {
                printf("Initial memory allocation failed\n");
                exit(0);
        }

        /* Reallocate the arrays memory space */
        intarray = (int *)realloc(intarray, 100 * sizeof(int));
        if (intarray == NULL)
                printf("The reallocation attempt failed\n");
        else
                printf("The reallocation was successful\n");
        exit(0);
}
```

Like the malloc and calloc functions, the realloc function returns a NULL pointer to indicate a memory allocation error.

The **free** function releases a previously allocated memory block. The program in Example 4.4 demonstrates how the free function might be used to deallocate a 25-element array of type float:

Example 4.4

```c
#include <stdio.h>
#include <stdlib.h>

float *fltarray;

main()
{
        /* Allocate space for the 25 element float array */
        fltarray = (float *)malloc(25 * sizeof(float));
        if (fltarray == NULL) {
                printf("Memory allocation failed\n");
                exit(1);
        }

        /* Release the array's allocated memory space */
        free(fltarray);
        exit(0);
}
```

With the dynamic memory management functions shown in Example 4.4 at its disposal, the WINDOWS toolbox can dynamically open and close text windows. Before it displays a text window, WINDOWS allocates a memory block large enough to hold the current contents of the text window. After successfully allocating the memory block, WINDOWS saves the text window's contents by using the savescreen function (see Chapter 2). When it is time to close the text window, WINDOWS restores the text window's former contents by using the restorescreen function (see Chapter 2). Redisplaying the former contents is followed by releasing the text window's dynamically allocated memory block.

SOURCE LISTING: window.c

Listing 4.1, **window.c**, presents the functions for dynamically opening and closing text windows, drawing text windows, displaying horizontal and vertical scroll bars, moving blocks of memory, scrolling text windows, and saving the initial display screen's contents.

Listing 4.1: window.c

```
/****************************************************************************
* window.c - For the WINDOWS Toolbox
*            Dynamic Window Routines
****************************************************************************/
#include <stdio.h>
#include <stdlib.h>
#ifndef ECOC88
#ifndef LATTICEC
#include <stdarg.h>
#endif
#endif
#include "windows.h"

static void reset_initial_video(void);

#ifdef WATCOMC
void draw_window(row1, col1, row2, col2, watt, bflg, ...)
#else
void draw_window(row1, col1, row2, col2, watt, bflg)
#endif
int row1, col1;
int row2, col2;
int watt;
int bflg;
{
    int batt;
    va_list arg_marker;

    va_start(arg_marker, bflg);
    clearscreen(row1, col1, row2, col2, watt);
    if (bflg != _NO_BORDER) {
        batt = va_arg(arg_marker, int);
        drawbox(row1, col1, row2, col2, bflg, batt);
    }
}
```

continued...

...from previous page

```
void draw_window(int, int, int, int, int, int, ...);

#ifdef WATCOMC
WINDOW *open_window(row1, col1, row2, col2, draw, ...)
#else
WINDOW *open_window(row1, col1, row2, col2, draw)
#endif
int row1, col1;
int row2, col2;
int draw;
{
    int watt, bflg, batt;
    va_list arg_marker;
    WINDOW *window;

    va_start(arg_marker, draw);
    window = malloc(sizeof(WINDOW));
    if (window == NULL) {
        printf("Not enough memory to open window\n");
        exit(1);
    }
    window->row1 = row1;
    window->col1 = col1;
    window->row2 = row2;
    window->col2 = col2;
    window->videoarray = malloc((col2 - col1 +1) * 2 * (row2 - row1 + 1));
    if (window->videoarray == NULL) {
        printf("Not enough memory to open window\n");
        exit(1);
    }
    savescreen(row1, col1, row2, col2, window->videoarray);
    if (draw) {
        watt = va_arg(arg_marker, int);
        bflg = va_arg(arg_marker, int);
        if (bflg == _NO_BORDER)
            draw_window(row1, col1, row2, col2, watt, _NO_BORDER);
```

continued...

...from previous page

```
        else {
            batt = va_arg(arg_marker, int);
            draw_window(row1, col1, row2, col2, watt, bflg, batt);
        }
    }
    return(window);
}


WINDOW *open_window(int, int, int, int, int, ...);

WINDOW *close_window(window)
WINDOW* window;
{
    if (window != NULL) {
    restorescreen(window->row1, window->col1, window->row2,
        window->col2, window->videoarray);
    free(window->videoarray);
    free(window);
    }
    return(NULL);
}


#ifdef DC88
#define DEFMEMMOVE
#endif

#ifdef LATTICEC
#define DEFMEMMOVE
#endif

#ifdef DEFMEMMOVE
static char *memmove(dst, src, n)
char *dst;
char *src;
unsigned int n;
{
```

continued...

...from previous page

```
    char *beg = src;

    if (src +n > dst) {
        src += n;
        dst += n;
        while (n--)
            *--dst = *--src;
    }
    else
        while (n--)
            *dst++ = *src++;
    return(beg);
}
#endif

void scroll_window(window, num, dir, att)
WINDOW *window;
int num;
int dir;
int att;
{
    int i, row1, col1, row2, col2, rows, cols;
    char *videoarray;

    switch (dir) {
        case _UP:
        case _DOWN:
        case _LEFT:
        case _RIGHT:
            row1 = window->row1 + 1;
            col1 = window->col1 + 1;
            row2 = window->row2 - 1;
            col2 = window->col2 - 1;
            break;
        case _UPA:
        case _DOWNA:
        case _LEFTA:
```

continued...

...from previous page

```
        case _RIGHTA:
                row1 = window->row1;
                col1 = window->col1;
                row2 = window->row2;
                col2 = window->col2;
    }
    cols = (col2 - col1 + 1) * 2;
    rows = row2 - row1 + 1;
    if ((videoarray = malloc(cols * rows)) == NULL) {
        printf("Not enough memory to allocate scroll buffer\n");
        exit(1);
    }
    savescreen(row1, col1, row2, col2, videoarray);
    switch (dir) {
        case _UP:
        case _UPA:
            for (i = row1 + num; i < row2 + 1; i++)
                memmove(videoarray + (i - num - row1) * cols,
                    videoarray + (i - row1) * cols, cols);
            break;
        case _DOWN:
        case _DOWNA:
            for (i = row2; i >= row1 + num; i--)
                memmove(videoarray + (i - row1) * cols,
                    videoarray + (i - num - row1) * cols, cols);
            break;
        case _LEFT:
        case _LEFTA:
            for (i = row1; i <= row2; i++)
                memmove(videoarray + (i - row1) * cols,
                    videoarray + (i - row1) * cols + num * 2,
                    cols - num * 2);
            break;
        default:
            for (i = row1; i <= row2; i++)
                memmove(videoarray + (i - row1) * cols + num * 2,
                    videoarray + (i - row1) * cols, cols - num * 2);
    }
```

continued...

...from previous page

```
        restorescreen(row1, col1, row2, col2, videoarray);
        if (att) {
            switch (dir) {
                case _UP:
                case _UPA:
                    clearscreen(row2 - num + 1, col1, row2, col2, att);
                    break;
                case _DOWN:
                case _DOWNA:
                    clearscreen(row1, col1, row1 + num - 1, col2, att);
                    break;
                case _LEFT:
                case _LEFTA:
                    clearscreen(row1, col2 - num + 1, row2, col2, att);
                    break;
                default:
                    clearscreen(row1, col1, row2, col1 + num - 1, att);
            }
        }
        free(videoarray);
}

void vertical_bar(window, current, total, att)
WINDOW *window;
int current;
int total;
int att;
{
        int marker;

        if (total == 0) {
            current = 0;
            total = 1;
        }
        fillone(window->row1 + 1, window->col2, 24, att);
        fillscreen(window->row1 + 2, window->col2, window->row2 - 2,
            window->col2, 177, att);
```

continued...

...from previous page

```
        fillone(window->row2 - 1, window->col2, 25, att);
        marker = (int)((long)(window->row2 - window->row1 - 4) * current / total
                + window->row1 + 2);
        fillone(marker, window->col2, 176, att);
}

void horizontal_bar(window, current, total, att)
WINDOW *window;
int current;
int total;
int att;
{
        int marker;

        if (total == 0) {
            current = 0;
            total = 1;
        }
        fillone(window->row2, window->col1 + 1, 27, att);
        fillscreen(window->row2, window->col1 + 2, window->row2,
            window->col2 - 2, 177, att);
        fillone(window->row2, window->col2 - 1, 26, att);
        marker = (int)((long)(window->col2 - window->col1 - 4) * current / total
                + window->col1 + 2);
        fillone(window->row2, marker, 176, att);
}

static WINDOW *window;
static int srow, scol, sstart, send;

void save_initial_video()
{
        settext80();
        getcurpos(&srow, &scol, &sstart, &send);
        cursoroff();
        window = open_window(1, 1, 25, 80, _DRAW, 7, _NO_BORDER);
        atexit(reset_initial_video);
}
```

continued...

...from previous page

```
static void reset_initial_video()
{
    close_window(window);
    setcurpos(srow, scol);
    setcursor(sstart, send);
}
```

Function Definition: draw_window

The **draw_window** function draws a text window onto the display screen. Its implementation is illustrated by the following pseudocode:

clear the text window's portion of the display screen
if (border is requested)
    draw the requested border type

Function Definition: open_window

The **open_window** function dynamically opens a text window. Its implementation is illustrated by the following pseudocode:

allocate memory for a WINDOW structure
if (memory allocation failed) {
    display an error message
    abort the program
}
save the window's coordinates
allocate a memory block for the window's current contents
if (memory allocation failed) {
    display an error message
    abort the program
}
save the window's current contents
if (draw window is requested)
    draw the window
return a pointer for the window's defining WINDOW structure

Function Definition: close_window

The **close_window** function closes a previously opened text window. Its implementation is illustrated by the following pseudocode:

```
if (window was previously allocated) {
    redisplay the window's former contents
    free the window's memory allocation
    free the window's WINDOW structure memory allocation
}
return a NULL pointer
```

Function Definition: memmove

The **memmove** function moves the contents of a memory area to another specified area of memory. Because the DeSmet DC88 C compiler's implementation of memmove doesn't function correctly and the Lattice C compiler doesn't provide a memmove function in its run-time library, the memmove function is conditionally compiled for the DeSmet DC88 and Lattice C compilers. The memmove function's implementation is illustrated by the following pseudocode:

```
if (end of the source area overlaps the destination) {
    point the source pointer to the end of its area
    point the destination pointer to the end of its area
    while (block move not done)
        decrement the pointers and move a byte
}
else {
    while (block move not done)
        move a byte and bump the pointers
}
return the starting source pointer
```

Function Definition: scroll_window

The **scroll_window** function scrolls the contents of a text window up, down, left, or right. Its implementation is illustrated by the following pseudocode:

```
get the text window's coordinates
allocate memory to buffer the text window's contents
if (memory allocation failed) {
    display an error message
    abort the program
}
move the text window's contents into the buffer
switch (direction) {
    case up:
        scroll the buffer up by the specified number of lines
    case down:
        scroll the buffer down by the specified number of lines
    case left:
        scroll the buffer left by the specified number of columns
    case right:
        scroll the buffer right by the specified number of columns
}
display the buffer's contents
if (clear the scrolled lines is requested) {
    switch (direction) {
        case up:
            clear the specified number of scroll lines at the text window's bottom
        case down:
            clear the specified number of scroll lines at the text window's top
        case left:
            clear the specified number of scroll columns at the text window's right
        case right:
            clear the specified number of scroll columns at the text window's left
    }
}
release the previously allocated buffer space
```

Function Definition: vertical_bar

The **vertical_bar** function displays a vertical scroll bar on the right side of a text window. Its implementation is illustrated by the following pseudocode:

```
trap any possible divide-by-zero errors
display an up arrow at the scroll bar's top
display the scroll bar's body
display a down arrow at the scroll bar's bottom
figure the scroll character's position
display the scroll character
```

Function Definition: horizontal_bar

The **horizontal_bar** function displays a horizontal scroll bar at the bottom of a text window. Its implementation is illustrated by the following pseudocode:

trap any possible divide-by-zero errors
display a left arrow at the beginning of the scroll bar
display the scroll bar's body
display a right arrow at the end of the scroll bar
figure the scroll character's position
display the scroll character

Function Definition: save_initial_video

The **save_initial_video** function initializes the WINDOWS operating environment, saves the initial cursor values, turns the cursor off, and saves the initial contents of the display screen. Its implementation is illustrated by the following pseudocode:

initialize the WINDOWS operating environment
get the cursor values
turn the cursor off
save and clear the display screen's contents by making it a text window
set up the reset_initial_video function call via the atexit() routine

Function Definition: reset_initial_video

The **reset_initial_video** function is used internally by the WINDOWS operating environment to restore the original display screen's values. A call to the **save_initial_video** function must occur before the WINDOWS operating environment can use the reset_initial_video function. The reset_initial_video function's implementation is illustrated by the following pseudocode:

restore the original display screen's contents by closing the previously opened text
    window
restore the original cursor position
restore the original cursor character's starting and ending lines

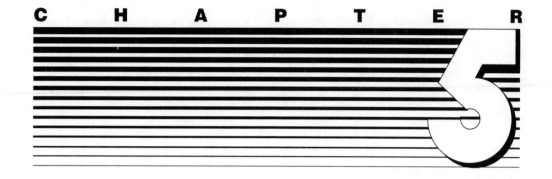

C H A P T E R 5

MENU FUNCTIONS

This chapter presents the WINDOWS toolbox menu functions. These menu functions implement three extremely useful menu types: pop-up menus, dialog box menus, and pull-down menus. Although other menu types do exist, these three are by far the most popular of the menu types found in today's state-of-the-art application programs. Not only do they increase operator efficiency, they also provide a much shorter training period for operators who are unfamiliar with an application program.

SOURCE LISTING: menus.c

Listing 5.1, **menus.c**, defines the global variables and a hotstring function used by all the WINDOWS menu functions. The global variable **_menu_att** is used by the menu functions as the default display attribute. The global variable **_menu_hotkey** is used by the menu functions as the display attribute for hotkey characters. The global variable **_menu_highlight** is used by the menu functions for highlighting a menu item.

Listing 5.1: menus.c

```
/*************************************************************************
* menus.c - For the WINDOWS Toolbox
*           Menu Global Variables and Functions
*************************************************************************/
#include "windows.h"

int _menu_att = 0x70, _menu_hotkey = 0x7f, _menu_highlight = 7;

void hotstring(row, col, hotkey, att, string)
int row;
int col;
int hotkey;
int att;
char *string;
{
    printstring(row, col, string);
    setone(row, col + hotkey, att);
}
```

POP-UP MENUS

Figure 5.1 illustrates a pop-up menu's components.

Figure 5.1   A pop-up menu

Essentially, a pop-up menu is a text window that lists a variety of possible menu selections. Following are more complete descriptions of a pop-up menu's components:

- **Menu Items**: A pop-up menu is composed of one or more menu items.

- **Highlighted Menu Item**: As Figure 5.1 illustrates, one of the menu's items will be highlighted. The highlighting can be moved from one item to the next by pressing either the Up Arrow key or Down Arrow key. The highlighted menu item can be selected by pressing the Enter key. Furthermore, help, if it's available, can be requested by pressing the F1 key.

- **Hotkeys**: Each of the pop-up menu items has an associated hotkey. Although Figure 5.1 shows the hotkeys as underlined characters (i.e., "S" for Save, "L" for Load, and "E" for Exit), a menu item's hotkey character will actually be displayed using a color different from the one used for the remainder of the menu item's characters. Selection of a pop-up menu item can be accomplished simply by pressing its corresponding hotkey.

SOURCE LISTING: popup.c

Listing 5.2, **popup.c**, presents the pop-up menu function.

Listing 5.2: popup.c

```
/*****************************************************************************
* popup.c - For the WINDOWS Toolbox
*           Popup Menu Routine
*****************************************************************************/
#include <stdio.h>
#include <stdlib.h>
#include <string.h>
#include "windows.h"

int popup(number, menu, row, col1)
int number;
MENU *menu;
int row;
int col1;
{
    int i, col2, key, flag = FALSE, mlen = 0, select, srow, scol;
    WINDOW *window1, *window2;

    getcurpos(&srow, &scol, &i, &key);
    if (i != 32) {
        flag = TRUE;
        cursoroff();
    }
    for (i = 0; i < number; i++)
        mlen = max(mlen, strlen(menu[i].string));
    mlen += 4;
    col1 -= mlen / 2;
    col2 = col1 + mlen - 1;
    window1 = open_window(row, col1, row + number + 1, col2,
        _DRAW, _menu_att, _SINGLE_LINE, _menu_att);
    for (i = 0; i < number; i++)
        hotstring(row + 1 + i, col1 + 2, menu[i].hotkey,
                _menu_hotkey, menu[i].string);
```

continued...

...from previous page

```
select = 0;
while (TRUE) {
     window2 = open_window(row + 1 + select, col1 + 1,
          row + 1 + select, col2 - 1, _NO_DRAW);
     setattrib(row + 1 + select, col1 + 1, row + 1 + select,
          col2 - 1, _menu_highlight);
     while (TRUE) {
          key = waitkey();
          switch (key) {
               case 13:
                    key = menu[select].string[menu[select].hotkey];
                    break;
               case 315:
                    if (menu[select].help != NULL)
                         (*menu[select].help)();
                    continue;
          }
          break;
     }
     window2 = close_window(window2);
     switch (key) {
          case 27:
               close_window(window1);
               setcurpos(srow, scol);
               if (flag)
                    cursoron();
               return(0);
          case 328:
               select = (--select + number) % number;
               continue;
          case 336:
               select = ++select % number;
               continue;
          default:
```

continued...

...from previous page

```
if (key > 31 && key < 128) {
        for (i = 0; i < number; i++) {
                if (toupper(key) == toupper(menu[i].string[menu[i].hotkey])) {
                        window1 = close_window(window1);
                        if (menu[i].function != NULL) {
                                (*menu[i].function)();
                                setcurpos(srow, scol);
                                if (flag)
                                        cursoron();
                                return(0);
                        }
                        setcurpos(srow, scol);
                        if (flag)
                                cursoron();
                        return(toupper(key));
                }
        }
    }
}
}
```

Function Definition: popup

The **popup** function implements pop-up style menus. Its implementation is illustrated by the following pseudocode:

get the current cursor values
if (cursor is on)
    turn the cursor off
figure the menu's width
figure the menu's left column
figure the menu's right column
open a text window for the menu
for (i = 0; i < number of menu items; i++) {
    display a menu item
}

continued...

...from previous page

```
highlighted menu item = first menu item
while (TRUE) {
    open a text window to save the highlighted menu item
    highlight the highlighted menu item
    while (TRUE) {
        get a key
        switch (key) {
            case ENTER:
                key = highlighted menu item's hotkey
                break
            case F1:
                call the highlighted menu item's help function
                continue
        }
        break
    }
    restore the highlighted menu item's appearance by closing its text window
    switch (key) {
        case ESC:
            erase the pop-up menu by closing its text window
            restore the cursor to its previous state
            return(0)
        case UP ARROW:
            move the highlighting up to the previous menu item
            continue
        case DOWN ARROW:
            move the highlighting down to the next menu item
            continue
        default:
            if (key is a printable character) {
                for (i = 0; i < number of items; i++) {
                    if (key = menu item[i]'s hotkey) {
                        erase the menu by closing its text window
                        if (function != NULL) {
                            call the function
                            restore the cursor values
                            return(0)
                        }
                        restore the cursor values
                        return(menu item's hotkey)
                    }
                }
            }
    }
}
```

DIALOG BOX MENUS

Figure 5.2 illustrates a dialog box menu's components.

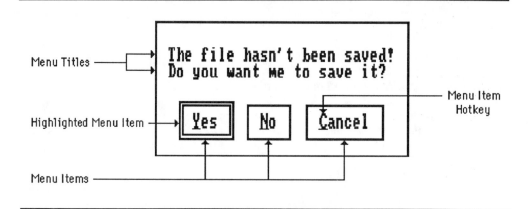

Figure 5.2   A dialog box menu

Basically, a dialog box menu is a text window that either displays a statement or asks a question, or both. In response, the operator must choose from a relatively short list of menu items. Following are more complete descriptions of a dialog box menu's components:

- **Titles**: A dialog box menu always has one or more titles. These titles are used to either display a statement or ask a question, or both.

- **Menu Items**: In addition to the titles, a dialog box menu will always have one or more menu items.

- **Highlighted Menu Item**: As Figure 5.2 illustrates, one of the dialog box menu's items will be highlighted. The highlighting can be moved from one menu item to the next by pressing the Left Arrow or Right Arrow keys. The highlighted menu items can be selected by pressing the Enter key.

- **Hotkeys:** Each of the dialog box menu items has an associated hotkey. Although Figure 5.2 shows the hotkeys as underlined characters (i.e., "Y" for Yes, "N" for No, and "C" for Cancel), a menu item's hotkey character will actually be displayed in a color different from the one used for the remainder of the menu item's characters. Selection of a dialog box menu item is accomplished simply by pressing its corresponding hotkey.

SOURCE LISTING: dialog.c

Listing 5.3, **dialog.c,** presents the dialog box menu function.

Listing 5.3: dialog.c

```
/****************************************************************************
* dialog.c - For the WINDOWS Toolbox
*            Dialog Box Menu Routine
****************************************************************************/
#include <stdio.h>
#include <stdlib.h>
#include <string.h>
#ifndef ECOC88
#ifndef LATTICEC
#include <stdarg.h>
#endif
#endif
#include "windows.h"

#ifdef WATCOMC
int dialog_menu(row, col, nchoices, menu, ntitles, ...)
#else
int dialog_menu(row, col, nchoices, menu, ntitles)
#endif
int row;
int col;
int nchoices;
MENU *menu;
int ntitles;
```

continued...

...from previous page

```
{
    int i, j, key, row1, col1, row2, col2, flag = FALSE, mlen = 0, chlen;
    int srow, scol, *tabs, select;
    char **titles;
    WINDOW *window;
    va_list arg_marker;

    getcurpos(&srow, &scol, &i, &key);
    if (i != 32) {
        flag = TRUE;
        cursoroff();
    }
    if ((titles = malloc(ntitles * sizeof(char *))) == NULL ||
            (tabs = malloc(nchoices * sizeof(int))) == NULL) {
        printf("Out of Memory\n");
        exit(1);
    }
    va_start(arg_marker, ntitles);
    for (i = 0; i < ntitles; i++) {
        titles[i] = va_arg(arg_marker, char *);
        mlen = max(mlen, strlen(titles[i]));
    }
    chlen = nchoices - 1;
    for (i = 0; i < nchoices; i++)
        chlen += strlen(menu[i].string) + 4;
    mlen = max(mlen, chlen);
    row1 = row - (ntitles + 7) / 2;
    row2 = row1 + ntitles + 6;
    col1 = col - (mlen + 4) / 2;
    col2 = col1 + mlen + 3;
    window = open_window(row1, col1, row2, col2, _DRAW, _menu_att,
        _SINGLE_LINE, _menu_att);
    for (i = 0; i < ntitles; i++)
        printcenter(row1 + i + 2, col, titles[i]);
    j = col - chlen / 2;
    for (i = 0; i < nchoices; i++) {
        tabs[i] = j;
```

continued...

...from previous page

```
        if (!i)
            drawbox(row2 - 3, j, row2 - 1,
                    j + strlen(menu[i].string) + 3,
                    _DOUBLE_LINE, _menu_att);
        else
            drawbox(row2 - 3, j, row2 - 1,
                    j + strlen(menu[i].string) + 3,
                    _SINGLE_LINE, _menu_att);
        hotstring(row2 - 2, j + 2, menu[i].hotkey,
            _menu_hotkey, menu[i].string);
        j += strlen(menu[i].string) + 5;
    }
    select = 0;
    while (TRUE) {
        if ((key = waitkey()) == 13)
            key = menu[select].string[menu[select].hotkey];
        switch (key) {
            case 331:
                if (nchoices != 1) {
                    drawbox(row2 - 3, tabs[select], row2 - 1,
                        tabs[select] + strlen(menu[select].string) + 3,
                        _SINGLE_LINE, _menu_att);
                    select = (--select + nchoices) % nchoices;
                    drawbox(row2 - 3, tabs[select], row2 - 1,
                        tabs[select] + strlen(menu[select].string) + 3,
                        _DOUBLE_LINE, _menu_att);
                }
                continue;
            case 333:
                if (nchoices != 1) {
                    drawbox(row2 - 3, tabs[select], row2 - 1,
                        tabs[select] + strlen(menu[select].string) + 3,
                        _SINGLE_LINE, _menu_att);
                    select = ++select % nchoices;
                    drawbox(row2 - 3, tabs[select], row2 - 1,
                        tabs[select] + strlen(menu[select].string) + 3,
                        _DOUBLE_LINE, _menu_att);
                }
                continue;
```

continued...

...from previous page

```
default:
    if (key > 31 && key < 128) {
        for (i = 0; i < nchoices; i++) {
            if (toupper(key) == toupper(menu[i].string[menu[i].hotkey])) {
                close_window(window);
                free(titles);
                free(tabs);
                if (menu[i].function != NULL) {
                    (*menu[i].function)();
                    setcurpos(srow, scol);
                    if (flag)
                        cursoron();
                    return(0);
                }
                setcurpos(srow, scol);
                if (flag)
                    cursoron();
                return(toupper(key));
            }
        }
    }
}
```

Function Definition: dialog_menu

The **dialog_menu** function implements dialog box style menus. Its implementation is illustrated by the following pseudocode:

get the current cursor values
if (cursor is on)
    turn the cursor off
allocate memory for an array of title string pointers and an array of menu item tab
    positions
if (insufficient memory) {
    display an error message
    abort the program
}
set the title pointers
figure the menu's width
figure the menu's top row
figure the menu's bottom row
figure the menu's left column
figure the menu's right column
open up a text window for the menu
for (i = 0; i < number of titles; i++) {
    display a title
}
for (i = 0; i < number of items; i++) {
    save the menu item's tab position
    if (first menu item)
        draw a highlight box
    else
        draw a regular box
    display the menu item
    figure the next tab position
}
highlighted menu item = first menu item
while (TRUE) {
    get a key
    if (key == ENTER)
        key = highlighted menu item's hotkey
    switch (key) {
        case LEFT ARROW:
            move highlight left to the previous menu item
            continue
        case RIGHT ARROW:
            move highlight right to the next menu item
            continue

    continued...

...from previous page

```
default:
    if (key is a printable character) {
        for (i = 0; i  number of items; i + +) {
            if (key = = menu item[i]'s hotkey) {
                erase the menu by closing its text window
                deallocate the array of title pointers
                deallocate the array of tab positions
                if (function ! = NULL) {
                    call the item's function
                    restore the cursor values
                    return(0)
                }
                restore the cursor values
                return(menu item's hotkey)
            }
        }
    }
}
}
```

PULL-DOWN MENUS

Pull-down menus are the menu system of choice among today's programmers and operators. Although a lot goes into creating a pull-down menu system, all pull-down menu systems are composed of two basic components: the pull-down menu bar and the associated pull-down menus.

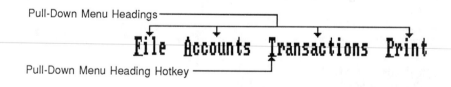

Figure 5.3   A pull-down menu bar

Figure 5.3 illustrates a pull-down menu bar's components. Following is a more complete description of these components:

- **Pull-down Menu Headings**: A pull-down menu bar is made up of one or more pull-down menu headings. Essentially, a pull-down menu heading categorizes its corresponding pull-down menu's items.

- **Hotkeys**: Each of the pull-down menu headings has an associated hotkey. Although Figure 5.3 shows the hotkeys as underlined characters (i.e., "F" for File, "A" for Accounts, "T" for Transactions, and "P" for Print), a pull-down menu heading's hotkey character will actually be displayed in a color different from the one used for the remainder of the pull-down menu heading's characters. Pulling a menu down is accomplished simply by pressing its corresponding hotkey.

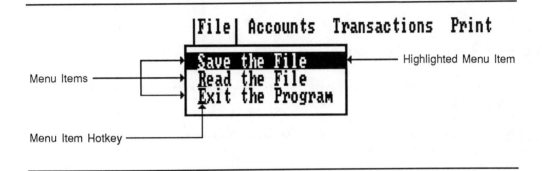

Figure 5.4   A pull-down menu

When a pull-down menu is pulled down, its appearance is similar to that of a pop-up menu. Figure 5.4 illustrates a pull-down menu's components. Following are more complete descriptions of these components:

- **Menu Items**: A pull-down menu is composed of one or more menu items.

- **Highlighted Menu Item**: In Figure 5.4, one of the pull-down menu's items is highlighted. The highlighting can be moved from one menu item to the next by pressing either the Up Arrow key or the Down Arrow key. The highlighted menu item can be selected by pressing the Enter key. Furthermore, help, if it's available, can be requested by pressing the F1 key.

- **Hotkeys:** Each of the pull-down menu items has an associated hotkey. Although Figure 5.4 illustrates the hotkeys as underlined characters (i.e., "S" for Save, "R" for Read, and "E" for Exit), a pull-down menu item's hotkey character will actually be displayed in a color different from the one used for the remainder of the pull-down menu item's characters. Selection of a pull-down menu item can be accomplished simply by pressing its corresponding hotkey.

SOURCE LISTING: pulldown.c

Listing 5.4, **pulldown.c,** presents the WINDOWS pull-down menu functions.

Listing 5.4: pulldown.c

```
/*****************************************************************************
* pulldown.c - For the WINDOWS Toolbox
*              Pulldown Menu Routines
*****************************************************************************/
#include <stdio.h>
#include <dos.h>
#include <stdlib.h>
#include <string.h>
#include "windows.h"

static int srow, scol, flag, *columns;
static char *hotkeys;
static MENU_HEAD *cptr;

void pulldown_bar(number, head, row)
int number;
MENU_HEAD *head;
int row;
{
    int i, col;
```

continued...

...from previous page

```
flag = FALSE;
getcurpos(&srow, &scol, &i, &col);
if (i != 32) {
    flag = TRUE;
    cursoroff();
}
if (cptr != head) {
    clearscreen(row, 1, row, 80, _menu_att);
    col = 3;
    for (i = 0; i < number; i++) {
        if (columns == NULL) {
            if ((columns = malloc(number * sizeof(int))) == NULL) {
                printf("Out of Memory\n");
                exit(1);
            }
        }
        else {
            if ((columns = realloc(columns, number * sizeof(int))) ==
                NULL) {
                printf("Out of Memory\n");
                exit(1);
            }
        }
        if (hotkeys == NULL) {
            if ((hotkeys = malloc((number + 1) * sizeof(char))) == NULL) {
                printf("Out of Memory\n");
                exit(1);
            }
        }
        else {
            if ((hotkeys = realloc(hotkeys, (number + 1) * sizeof(char)))
                == NULL) {
                printf("Out of Memory\n");
                exit(1);
            }
        }
```

continued...

...from previous page

```
                columns[i] = col;
                hotkeys[i] = toupper(head[i].heading[head[i].hotkey]);
                hotstring(row, col, head[i].hotkey, _menu_hotkey, head[i].heading);
                col += strlen(head[i].heading) + 2;
            }
            hotkeys[number] = '\0';
            cptr = head;
        }
        setcurpos(srow, scol);
        if (flag)
            cursoron();
    }


int pulldown(number, head, row, ikey, menu_help)
int number;
MENU_HEAD *head;
int row;
int ikey;
void (*menu_help)();
{
    int i, key, col, menu, rcol, select;
    char *match;
    MENU *mptr;
    WINDOW *window1, *window2;
    static char alts[27] = "QWERTYUIOPASDFGHJKLZXCVBNM";

    pulldown_bar(number, head, row);
    key = ikey ? ikey : waitkey();
    if (menu_help != NULL && key == 315) {
        cursoroff();
        (*menu_help)();
        setcurpos(srow, scol);
        if (flag)
            cursoron();
        return(0);
    }
```

continued...

...from previous page

```
if (key >= 272 && key <= 281)
    menu = alts[key - 272];
else {
    if (key >= 286 && key <= 294)
        menu = alts[key - 276];
    else {
        if (key >= 300 && key <= 306)
            menu = alts[key - 281];
        else
            return(key);
    }
}
if (!(match = strchr(hotkeys, menu)))
    return(key);
cursoroff();
menu = match - hotkeys;
while (TRUE) {
    mptr = head[menu].mptr;
    col = columns[menu];
    rcol = strlen(head[menu].heading);
    for (i = 0; i < head[menu].number; i++)
        rcol = max(rcol, strlen(mptr[i].string));
    rcol += col + 1;
    window1 = open_window(row, col - 2, row + 2 + head[menu].number,
        rcol, _NO_DRAW);
    draw_window(row + 1, col - 2, row + 2 + head[menu].number,
        rcol, _menu_att, _SINGLE_LINE, _menu_att);
    printone(row, col - 1, 0xb3);
    printone(row, col + strlen(head[menu].heading), 0xb3);
    printone(row + 1, col - 1, 0xc1);
    printone(row + 1, col + strlen(head[menu].heading), 0xc1);
    for (i = 0; i < head[menu].number; i++)
            hotstring(row + 2 + i, col, mptr[i].hotkey,
                _menu_hotkey, mptr[i].string);
    select = 0;
    while (TRUE) {
        window2 = open_window(row + 2 + select, col - 1,
            row + 2 + select, rcol - 1, _NO_DRAW);
```

continued...

...from previous page

```
setattrib(row + 2 + select, col - 1, row + 2 + select,
    rcol - 1, _menu_highlight);
while (TRUE) {
    key = waitkey();
    switch (key) {
        case 13:
            key = mptr[select].string[mptr[select].hotkey];
            break;
        case 315:
            if (mptr[select].help != NULL)
                (*mptr[select].help)();
            continue;
    }
    break;
}
window2 = close_window(window2);
switch (key) {
    case 27:
        window1 = close_window(window1);
        setcurpos(srow, scol);
        if (flag)
            cursoron();
        return(0);
    case 328:
        select = (--select + head[menu].number) %
            head[menu].number;
        continue;
    case 331:
        window1 = close_window(window1);
        menu = (--menu + number) % number;
        break;
    case 333:
        window1 = close_window(window1);
        menu = ++menu % number;
        break;
    case 336:
        select = ++select % head[menu].number;
        continue;
```

continued...

...from previous page

```
            default:
                if (key > 31 && key < 128) {
                    for (i = 0; i < head[menu].number; i++) {
                        if (toupper(key) == toupper(mptr[i].string[mptr[i].hotkey]))
{
                            window1 = close_window(window1);
                            (*mptr[i].function)();
                            setcurpos(srow, scol);
                            if (flag)
                                cursoron();
                            return(0);
                        }
                    }
                }
                continue;
        }
        break;
    }
}
}
```

Function Definition: pulldown_bar

The **pulldown_bar** function displays pull-down menu bars. Its implementation is illustrated by the following pseudocode:

get the cursor values
if (cursor is on)
    turn the cursor off
if (the pull-down menu isn't the same as the last one) {
    clear the menu bar's row
    for (i = 0; i < number of headings; i++) {
        reallocate the array of hotkeys
        if (the reallocation failed) {
            display an error message
            abort the program
        }
        save the heading's hotkey
        display the menu heading
    }
    flag the end of the hotkey string
    save the pull-down menu pointer
}
restore the cursor values

Function Definition: pulldown

The **pulldown** function implements the pull-down menu system. Its implementation is illustrated by the following pseudocode:

display the menu bar
if (an initial key was passed)
    key = initial key
else
    key = next key pressed
*if (key isn't an **ALT** key)*
    return(key)
if (key isn't a heading hotkey)
    return(key)
turn off the cursor
menu = hotkey menu
while (TRUE) {
    figure the menu's width
    open a text window for the menu
    draw the menu's window
    draw the rest of the menu's frame

    continued...

...from previous page

```
for (i = 0; i < number of menu items; i + +) {
    display a menu item
}
highlighted menu item = first menu item
while (TRUE) {
    open a text window to save the highlighted menu item
    highlight the highlighted menu item
    while (TRUE) {
        get a key
        switch (key) {
            case ENTER:
                key = highlighted menu item's hotkey
                break;
            case F1:
                call the highlighted menu item's help function
                continue
        }
        break
    }
    restore the highlighted menu item's appearance by closing its text window
    switch (key) {
        case ESC:
            erase the pull-down menu by closing its text window
            restore the cursor values
            return(0)
        case UP ARROW:
            move the highlighting up to the previous menu item
            continue
        case LEFT ARROW:
            erase the pull-down menu by closing its text window
            heading hotkey = previous heading's hotkey
            break
        case RIGHT ARROW:
            erase the pull-down menu by closing its text window
            heading hotkey = next heading's hotkey
            break
        case DOWN ARROW:
            move the highlighting down to the next menu item
            continue
```

continued...

...from previous page

```
default:
    if (key is printable) {
        for (i = 0; i < number of items; i + +) {
            if (key = = menu item[i]'s hotkey) {
                erase the pull-down menu y closing its text window
                call the item's function
                restore the cursor values
                return(0)
            }
        }
    }
    continue
}
break
    }
}
```

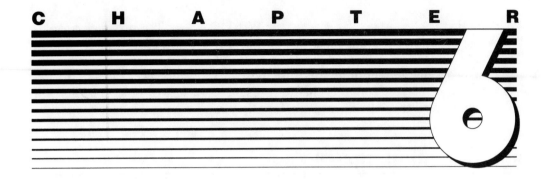

ERROR-HANDLING FUNCTIONS

To maintain the elegant display screens the WINDOWS toolbox provides, a WIN-DOWS application program must not permit any uncontrolled display output. The chief causes of uncontrolled display output are run-time errors, hardware errors, and program interruptions. Because these three occurrences can wreak total havoc with a display screen, this chapter presents a variety of functions that will effectively trap all three belligerents before they can do any serious damage.

RUN-TIME ERROR TRAPPING

Although it is practically impossible for a program to trap every type of run-time error that can occur, a well thought out application program should have no trouble dealing with all but the most esoteric of run-time errors. Such problems as divide-by-zero and file-handling errors can be effectively trapped with considerable ease. Divide-by-zero errors can be trapped simply by having the application perform divisor checks before carrying out any division operations. File-handling errors, such as the inability to locate a file, can usually be handled by displaying an appropriate error message and having the operator try the operation again. In addition to file-handling errors, there are a host of other run-time problems that can be easily handled simply by telling the operator that an error has occurred. Accordingly, the WINDOWS toolbox provides an error-handling function for displaying error messages.

HARDWARE ERROR TRAPPING

Although most run-time errors can be effectively handled with an appropriate error message, hardware error handling is a much more difficult task to implement effectively. Whenever a hardware error occurs, MS-DOS calls the INT 24H critical error handler. On entry to the INT 24H critical error handler, MS-DOS will indicate the error device type by setting bit seven of register AH for nondisk errors or clearing bit seven of register AH for disk input/output errors; registers BP:SI will point to the error device's header control block; and the lower byte of register DI will hold one of the following error codes:

Error Code	Error Type
00H	Write-protect error
01H	Unknown unit
02H	Drive not ready
03H	Unknown command
04H	Data error
05H	Bad request structure length
06H	Seek error
07H	Unknown media type
08H	Sector not found
09H	Printer out of paper
0AH	Write fault
0BH	Read fault
0CH	General failure

Essentially, the critical error handler must decide to ignore the error, retry the error-causing operation, or terminate the program. Once a decision is made, the critical error handler passes the decision back to MS-DOS by returning one of the following values in register AL:

Decision Code	Action to Be Taken
00H	Ignore the error
01H	Retry the operation
02H	Terminate the program through the [Ctrl/C] handler (INT 23H)

Although MS-DOS provides a default INT 24H critical error handler, it is totally unsuitable for the WINDOWS operating environment. Its unsuitability stems from its offensive habit of displaying the **Abort, Retry, Ignore?** message as part of its error trapping routine. Figure 6.1 illustrates the destruction this message might cause if a drive door was inadvertently left open by the operator. Obviously, the WINDOWS display screen is ruined by the critical error handler's message.

Pull-Down Menu Bar Overlayed by the MS-DOS Hardware Error Handler ─────┐

```
Not ready error reading drive A Print◄┘
Abort, Retry, Ignore?
```

Figure 6.1   The MS-DOS hardware error handler

Because the MS-DOS critical error handler is so incompatible with the WIN-DOWS operating environment, WINDOWS must be able to provide its own INT 24H critical error-handling routine. Fortunately, some C compilers provide the _harderr and _hardresume functions (these functions may also be called harderr and hardresume by some compilers), which provide an effective means for setting up an INT 24H critical error handler. Basically, the _harderr function is used by an application program to pass the address of the new INT 24H critical error handler to MS-DOS. Because the WINDOWS INT 24H critical error handler is called **error_handler**, its address can be easily passed to MS-DOS by executing a _harderr(error_handler); function call. With its address passed to MS-DOS, the error_handler function will effectively handle all critical errors by displaying a dialog box menu on the screen. This dialog box menu asks the operator to make a decision about how the error situation should be resolved. The error_handler function will then pass the operator's decision back to MS-DOS via the _hardresume function.

SOURCE LISTING: error.c

Listing 6.1, **error.c**, defines the WINDOWS error-handling functions. Because many of the C compilers that WINDOWS supports don't offer the _harderr and _hardresume functions in their run-time libraries, the error_handler function is conditionally compiled only for the C compilers that support the INT 24H related library functions.

Listing 6.1: error.c

```c
/***************************************************************************
* error.c - For the WINDOWS Toolbox
*           Error Handling Routines
***************************************************************************/
#include <stdio.h>
#include <dos.h>
#include "windows.h"

void display_error(string)
char *string;
{
    static MENU menu[] = {"OK"} ;

    dialog_menu(13, 40, 1, menu, 1, string);
}


#ifdef HARDERROR
#ifdef MICROSOFTC
void far error_handler(unsigned deverror, unsigned errcode, unsigned far *devhdr)
#define ERRORCODE errcode
#else
void far error_handler(unsigned error, unsigned ax, unsigned bp, unsigned si)
#define ERRORCODE error
#endif
{
    static char *errors[13] = {
        {"Attempt to write to a write-protected disk"},
        {"Unknown unit"},
        {"Drive not ready"},
        {"Unknown command"},
        {"CRC error in data"},
        {"Bad drive-request structure length"},
        {"Seek error"},
        {"Unknown media type"},
        {"Sector not found"},
        {"Printer out of paper"},
        {"Write fault"},
        {"Read fault"},
        {"General failure"} };
```

continued...

...from previous page

```
static MENU menu[3] = { {"Ignore the error", 0, NULL},
    {"Retry the operation", 0, NULL},
    {"Abort the program", 0, NULL} };

switch (dialog_menu(13, 40, 3, menu, 1, errors[ERRORCODE])) {
    case 'I':
        _hardresume(_HARDERR_IGNORE);
    case 'R':
        _hardresume(_HARDERR_RETRY);
    case 'A':
        _hardresume(_HARDERR_ABORT);
    }
}
#endif
```

Function Definition: display_error

The **display_error** function uses the **dialog_menu** function to display an error message. Its implementation is illustrated by the following pseudocode:

call dialog_menu to display the error message and wait for the response

Function Definition: error_handler

The **error_handler** function is an INT 24H critical error handler. To perform its intended function, the error_handler function's address must be passed to MS-DOS via a _harderr function call. The error_handler function's implementation is illustrated by the following pseudocode:

display an error message and get the operator's response via a dialog box menu
return(the appropriate decision code)

[CTRL/C] AND [CTRL/BREAK] TRAPPING

Whenever either the **[Ctrl/C]** or the **[Ctrl/Break]** key combination is pressed, MS-DOS calls its INT 23H [Ctrl/C] handler. By default, the MS-DOS INT 23H [Ctrl/C] handler will cause an application program to abort to MS-DOS. Although a program abort might not be a very important event for some programs, aborting application programs that have open data files could lead to disastrous consequences. To correct this situation, some C compilers supply their own INT 23H [Ctrl/C] handler. In the case of Power C, the INT 23H [Ctrl/C] handler ignores all [Ctrl/C] interruptions. Thus, ill-timed program aborts are completely eliminated. Unfortunately, most C compilers take the attitude that the programmer is on his own when it comes to [Ctrl/C] handling. Luckily, developing an INT 23H [Ctrl/C] handler is a fairly simple task.

As mentioned above, MS-DOS traps [Ctrl/C] and [Ctrl/Break] key combinations by calling the INT 23H [Ctrl/C] handler. Upon return from this handler, MS-DOS will terminate the currently executing application program if the carry flag is set; otherwise, MS-DOS will return control back to the application program. Therefore, a user-developed INT 23H [Ctrl/C] handler only needs to return with a cleared carry flag to eliminate unwanted program terminations. The following is a simple INT 23H [Ctrl/C] handler that clears the carry flag:

Example 6.1

```
void interrupt far ctrl_c_handler(es, ds, di, si, bp, sp, bx,
    dx, cx, ax, ip,   cs, flags)
unsigned es, ds, di, si, bp, sp, bx, dx, cx, ax, ip, cs, flags;
{
    flags &= 0xfffe;
}
```

To set up the **ctrl_c_handler** function as the new INT 23H [Ctrl/C] handler, an application program must pass its address by performing a **_dos_setvect(0x23, ctrl_c_handler);** function call. This function call will replace the current INT 23H [Ctrl/C] handler's address with ctrl_c_handler's address.

Although it would be logical to assume that the former INT 23H [Ctrl/C] handler's address should be saved and then restored at program termination, MS-DOS relieves the application program of this responsibility by automatically saving the current INT 23H [Ctrl/C] handler's address before executing an application program. Upon termination of the application program, MS-DOS automatically restores INT 23H to its previous handler. Thus, the application program is relieved of the responsibility for restoring the INT 23H [Ctrl/C] handler.

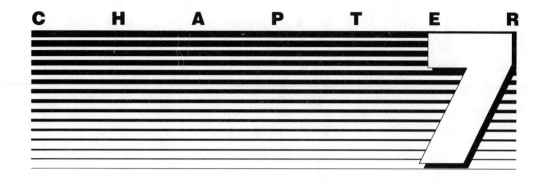

C H A P T E R

7

SIMPLE LEDGER

The previous six chapters have been devoted to constructing the WINDOWS tool-box. To show you how the WINDOWS toolbox is used in an actual application program's implementation, this chapter presents a sample WINDOWS application program called SIMPLE LEDGER. As its name implies, SIMPLE LEDGER is a rudimentary general ledger accounting system. Although its features are quite basic, SIMPLE LEDGER can be used to successfully maintain a general ledger for almost any small business.

SIMPLE LEDGER ACCOUNT CLASSIFICATIONS

Even though the WINDOWS toolbox makes SIMPLE LEDGER a fairly uncom-plicated program to operate, an elementary understanding of accounting is re-quired to put the program into practical use. Furthermore, the SIMPLE LEDGER account classifications must be understood to properly build a general ledger's chart of accounts. Figure 7.1 illustrates how SIMPLE LEDGER breaks down a general ledger's accounts into ten distinct classifications. Although these ten classifications are fairly straightforward, the **Beginning Inventories** and **Ending Inventories** classifications require some clarification.

To correctly determine the cost of goods sold on an income statement, SIMPLE LEDGER needs to know both the starting value and the ending value for a business's inventories. Accordingly, SIMPLE LEDGER requires the operator to maintain two separate accounts for each of the business's inventories. Although this duplication of inventory accounts may seem to be an unacceptable account-ing practice, SIMPLE LEDGER knows which inventory figure is appropriate for a particular financial report; therefore, the equality of debits and credits is never corrupted by SIMPLE LEDGER's use of duplicate inventory accounts.

Number Range	Account Type	Examples
10000 - 17999	Current Asset	Cash, Accounts Receivable, Marketable Securities, etc.
18000 - 18999	Beginning Inventory	Merchandise Inventory, Raw Materials, Unfinished Goods, Finished Goods, etc.
19000 - 19999	Ending Inventory	Merchandise Inventory, Raw Materials, Unfinished Goods, Finished Goods, etc.
20000 - 29999	Plant Asset	Land, Buildings, Equipment, etc.
30000 - 39999	Current Liability	Accounts Payable, Notes Payable, etc.
40000 - 49999	Long-Term Liability	Notes Payable, Mortgage Payable, etc.
50000 - 59999	Capital	Capital, Common Stock, Treasury Stock, Preferred Stock, etc.
60000 - 69999	Revenue	Sales, Sales Discounts, Sales Allowances, etc.
70000 - 79999	Purchases	Purchases, Purchases Discounts, etc.
80000 - 89999	Expense	Wages, Salaries, Utilities, Travel, etc.
90000 - 99999	Other Revenue or Expense	Interest, Income Taxes, Cash Short and Over, etc.

Figure 7.1   SIMPLE LEDGER account classifications

SOURCE LISTING: ledger.c

Listing 7.1, **ledger.c**, is the source code for SIMPLE LEDGER. This demonstration program illustrates many of functions that are found in the WINDOWS toolbox: pull-down menus for program navigation, extensive use of windows for screen displays, and dialog box menus for operator prompts. Additionally, ledger.c features a number of data entry routines you may find useful for inclusion in your own application programs.

Listing 7.1: ledger.c

```c
/***************************************************************************
* ledger.c - For the WINDOWS Toolbox
*            SIMPLE LEDGER - A Demonstration Program
***************************************************************************/
#include <stdio.h>
#include <stdlib.h>
#include <string.h>
#ifndef DC88
#include <time.h>
#else
#include <math.h>
#endif

#include "windows.h"

#define print_cr() report_line[0] = '\0';\
                print_line()

typedef struct {
    long number;
    char name[31];
    double balance;
} ACCOUNT;

typedef struct {
    long acct_no;
    char date[9], description[31];
    double amount;
} TRANSACTION;

void ol_func(void);
void cl_func(void);
void ep_func(void);
void ea_func(void);
void et_func(void);
void ca_func(void);
void tb_func(void);
void glar_func(void);
```

continued...

...from previous page

```
void fs_func(void);
void ea_func(void);
void et_func(void);
int inputstring(int, int, int, int, char *);
int inputdollars(int, int, int, int, double *);
int inputnumber(int, int, int, int, long *);
void setbit(char *, int);
void resetbit(char *, int);
int testbit(char *, int);
int nextbit(char *, int);
int compare(ACCOUNT *, ACCOUNT *);
void savenums(void);
void saveaccts(void);
void savetrans(void);
void start_report(void);
void print_heading(void);
void print_line(void);
double print_accounts(long, long, int);

static MENU file[] = {
    {"Open a Ledger", 0, ol_func},
    {"Close a Ledger", 0, cl_func},
    {"Exit the Program", 0, ep_func} };

static MENU print[] = {
    {"Print a Chart of Accounts", 8, ca_func},
    {"Print a Trial Balance", 8, tb_func},
    {"Print a General Ledger Activity Report", 8, glar_func},
    {"Print the Financial Statements", 10, fs_func} };

static MENU_HEAD heads[] = {
    {"File", 0, 3, file},
    {"Print", 0, 4, print} };

static char company_name[31], report_title[81], report_line[81];
static int num_accts, num_trans, gen_att = 0x70;
static int report_page, report_lines;
static ACCOUNT account[100];
static TRANSACTION transaction[200];
```

continued...

...from previous page

```
static char cnname[13], aname[13], tname[13];
static WINDOW *rwindow;
FILE *cname, *accounts, *transactions;

main(int argc, char *argv[])
{
    int number;
    boolean mono = FALSE;

    printf(" ");
    setcursor(6, 7);
    save_initial_video();
    if (argc == 2) {
        if (toupper(argv[1][0]) == 'B')
            mono = TRUE;
    }
    if (!mono) {
        _menu_att = 0x30;
        _menu_hotkey = 0x34;
        _menu_highlight = 0x47;
        gen_att = 0x17;
    }
    pulldown_bar(2, heads, 1);
    hotstring(1, 16, 0, _menu_hotkey, "Accounts");
    hotstring(1, 26, 0, _menu_hotkey, "Transactions");
    clearscreen(25, 1, 25, 80, _menu_att);
    while (TRUE) {
        printcenter(25, 40, company_name);
        switch (pulldown(2, heads, 1, 0, NULL)) {
            case 0:
                if (rwindow != NULL)
                    close_window(rwindow);
                break;
            case 286:
                number = num_accts;
                ea_func();
                if (num_accts || number) {
                    savenums();
                    saveaccts();
                }
                break;
```

continued...

...from previous page

```
                case 276:
                        number = num_trans;
                        et_func();
                        if (num_trans || number) {
                                savenums();
                                savetrans();
                        }
                }
        }
}

void ol_func(void)
{
    char string[9], title[31];
    WINDOW *window;
    static MENU menu[] = {
        {"Open a New Ledger"},
        {"New Ledger Name"},
        {"Cancel"} };

    cl_func();
    while (TRUE) {
        window = open_window(11, 27, 15, 53, _DRAW, gen_att,
            _SINGLE_LINE, gen_att);
        printstring(13, 29, "Open Ledger:");
        drawbox(12, 42, 14, 51, _SINGLE_LINE, gen_att);
        string[0] = '\0';
        while (TRUE) {
            switch(inputstring(FALSE, 13, 43, 8, string)) {
                case 13:
                        if (string[0])
                                break;
                        else
                                continue;
                case 27:
                        close_window(window);
                        return;
```

continued...

...from previous page

```
                default:
                        continue;
            }
            break;
        }
    close_window(window);
    sprintf(cnname, "%s.l1", string);
    sprintf(aname, "%s.l2", string);
    sprintf(tname, "%s.l3", string);
    if ((cname = fopen(cnname, "r+b")) != NULL)
        break;
    sprintf(title, "Couldn't Find Ledger: %s", string);
    switch (dialog_menu(13, 40, 3, menu, 1, title)) {
        case 'C':
                return;
        case 'N':
                continue;
    }
    window = open_window(11, 15, 15, 64, _DRAW, gen_att,
        _SINGLE_LINE, gen_att);
    printstring(13, 17, "Company Name:");
    drawbox(12, 31, 14, 62, _SINGLE_LINE, gen_att);
    company_name[0] = '\0';
    while (TRUE) {
        switch(inputstring(FALSE, 13, 32, 30, company_name)) {
            case 13:
                    if (company_name[0])
                            break;
                    else
                            continue;
            case 27:
                    close_window(window);
                    return;
            default:
                    continue;
        }
        break;
    }
```

continued...

...from previous page

```
close_window(window);
window = open_window(12, 27, 14, 52, _DRAW, gen_att,
     _SINGLE_LINE, gen_att);
printstring(13, 29, "Initializing the Files");
if (!((cname = fopen(cnname, "w+b")) != NULL &&
     fwrite(company_name, 1, 31, cname) == 31 &&
     fwrite(&num_accts, sizeof(int), 1, cname) == 1 &&
     fwrite(&num_trans, sizeof(int), 1, cname) == 1)) {
          if (cname != NULL)
               fclose(cname);
          cname = NULL;
          company_name[0] = '\0';
          close_window(window);
          display_error("Couldn't Successfully Open the Ledger");
          return;
}
if (!((accounts = fopen(aname, "w+b")) != NULL &&
     fwrite(account, sizeof(ACCOUNT), 100, accounts) == 100)) {
          fclose(cname);
          if (accounts != NULL)
               fclose(accounts);
          cname = NULL;
          company_name[0] = '\0';
          close_window(window);
          display_error("Couldn't Successfully Open the Ledger");
          return;
}
if (!((transactions = fopen(tname, "w+b")) != NULL &&
     fwrite(transaction, sizeof(TRANSACTION), 200,
          transactions) == 200)) {
          fclose(cname);
          fclose(accounts);
          if (transactions != NULL)
               fclose(transactions);
          cname = NULL;
          company_name[0] = '\0';
          close_window(window);
          display_error("Couldn't Successfully Open the Ledger");
          return;
```

continued...

7 SIMPLE LEDGER

...from previous page

```
        }
        close_window(window);
        return;
    }
    window = open_window(12, 29, 14, 50, _DRAW, gen_att,
        _SINGLE_LINE, gen_att);
    printstring(13, 31, "Opening the Ledger");
    if (!(fread(company_name, 1, 31, cname) == 31 &&
        fread(&num_accts, sizeof(int), 1, cname) == 1 &&
        fread(&num_trans, sizeof(int), 1, cname) == 1)) {
            fclose(cname);
            cname = NULL;
            company_name[0] = '\0';
            num_trans = 0;
            close_window(window);
            display_error("Couldn't Successfully Open the Ledger");
            return;
    }
    if (!((accounts = fopen(aname, "r+b")) != NULL &&
        fread(account, sizeof(ACCOUNT), num_accts,
            accounts) == num_accts)) {
            fclose(cname);
            if (accounts != NULL)
                fclose(accounts);
            cname = NULL;
            company_name[0] = '\0';
            num_trans = 0;
            close_window(window);
            display_error("Couldn't Successfully Open the Ledger");
            return;
    }
    if (!((transactions = fopen(tname, "r+b")) != NULL &&
        fread(transaction, sizeof(TRANSACTION), num_trans,
            transactions) == num_trans)) {
            fclose(cname);
            fclose(accounts);
            if (transactions != NULL)
                fclose(transactions);
```

continued...

...from previous page

```
            cname = NULL;
            company_name[0] = '\0';
            num_trans = 0;
            close_window(window);
            display_error("Couldn't Successfully Open the Ledger");
            return;
        }
        close_window(window);
}

void cl_func(void)
{
        int i;

        if (cname != NULL) {
            fclose(cname);
            fclose(accounts);
            fclose(transactions);
            cname = accounts = transactions = NULL;
            company_name[0] = '\0';
            clearscreen(25, 1, 25, 80, _menu_att);
            num_accts = num_trans = 0;
        }
}

void ep_func(void)
{
        cl_func();
        exit(0);
}

void ea_func(void)
{
        int i, field, current_account = 0, key;
        ACCOUNT acct;
        WINDOW *window1, *window2;
```

continued...

...from previous page

```
if (cname == NULL)
    return;
window1 = open_window(7, 14, 19, 65, _DRAW, gen_att,
    _SINGLE_LINE, gen_att);
printstring(9, 16, "Account Number");
drawbox(8, 32, 10, 38, _SINGLE_LINE, gen_att);
printstring(12, 16, "Account Name");
drawbox(11, 32, 13, 63, _SINGLE_LINE, gen_att);
printstring(15, 16, "Account Balance");
drawbox(14, 32, 16, 43, _SINGLE_LINE, gen_att);
while (TRUE) {
    clearscreen(18, 15, 18, 64, gen_att);
    if (num_accts) {
        printcenter(18, 40, "ESC - Cancel  A - Add  E - Edit  D - Delete");
        inputnumber(TRUE, 9, 33, 5, &account[current_account].number);
        inputstring(TRUE, 12, 33, 30, account[current_account].name);
        inputdollars(TRUE, 15, 33, 10, &account[current_account].balance);
    }
    else {
        printcenter(18, 40, "ESC - Cancel  A - Add");
        clearscreen(9, 33, 9, 37, gen_att);
        clearscreen(12, 33, 12, 62, gen_att);
        clearscreen(15, 33, 15, 42, gen_att);
    }
    while (TRUE) {
        key = waitkey();
        if (key == 27) {
            close_window(window1);
            return;
        }
        if (key == 328) {
            if (current_account) {
                current_account--;
                break;
            }
            continue;
        }
```

continued...

...from previous page

```
if (key == 336) {
    if (current_account + 1 < num_accts) {
        current_account++;
        break;
    }
    continue;
}
if (key < 32 || key > 127)
    continue;
switch (toupper(key)) {
    case 'A':
        if (num_accts == 100)
            continue;
        acct.number = acct.balance = 0;
        acct.name[0] = '\0';
        clearscreen(18, 15, 18, 64, gen_att);
        printcenter(18, 40, "ESC - Cancel");
        clearscreen(12, 33, 12, 62, gen_att);
        clearscreen(15, 33, 15, 42, gen_att);
        while (TRUE) {
            while (acct.number < 10000 || acct.number > 99999) {
                if (inputnumber(FALSE, 9, 33, 5, &acct.number)
                    == 27) {
                    close_window(window1);
                    return;
                }
            }
            for (i = 0; i < num_accts; i++) {
                if (account[i].number == acct.number) {
                    window2 = open_window(20, 14, 20, 65,
                        _DRAW, _menu_highlight, _NO_BORDER);
                    putchar(7);
                    printcenter(20, 40,
                        "Account already exists!");
                    waitkey();
                    window2 = close_window(window2);
                    break;
                }
            }
```

continued...

...from previous page

```
                              }
                              if (i == num_accts)
                                   break;
                              acct.number = 0;
                         }
                         field = 1;
                         clearscreen(18, 15, 18, 64, gen_att);
                         printcenter(18, 40, "ESC - Cancel   F10 - Process");
                         while (TRUE) {
                              if (field == 1)
                                   key = inputstring(FALSE, 12, 33, 30, acct.name);
                              else
                                   key = inputdollars(FALSE, 15, 33, 10, &acct.balance);
                              switch (key) {
                                   case 27:
                                        close_window(window1);
                                        return;
                                   case 13:
                                   case 336:
                                        if (field == 1)
                                             field = 2;
                                        continue;
                                   case 324:
                                        account[num_accts].number = acct.number;
                                        strcpy(account[num_accts].name, acct.name);
                                        account[num_accts++].balance = acct.balance;
                                        qsort(account, num_accts, sizeof(ACCOUNT),
                                             compare);
                                        for (i = 0; i < num_accts; i++) {
                                             if (account[i].number == acct.number) {
                                                       current_account = i;
                                                       break;
                                             }
                                        }
                                        break;
                                   case 328:
                                        if (field == 2)
                                             field = 1;
                                        continue;
```

continued...

...from previous page

```
                    default:
                        continue;
                }
                break;
            }
            break;
        case 'D':
            if (!num_accts)
                break;
            if (!--num_accts)
                break;
            for (i = current_account; i < num_accts; i++) {
                account[i].number = account[i + 1].number;
                strcpy(account[i].name, account[i + 1].name);
                account[i].balance = account[i + 1].balance;
            }
            if (current_account == num_accts)
                current_account--;
            break;
        case 'E':
            strcpy(acct.name, account[current_account].name);
            acct.balance = account[current_account].balance;
            field = 1;
            clearscreen(18, 15, 18, 64, gen_att);
            printcenter(18, 40, "ESC - Cancel  F10 - Process");
            while (TRUE) {
                if (field == 1)
                    key = inputstring(FALSE, 12, 33, 30, acct.name);
                else
                    key = inputdollars(FALSE, 15, 33, 10, &acct.balance);
                switch (key) {
                    case 27:
                        close_window(window1);
                        return;
                    case 13:
                    case 336:
                        if (field == 1)
                            field = 2;
                        continue;
```

continued...

...from previous page

```
                                      case 324:
                                          strcpy(account[current_account].name,
                                              acct.name);
                                          account[current_account].balance =
                                              acct.balance;
                                          break;
                                      case 328:
                                          if (field == 2)
                                              field = 1;
                                          continue;
                                      default:
                                          continue;
                              }
                              break;
                      }
                      break;
                  default:
                      continue;
              }
              break;
          }
      }
}

void et_func(void)
{
    int i, field, current_trans = 0, key;
    double total = 0;
    ACCOUNT acct, *acct_ptr;
    TRANSACTION trans;
    WINDOW *window1, *window2;

    if (!num_accts)
        return;
    for (i = 0; i < num_trans; i++)
        total += transaction[i].amount;
    window1 = open_window(4, 14, 22, 65, _DRAW, gen_att,
        _SINGLE_LINE, gen_att);
```

continued...

...from previous page

```
printstring(6, 16, "Account Number");
drawbox(5, 32, 7, 38, _SINGLE_LINE, gen_att);
printstring(9, 16, "Account Name");
drawbox(8, 32, 10, 63, _SINGLE_LINE, gen_att);
printstring(12, 16, "Date");
drawbox(11, 32, 13, 41, _SINGLE_LINE, gen_att);
printstring(15, 16, "Description");
drawbox(14, 32, 16, 63, _SINGLE_LINE, gen_att);
printstring(18, 16, "Amount");
drawbox(17, 32, 19, 43, _SINGLE_LINE, gen_att);
drawbox(17, 52, 19, 63, _SINGLE_LINE, gen_att);
while (TRUE) {
    clearscreen(21, 15, 21, 64, gen_att);
    if (num_trans) {
        printcenter(21, 40, "ESC - Cancel  A - Add  E - Edit  D - Delete");
        acct.number = transaction[current_trans].acct_no;
        inputnumber(TRUE, 6, 33, 5, &acct.number);
        acct_ptr = bsearch(&acct, account, num_accts,
            sizeof(ACCOUNT), compare);
        inputstring(TRUE, 9, 33, 30, acct_ptr->name);
        inputstring(TRUE, 12, 33, 8, transaction[current_trans].date);
        inputstring(TRUE, 15, 33, 30,
            transaction[current_trans].description);
        inputdollars(TRUE, 18, 33, 10,
            &transaction[current_trans].amount);
        inputdollars(TRUE, 18, 53, 10, &total);
    }
    else {
        printcenter(21, 40, "ESC - Cancel  A - Add");
        clearscreen(6, 33, 6, 37, gen_att);
        clearscreen(9, 33, 9, 62, gen_att);
        clearscreen(12, 33, 12, 40, gen_att);
        clearscreen(15, 33, 15, 62, gen_att);
        clearscreen(18, 33, 18, 42, gen_att);
        clearscreen(18, 53, 18, 62, gen_att);
    }
```

continued...

...from previous page

```
while (TRUE) {
    key = waitkey();
    if (key == 27) {
        close_window(window1);
        return;
    }
    if (key == 328) {
        if (current_trans) {
            current_trans--;
            break;
        }
        continue;
    }
    if (key == 336) {
        if (current_trans + 1 < num_trans) {
            current_trans++;
            break;
        }
        continue;
    }
    if (key < 32 || key > 127)
        continue;
    switch (toupper(key)) {
        case 'A':
            if (num_trans == 200)
                continue;
            trans.acct_no = trans.amount = 0;
            if (num_trans) {
                strcpy(trans.date, transaction[num_trans - 1].date);
                strcpy(trans.description,
                    transaction[num_trans - 1].description);
            }
            else
                trans.date[0] = trans.description[0] = '\0';
            clearscreen(21, 15, 21, 64, gen_att);
            printcenter(21, 40, "ESC - Cancel");
            clearscreen(6, 33, 6, 37, gen_att);
            clearscreen(9, 33, 9, 62, gen_att);
            inputstring(TRUE, 12, 33, 8, trans.date);
```

continued...

...from previous page

```
inputstring(TRUE, 15, 33, 30, trans.description);
clearscreen(18, 33, 18, 42, gen_att);
while (TRUE) {
    while (trans.acct_no < 10000 ||
          trans.acct_no > 99999) {
        if (inputnumber(FALSE, 6, 33, 5,
            &trans.acct_no) == 27) {
                close_window(window1);
                return;
        }
    }
    acct.number = trans.acct_no;
    if ((acct_ptr = bsearch(&acct, account, num_accts,
        sizeof(ACCOUNT), compare)) == NULL) {
        window2 = open_window(23, 14, 23, 65,
            _DRAW, _menu_highlight, _NO_BORDER);
        putchar(7);
        printcenter(23, 40,
            "That account number doesn't exist");
        waitkey();
        window2 = close_window(window2);
        trans.acct_no = 0;
    }
    else
        break;
}
inputstring(TRUE, 9, 33, 30, acct_ptr->name);
field = 3;
clearscreen(21, 15, 21, 64, gen_att);
printcenter(21, 40, "ESC - Cancel  F10 - Process");
while (TRUE) {
    switch (field) {
        case 1:
            key = inputstring(FALSE, 12, 33, 8,
                trans.date);
            break;
        case 2:
            key = inputstring(FALSE, 15, 33, 30,
                trans.description);
            break;
```

continued...

...from previous page

```
                  case 3:
                      key = inputdollars(FALSE, 18, 33, 10,
                          &trans.amount);
              }
              switch (key) {
                  case 27:
                      close_window(window1);
                      return;
                  case 13:
                  case 336:
                      if (field == 1 || field == 2)
                          field++;
                      continue;
                  case 324:
                      transaction[num_trans].acct_no =
                          trans.acct_no;
                      strcpy(transaction[num_trans].date,
                          trans.date);
                      strcpy(transaction[num_trans].description,
                          trans.description);
                      transaction[num_trans].amount =
                          trans.amount;
                      total += trans.amount;
                      current_trans = num_trans;
                      num_trans++;
                      break;
                  case 328:
                      if (field == 2 || field == 3)
                          field--;
                      continue;
                  default:
                      continue;
              }
              break;
          }
          break;
```

continued...

...from previous page

```
case 'D':
    if (!num_trans)
        break;
    if (!--num_trans) {
        total = 0;
        break;
    }
    total -= transaction[current_trans].amount;
    for (i = current_trans; i < num_trans; i++) {
        transaction[i].acct_no = transaction[i + 1].acct_no;
        strcpy(transaction[i].date, transaction[i + 1].date);
        strcpy(transaction[i].description,
            transaction[i + 1].description);
        transaction[i].amount = transaction[i + 1].amount;
    }
    if (current_trans == num_trans)
        current_trans--;
    break;
case 'E':
    strcpy(trans.date, transaction[current_trans].date);
    strcpy(trans.description,
        transaction[current_trans].description);
    trans.amount = transaction[current_trans].amount;
    field = 1;
    clearscreen(21, 15, 21, 64, gen_att);
    printcenter(21, 40, "ESC - Cancel  F10 - Process");
    while (TRUE) {
        switch (field) {
            case 1:
                key = inputstring(FALSE, 12, 33, 8,
                    trans.date);
                break;
            case 2:
                key = inputstring(FALSE, 15, 33, 30,
                    trans.description);
                break;
            case 3:
                key = inputdollars(FALSE, 18, 33, 10,
                    &trans.amount);
```

continued...

...from previous page

```
                                }
                                switch (key) {
                                    case 27:
                                        close_window(window1);
                                        return;
                                    case 13:
                                    case 336:
                                        if (field == 1 || field == 2)
                                            field++;
                                        continue;
                                    case 324:
                                        strcpy(transaction[current_trans].date,
                                            trans.date);
                                        strcpy(transaction[current_trans].description,
                                            trans.description);
                                        total += -transaction[current_trans].amount +
                                            trans.amount;
                                        transaction[current_trans].amount =
                                            trans.amount;
                                        break;
                                    case 328:
                                        if (field == 2 || field == 3)
                                            field--;
                                        continue;
                                    default:
                                        continue;
                                }
                                break;
                        }
                        break;
                    default:
                        continue;
                }
                break;
            }

        }
    }
```

continued...

...from previous page

```
void ca_func(void)
{
    int i;

    if (!num_accts)
        return;
    sprintf(report_title, "Chart of Accounts");
    start_report();
    for (i = 0; i < num_accts; i++) {
        sprintf(report_line, "%5lu %-30s %10.2f ", account[i].number,
            account[i].name, account[i].balance);
        while (TRUE) {
            if (account[i].number < 18000) {
                strcat(report_line, " Current Asset");
                break;
            }
            if (account[i].number < 19000) {
                strcat(report_line, " Beginning Inventory");
                break;
            }
            if (account[i].number < 20000) {
                strcat(report_line, " Ending Inventory");
                break;
            }
            if (account[i].number < 30000) {
                strcat(report_line, " Plant Asset");
                break;
            }
            if (account[i].number < 40000) {
                strcat(report_line, " Current Liability");
                break;
            }
            if (account[i].number < 50000) {
                strcat(report_line, " Long-Term Liability");
                break;
            }
            if (account[i].number < 60000) {
                strcat(report_line, " Capital");
                break;
            }
```

continued...

...from previous page

```
                    if (account[i].number < 70000) {
                        strcat(report_line, " Revenue");
                        break;
                    }
                    if (account[i].number < 80000) {
                        strcat(report_line, " Purchase");
                        break;
                    }
                    if (account[i].number < 90000) {
                        strcat(report_line, " Expense");
                        break;
                    }
                    strcat(report_line, " Other Revenue or Expense");
                    break;
            }
            print_line();
        }
        fprintf(stdprn, "%c", 12);;
}

void tb_func(void)
{
    int i;
    double debits = 0, credits = 0;

    if (!num_accts)
        return;
    sprintf(report_title, "Trial Balance");
    start_report();
    for (i = 0; i < num_accts; i++) {
        if (account[i].number < 19000 || account[i].number > 19999) {
            if (account[i].balance >= 0) {
                debits += account[i].balance;
                sprintf(report_line, "%5lu %-30s %10.2f", account[i].number,
                    account[i].name, account[i].balance);
                print_line();
            }
        }
    }
```

continued...

...from previous page

```
    for (i = 0; i < num_accts; i++) {
        if (account[i].number < 19000 || account[i].number > 19999) {
            if (account[i].balance < 0) {
                credits += account[i].balance;
                sprintf(report_line, "%5lu %-30s %21.2f", account[i].number,
                    account[i].name, -account[i].balance);
                print_line();
            }
        }
    }
    sprintf(report_line, "%37s--------- ----------", "");
    print_line();
    sprintf(report_line, "%37s%10.2f %10.2f", "", debits, -credits);
    print_line();
    sprintf(report_line, "%37s========= ==========", "");
    print_line();
    fprintf(stdprn, "%c", 12);;
}

void glar_func(void)
{
    int i, j, k;
    ACCOUNT acct, *acct_ptr;
    static double acct_bal[100];

    if (!num_accts || !num_trans)
        return;
    sprintf(report_title, "Journal Entries");
    start_report();
    for (i = 0; i < num_trans; i++) {
        acct.number = transaction[i].acct_no;
        acct_ptr = bsearch(&acct, account, num_accts, sizeof(ACCOUNT),
            compare);
        if (transaction[i].amount >= 0)
            sprintf(report_line, "%8s %5lu %-30s %10.2f", transaction[i].date,
                transaction[i].acct_no, acct_ptr->name,
                transaction[i].amount);
```

continued...

...from previous page

```
        else
                sprintf(report_line, "%8s %5lu %-30s %21.2f", transaction[i].date,
                    transaction[i].acct_no, acct_ptr->name,
                    -transaction[i].amount);
            print_line();
    }
    fprintf(stdprn, "%c", 12);;
    close_window(rwindow);
    sprintf(report_title, "Account Activity Report");
    start_report();
    for (i = 0; i < num_accts; i++) {
        acct_bal[i] = account[i].balance;
        for (j = 0; j < num_trans; j++) {
            if (account[i].number == transaction[j].acct_no) {
                sprintf(report_line, "Account Number: %5lu",
                    account[i].number);
                print_line();
                sprintf(report_line, "Account Name  : %s", account[i].name);
                print_line();
                for (k = 0; k < 61; k++)
                    fprintf(stdprn, "=");
                print_cr();
                sprintf(report_line, "%-8s %-30s %10s %10s", "Date",
                    "Description", "Amount", "Balance");
                print_line();
                for (k = 0; k < 61; k++)
                    fprintf(stdprn, "-");
                print_cr();
                sprintf(report_line, "%8s %-30s %21.2f", "",
                    "Beginning Balance", acct_bal[i]);
                print_line();
                for (k = j; k < num_trans; k++) {
                    if (account[i].number == transaction[k].acct_no) {
                        acct_bal[i] += transaction[k].amount;
                        sprintf(report_line, "%8s %-30s %10.2f %10.2f",
                            transaction[k].date, transaction[k].description,
                            transaction[k].amount, acct_bal[i]);
                        print_line();
                    }
                }
            }
```

continued...

...from previous page

```
                sprintf(report_line, "%8s %-30s %21.2f", "",
                    "Ending Balance", acct_bal[i]);
                print_line();
                for (k = 0; k < 61; k++)
                    fprintf(stdprn, "=");
                print_cr();
                print_cr();
                break;
            }
        }
    }
    fprintf(stdprn, "%c", 12);;
    for (i = 0; i < num_accts; i++)
        account[i].balance = acct_bal[i];
    num_trans = 0;
    savenums();
    saveaccts();
}

void fs_func(void)
{
    double reg1, reg2, net_income;

    if (!num_accts)
        return;
    sprintf(report_title, "Income Statement");
    start_report();
    sprintf(report_line, "Revenues:");
    print_line();
    reg1 = print_accounts(60000, 69999, -1);
    sprintf(report_line, "%-30s %21.2f", "Total Revenues", reg1);
    print_line();
    print_cr();
    sprintf(report_line, "Cost of Goods Sold:");
    print_line();
    print_cr();
    sprintf(report_line, "Beginning Inventories:");
    print_line();
    reg2 = print_accounts(18000, 18999, 1);
```

continued...

...from previous page

```
sprintf(report_line, "%-30s %10.2f", "Total Beginning Inventories", reg2);
print_line();
print_cr();
sprintf(report_line, "Plus Purchases:");
print_line();
reg2 += print_accounts(70000, 79999, 1);
sprintf(report_line, "%-30s %10.2f", "Goods Available for Sale", reg2);
print_line();
print_cr();
sprintf(report_line, "Less Ending Inventories:");
print_line();
reg2 -= print_accounts(19000, 19999, 1);
sprintf(report_line, "%-30s %21.2f", "Total Cost of Goods Sold", reg2);
print_line();
sprintf(report_line, "%30s %21s", "", "----------");
print_line();
reg1 -= reg2;
sprintf(report_line, "%-30s %21.2f", "Gross Profit", reg1);
print_line();
print_cr();
sprintf(report_line, "Operating Expenses:");
print_line();
reg2 = print_accounts(80000, 89999, 1);
sprintf(report_line, "%-30s %21.2f", "Total Operating Expenses", reg2);
print_line();
sprintf(report_line, "%30s %21s", "", "----------");
print_line();
reg1 -= reg2;
sprintf(report_line, "%-30s %21.2f", "Income from Operations", reg1);
print_line();
print_cr();
sprintf(report_line, "Other Revenues & Expenses:");
print_line();
reg2 = print_accounts(90000, 99999, -1);
sprintf(report_line, "%-30s %21.2f", "Totl Other Revenues & Expenses",
        reg2);
print_line();
sprintf(report_line, "%30s %21s", "", "----------");
```

continued...

...from previous page

```
print_line();
reg1 -= reg2;
sprintf(report_line, "%-30s %21.2f", "Net Income", reg1);
print_line();
sprintf(report_line, "%30s %21s", "", "==========");
print_line();
fprintf(stdprn, "%c", 12);
net_income = reg1;
close_window(rwindow);
sprintf(report_title, "Balance Sheet");
start_report();
sprintf(report_line, "Assets:");
print_line();
print_cr();
sprintf(report_line, "Current Assets:");
print_line();
reg1 = print_accounts(10000, 17999, 1) +
    print_accounts(19000, 19999, 1);
sprintf(report_line, "%-30s %21.2f", "Total Current Assets", reg1);
print_line();
print_cr();
sprintf(report_line, "Plant Assets:");
print_line();
reg2 = print_accounts(20000, 29999, 1);
sprintf(report_line, "%-30s %21.2f", "Total Plant Assets", reg2);
print_line();
sprintf(report_line, "%30s %21s", "", "----------");
print_line();
reg1 += reg2;
sprintf(report_line, "%-30s %21.2f", "Total Assets", reg1);
print_line();
sprintf(report_line, "%30s %21s", "", "==========");
print_line();
print_cr();
sprintf(report_line, "Liabilities:");
print_line();
print_cr();
sprintf(report_line, "Current Liabilities:");
print_line();
```

continued...

...from previous page

```
        reg1 = print_accounts(30000, 39999, -1);
        sprintf(report_line, "%-30s %21.2f", "Total Current Liabilities", reg1);
        print_line();
        print_cr();
        sprintf(report_line, "Long-Term Liabilities:");
        print_line();
        reg2 = print_accounts(40000, 49999, -1);
        sprintf(report_line, "%-30s %21.2f", "Total Plant Assets", reg2);
        print_line();
        sprintf(report_line, "%30s %21s", "", "----------");
        print_line();
        reg1 += reg2;
        sprintf(report_line, "%-30s %21.2f", "Total Liabilities", reg1);
        print_line();
        print_cr();
        sprintf(report_line, "Capital:");
        print_line();
        reg2 = print_accounts(50000, 59999, -1);
        sprintf(report_line, "%-30s %10.2f", "Net Income", net_income);
        print_line();
        sprintf(report_line, "%30s ----------", "");
        print_line();
        reg2 += net_income;
        sprintf(report_line, "%-30s %21.2f", "Total Capital", reg2);
        print_line();
        sprintf(report_line, "%30s %21s", "", "----------");
        print_line();
        reg1 += reg2;
        sprintf(report_line, "%-30s %21.2f", "Total Liabilities and Capital",
            reg1);
        print_line();
        sprintf(report_line, "%30s %21s", "", "==========");
        print_line();
        fprintf(stdprn, "%c", 12);
}
```

continued...

...from previous page

```
int inputstring(int flag, int row, int col, int length, char *string)
{
    int key;

    while (TRUE) {
        setcurpos(row, col);
        printf("%-*s", length, string);
        if (flag)
            return(0);
        setcurpos(row, col + strlen(string) - (strlen(string) == length));
        cursoron();
        key = waitkey();
        cursoroff();
        switch (key) {
            case 8:
                if (strlen(string))
                    string[strlen(string) - 1] = '\0';
                break;
            case 327:
                string[0] = '\0';
                break;
            default:
                if (key > 31 && key < 128) {
                    if (strlen(string) != length) {
                        string[strlen(string) + 1] = '\0';
                        string[strlen(string)] = key;
                    }
                }
                else
                    return(key);
        }
    }
}

int inputdollars(int flag, int row, int col, int length, double *dptr)
{
    int i, key, decimal_count = 2;
    boolean decimal = TRUE, sign;
    char string[81];
```

continued...

...from previous page

```
if (*dptr > -.01 && *dptr < .01)
    *dptr = 0;
sign = *dptr < 0 ? TRUE : FALSE;
sprintf(string, "%*.2f", length, *dptr);
if (string[length - 2] == '0' && string[length - 1] == '0')
    decimal = FALSE;
while (TRUE) {
    if (*dptr == 0 && sign)
        sprintf(string, "%*s", length, "-0.00");
    else {
        if (sprintf(string, "%*.2f", length, *dptr) > length) {
            for (i = 0; i < length; i++)
                string[i] = '*';
            string[length] = '\0';
        }
    }
    printstring(row, col, string);
    if (flag)
        return(0);
#ifndef DC88
    setcurpos(row, decimal ? col + length - (decimal_count ? 1 : 2)
        : col + length - 4);
#else
    if (decimal)
        setcurpos(row, col + length - (decimal_count ? 1 : 2));
    else
        setcurpos(row, col + length - 4);
#endif
    cursoron();
    key = waitkey();
    cursoroff();
    switch (key) {
        case 8:
            if (*dptr) {
                if (decimal) {
                    switch (decimal_count) {
                        case 0:
                            decimal = FALSE;
                            break;
```

continued...

...from previous page

```
                          default:
                               string[length + decimal_count - 3] = '0';
                               *dptr = atof(string);
                               decimal_count--;
                    }
          }
          else {
               string[length - 4] = '0';
               #ifndef DC88
               *dptr = atof(string) / 10;
               #else
               *dptr = atof(string);
               *dptr /= 10;
               #endif
          }
          if (*dptr == 0)
               sign = FALSE;
     }
     break;
case '.':
     if (!decimal) {
          decimal = TRUE;
          decimal_count = 0;
     }
     break;
case '-':
     *dptr = - *dptr;
     sign = !sign;
     break;
case 327:
     *dptr = 0;
     decimal = sign = FALSE;
     break;
default:
     if (key >= '0' && key <= '9') {
          if (decimal) {
               switch (decimal_count) {
```

continued...

...from previous page

```
                              case 0:
                                    string[length - 2] = key;
                                    *dptr = atof(string);
                                    decimal_count++;
                                    break;
                              case 1:
                                    string[length - 1] = key;
                                    *dptr = atof(string);
                                    decimal_count++;
                        }
                  }
                  else {
                        if (string[1] == ' ' || string[1] == '-') {
                              for (i = 0; i < length - 4; i++)
                                    string[i] = string[i + 1];
                              string[length - 4] = key;
                              *dptr = atof(string);
                        }
                  }
                  if (*dptr >= 0 && sign)
                        *dptr = - *dptr;
            }
            else
                  return(key);
        }
      }
}

int inputnumber(int flag, int row, int col, int length, long *lptr)
{
      int i, key;
      char string[81];

      while (TRUE) {
            if (*lptr) {
                  if (sprintf(string, "%*lu", length, *lptr) > length) {
                        for (i = 0; i < length; i++)
                              string[i] = '*';
                        string[length] = '\0';
                  }
            }
```

continued...

...from previous page

```
            else
                sprintf(string, "%*s", length, "");
            printstring(row, col, string);
            if (flag)
                return(0);
            setcurpos(row, col + length - 1);
            cursoron();
            key = waitkey();
            cursoroff();
            switch (key) {
                case 8:
                    if (*lptr)
                        *lptr = (*lptr - (string[length - 1] - '0')) / 10;
                    break;
                case 327:
                    *lptr = 0;
                    break;
                default:
                    if (key >= '0' && key <= '9') {
                        if (string[0] == ' ')
                            *lptr = *lptr * 10 + (key - '0');
                    }
                    else
                        return(key);
            }
        }
}

int compare(ACCOUNT *acct1, ACCOUNT *acct2)
{
    if (acct1->number < acct2->number)
        return(-1);
    if (acct1->number > acct2->number)
        return(1);
    return(0);
}

void savenums(void)
{
```

continued...

...from previous page

```
    if (!(!fseek(cname, 31, SEEK_SET) &&
        fwrite(&num_accts, sizeof(int), 1, cname) == 1 &&
        fwrite(&num_trans, sizeof(int), 1, cname) == 1)) {
        display_error("Disk write error");
    }
}

void saveaccts(void)
{
    if (!(!fseek(accounts, 0, SEEK_SET) &&
        fwrite(account, sizeof(ACCOUNT), num_accts,
        accounts) == num_accts))
        display_error("Disk write error");
}

void savetrans(void)
{
    if (!(!fseek(transactions, 0, SEEK_SET) &&
        fwrite(transaction, sizeof(TRANSACTION), num_trans,
        transactions) == num_trans))
        display_error("Disk write error");
}

void start_report(void)
{
    int col1, col2;
    char mess[81];

    sprintf(mess, "Please wait while I print the %s", report_title);
    col1 = 40 - (strlen(mess) + 4) / 2;
    col2 = col1 + strlen(mess) + 3;
    rwindow = open_window(12, col1, 14, col2, _DRAW, gen_att,
        _SINGLE_LINE, gen_att);
    printstring(13, col1 + 2, mess);
    report_page = 0;
    print_heading();
}
```

continued...

...from previous page

```
void print_heading(void)
{
     #ifndef DC88
     char *tstring;
     time_t ltime;
     #else
     char tstring[9];
     #endif

     fprintf(stdprn, "\n");
     fprintf(stdprn, "%s\n", company_name);
     fprintf(stdprn, "%s\n", report_title);
     #ifndef DC88
     time(&ltime);
     tstring = ctime(&ltime);
     fprintf(stdprn, "%3.3s %2.2s, %4.4s\n", tstring + 4, tstring + 8,
          tstring + 20);
     #else
     dates(tstring);
     if (tstring[0] = ' ')
          tstring[0] = '0';
     fprintf(stdprn, "%s\n", tstring);
     #endif
     fprintf(stdprn, "Page: %d\n", ++report_page);
     fprintf(stdprn, "\n");
     report_lines = 6;
}

void print_line(void)
{
     fprintf(stdprn, "%s\n", report_line);
     if (++report_lines == 60) {
          fprintf(stdprn, "%c", 12);;
          print_heading();
     }
}
```

continued...

...from previous page

```
double print_accounts(long facct, long lacct, int sign)
{
    int i;
    double total = 0;

    for (i = 0; i < num_accts; i++) {
        if (account[i].number >= facct && account[i].number <= lacct) {
            sprintf(report_line, "%-30s %10.2f", account[i].name,
                account[i].balance * sign);
            print_line();
            total += account[i].balance * sign;
        }
    }
    if (facct != 10000 && facct != 50000) {
        sprintf(report_line, "%30s ----------", "");
        print_line();
    }
    return(total);
}
```

Function Definition: main

As with all C programs, the **main** function is the main program loop. Its implementation is illustrated by the following pseudocode:

```
initialize WINDOWS and save the current display screen
if (parameter = = 'B')
    set monochrome flag to TRUE
if (!monochrome)
    set attributes for a color display
display the pull-down menu bar
display the Accounts menu item
display the Transactions menu item
clear the bottom display line
while (TRUE) {
    display the company name on the bottom line
    switch (pull-down menu return key) {
        case pull-down menu item was selected:
            if (pull-down function was a report function)
                close the report window
            break
        case Accounts selected:
            edit the accounts
            if (number of accounts has changed)
                save the accounts
            break
        case Transactions selected:
            edit the transactions
            if (number of transactions has changed)
                save the transactions
    }
}
```

Function Definition: ol_func

The **ol_func** function is used to open a general ledger. Its implementation is illustrated by the following pseudocode:

```
close any currently open ledger
while (TRUE) {
    open and display the data entry window
    while (TRUE) {
        switch (data entry return key) {
            case ENTER:
                if (a ledger name was entered)
                    break
                else
                    go do it again
            case ESC:
                close the data entry window
                return to the pull-down menu function
            default:
                loop till either ENTER or ESC is pressed
        }
    }
    close the data entry window
    set the filenames
    if (the ledger exists)
        break
    switch (return key from "Couldn't Find Ledger" dialog menu) {
        case 'C':
            return to the pull-down menu function
        case 'N':
            go get a new ledger name
    }
    open and display a data entry window
    while (TRUE) {
        switch (data entry return key) {
            case ENTER:
                if (a company name was entered)
                    break
                else
                    go get a company name
            case ESC:
                close the data entry window
                return to the pull-down menu function
            default:
                loop till either ENTER or ESC is pressed
        }
    }
}
```

continued...

...from previous page

> *close the data entry window*
> *open and display a message window*
> *open and initialize the company data file*
> *open and initialize the accounts file*
> *open and initialize the transactions file*
> *close the message window*
> *return to the pull-down function*

}
read the company data file
open and read the accounts file
open and read the transactions file
close the data entry window

Function Definition: cl_func

The **cl_func** function closes an open general ledger. Its implementation is illustrated by the following pseudocode:

if (a ledger is open) {
> *close the company data file*
> *close the accounts file*
> *close the transactions file*
> *set the streams to* **NULL**
> *set the company name to a null string*
> *erase the company name on the bottom line*
> *set the number of accounts and the number of transactions to zero*

}

Function Definition: ep_func

The **ep_func** function exits from SIMPLE LEDGER to MS-DOS. Its implementation is illustrated by the following pseudocode:

close any currently open ledger
exit to DOS and signal no errors

Function Definition: ea_func

The **ea_func** function is used to add, edit, and delete general ledger accounts. Its implementation is illustrated by the following pseudocode:

```
if (a ledger isn't open)
    return to the main program loop
open and display a data entry window
while (TRUE) {
    erase the control keys
    if (the ledger isn't empty) {
        display the control keys
        display the current account's number
        display the current account's name
        display the current account's balance
    }
    else {
        display the control keys
        erase the data entry fields
    }
    while (TRUE) {
        get a key
        if (ESC)
            close the data entry window
            return to the main program loop
        if (UP ARROW) {
            if (current account ! = first account) {
                back up to the previous account
                go display the new current account
            }
            go get another key
        }
        if (DOWN ARROW) {
            if (current account ! = last account) {
                bump to the next account
                go display the new current account
            }
            go get another key
        }
        if (key isn't printable)
            go get another key
```

continued...

...from previous page

```
switch (key) {
    case 'A':
        if (ledger is full)
            go get another key
        set account number to zero
        set account balance to zero
        set account name to a null string
        erase the control keys
        display the control keys
        get a valid account number
        get the account name and account balance
        go get another key
    case 'D':
        if (the ledger is empty)
            go get another key
        decrement the number of accounts
        if (the ledger is empty)
            go get another key
        reposition the remaining accounts
        go get another key
    case 'E':
        account name = current account name
        account balance = current account balance
        erase the control keys
        display the control keys
        get the new account name
        get the new account balance
        save the new account name
        save the new account balance
        go get another key
    default:
        go get another key
    }
  }
}
```

Function Definition: et_func

The **et_func** function is used to add, edit, and delete transactions. Its implementation is illustrated by the following pseudocode:

```
if (the ledger is empty)
    return to the main program loop
figure the debits/credits difference
open and display the data entry window
while (TRUE) {
    erase the control keys
    if (there are any transactions) {
        display the control keys
        display the current transaction's account number
        display the current transaction's account name
        display the current transaction's date
        display the current transaction's description
        display the current transaction's amount
        display the current debits/credits difference
    }
    else {
        display the control keys
        erase the data entry fields
    }
    while (TRUE) {
        get a key
        if (ESC) {
            close the data entry window
            return to the main program loop
        }
        if (UP ARROW) {
            if (current transaction ! = first
                transaction) {
                back up to the previous transaction
                go display the new current transaction
            }
            go get another key
        }
        if (DOWN ARROW) {
            if (current transaction ! = last
                transaction) {
                bump to the next transaction
                go display the new current transaction
```

continued...

...from previous page

```
        }
        go get another key
}
if (the key isn't printable)
    go get another key
switch (key) {
    case 'A':
        if (transaction file is full)
            go get another key
        set the transaction account number to zero
        set the transaction amount to zero
        if (not the first transaction) {
            set the transaction date to the last date
            set the transaction description to the last description

        }
        else {
            set the transaction date to a null string
            set the transaction description to a null string

        }
        erase the control keys
        display the control key
        get the transaction account number
        get the transaction date
        get the transaction description
        get the transaction amount
    case 'D':
        if (there aren't any transactions)
            go get another key
        decrement the number of transactions
        if (there aren't any transactions)
            go get another key
        adjust the debit/credit difference
        reposition the remaining transactions
    case 'E':
        transaction date = current transaction date
        transaction description = current transaction description
        transaction amount = current transaction amount
        erase the control keys
        display the control keys
        get the new transaction date
        get the new transaction description
        get the new transaction amount
```

continued...

...from previous page

```
                save the new transaction date
                save the new transaction description
                save the new transaction amount
            default:
                go get another key
      }
    }
}
```

Function Definition: ca_func

The **ca_func** function prints a chart of accounts. Its implementation is illustrated by the following pseudocode:


```
if (the ledger is empty)
     return to the pull-down menu function
set the report title
start the report
for (i = 0; i < number of accounts; i + +) {
     set the report line for the account number, account name, and account balance
     add the classification to the report line
     print the report line
}
do a form feed
```


Function Definition: tb_func

The **tb_func** function prints a trial balance. Its implementation is illustrated by the following pseudocode:

```
set total debits to zero
set total credits to zero
if (the ledger is empty)
     return to the pull-down menu function
set the report title
start the report
for (i = 0; i < number of accounts; i + +) {
     if (account isn't an ending inventory account) {
          if (account has a debit balance) {
               debits + = account balance
               set the report line to the account number, account name, and account
                    balance
               print the report line
          }
     }
}
for (i = 0; i < number of accounts; i + +) {
     if (account isn't an ending inventory account) {
          if (account has a credit balance) {
               credits + = account balance
               set the report line to the account number, account name, and account
                    balance
               print the report line
          }
     }
}
print the total debits and credits
do a form feed
```

Function Definition: glar_func

The **glar_func** function prints a general ledger activity report, posts the transactions to their respective accounts, and closes out the transactions file. Its implementation is illustrated by the following pseudocode:

```
if (the ledger is empty || there aren't any transactions)
    return to the pull-down menu function
set the report title
start up the report
for (i = 0; i < number of transactions; i+ +) {
    set the report line to the transaction's account number and amount
    print the report line
}
do a form feed
close the report window
set the report title
start up the report
for (i = 0; i < number of accounts; i+ +) {
    new account balance = current account balance
    for (j = 0; j < number of transactions; j+ +) {
        if (account number = = transaction's account
            number) {
        print the account number
        print the account name
        print the beginning balance
        for (k = j; k < number of transactions; k+ +) {
            if (account number = = transaction's account
                number) {
                new account balance + = transaction amount
                set the report line for the transaction's date, description, amount,
                    and the new account balance
                print the report line
            }
        print the ending balance
    }
}
do a form feed
save the new account balances
set the number of transactions to zero
save the affected data files
```

Function Definition: fs_func

The **fs_func** function prints an income statement and a balance sheet. Its implementation is illustrated by the following pseudocode:

if (the ledger is empty)
    return to the pull-down menu function
set the report title
start the report
print the **Revenues** *heading*
print the **Revenues** *accounts*
print the **Total Revenues**
print the **Cost of Goods Sold** *heading*
print the **Beginning Inventories** *accounts*
print the total of the **Beginning Inventories** *accounts*
print the **Purchases** *accounts*
print the total **Goods Available for Sale**
print the **Ending Inventories** *accounts*
print the **Total Cost of Goods Sold**
print the **Gross Profit**
print the **Operating Expenses** *heading*
print the **Expenses** *accounts*
print the **Total Operating Expenses**
print the **Income from Operations**
print the **Other Revenues & Expenses** *heading*
print the **Other Revenues & Expenses** *accounts*
print the **Total Other Revenues & Expenses**
print the **Net Income**
close the report window
set the new report title
start the report
print the **Assets** *heading*
print the **Current Assets** *heading*
print the **Current Assets** *accounts*
print the **Ending Inventories** *accounts*
print the **Total Current Assets**
print the **Plant Assets** *heading*
print the **Plant Assets** *accounts*
print the **Total Plant Assets**
print the **Total Assets**
print the **Liabilities** *heading*
print the **Current Liabilities** *heading*
print the **Current Liabilities** *accounts*
print the **Total Current Liabilities**
print the **Long-Term Liabilities** *heading*
print the **Long-Term Liabilities** *accounts*
print the **Total Long-Term Liabilities**
print the **Total Liabilities**
print the **Capital** *heading*
print the **Capital** *accounts*
print the **Net Income**
print the **Total Capital**
print the **Total Liabilities and Capital**

Function Definition: inputstring

The **inputstring** function is used to enter string data. Its implementation is illustrated by the following pseudocode:

```
while (TRUE) {
    set the cursor position to the start of the data entry field
    display the string
    if (display only)
        return
    set the cursor position to the end of the string
    turn on the cursor
    get a key
    turn off the cursor
    switch (key) {
        case BACKSPACE:
            if (!null string)
                last string character = 0
            go get another key
        case HOME:
            set string to a null string
            go get another key
        default:
            if (key is printable) {
                if (field isn't full)
                    string = string + character
            }
            else
                return(key)
    }
}
```

Function Definition: inputdollars

The **inputdollars** function is used to enter dollar values. Its implementation is illustrated by the following pseudocode:

```
if (value is less than a penny)
    set value to zero
set the sign flag
set the decimal point flag
while (TRUE) {
    if (value = = -0.00)
        format the field for -0.00
    else {
        format the field
        if (field overflowed)
            set the field to all *s
    }
    display the data entry field
    if (display only)
        return
    set the cursor position to the next digit's position
    turn the cursor on
    get a key
    turn the cursor off
    switch (key) {
        case BACKSPACE:
            if (value ! = 0) {
                if (decimal point has been pressed) {
                    switch (decimal count) {
                        case no cents:
                                decimal point
                                        flag = FALSE
                                go get another key
                        default:
                                set last digit entered to 0
                                set the new value
                                decrement the decimal count
                    }
                }
                else {
                    set last digit entered to 0
                    value = new string value / 10
                }
                if (value = = 0)
                    sign = FALSE
            }
            go get another key
```

continued...

...from previous page

```
case '.':
    if (decimal point hasn't been pressed) {
        decimal point flag = TRUE
        decimal count = 0
    }
    go get another key
case '-':
    value = -value
    sign flag = !sign flag
    go get another key
case HOME:
    value = 0
    decimal point flag = FALSE
    sign flag = FALSE
    go get another key
default:
    if (key is a digit) {
        if (decimal point has been pressed) {
            switch (decimal count):
                case no pennies:
                    save key as tenths
                    set the new value
                    bump the decimal count
                    go get another key
                case tenths already entered:
                    save key as hundredths
                    set the new value
                    bump the decimal count
                    go get another key
        }
        else {
            if (data entry field isn't full) {
                save the new ones digit
                set the new value
            }
        }
        if (value > = 0 && sign flag = = TRUE)
            make the value negative
    }
    else
        return(key)
    }
}
```

Function Definition: inputnumber

The **inputnumber** function is used to enter account numbers. Its implementation is illustrated by the following pseudocode:

```
while (TRUE) {
    if (value ! = 0)
        format the display string
    else
        set the display string to a blank field
    display the data entry field
    if (display only)
        return
    set the cursor position to the end of the data entry field
    turn the cursor on
    get a key
    turn the cursor off
    switch (key) {
        case BACKSPACE:
            if (value ! = 0)
                set the ones digit to zero
                value = value / 10
            go get another key
        case HOME:
            value = 0
            go get another key
        default:
            if (key is a digit) {
                if (data entry field isn't full)
                    set the new value
            }
            else
                return(key)
    }
}
```

Function Definition: compare

The **compare** function is used by the **qsort** and **bsearch** functions to compare account structures. Its implementation is illustrated by the following pseudocode:

if (first account number < second account number)
    return(-1)
if (first account number > second account number)
    return(1)
return(0)

Function Definition: savenums

The **savenums** function saves the number of accounts and the number of transactions to the company data file. Its implementation is illustrated by the following pseudocode:

set the file position to the number of accounts
write the number of accounts
write the number of transactions

Function Definition: saveaccts

The **saveaccts** function saves the general ledger accounts to the accounts file. Its implementation is illustrated by the following pseudocode:

set the file position to the start of the accounts file
write the accounts

Function Definition: savetrans

The **savetrans** function saves the general ledger transactions to the transactions file. Its implementation is illustrated by the following pseudocode:

set the file position to the start of the transactions file
write the transactions

Function Definition: start_report

The **start_report** function opens the report window and prints the first heading. Its implementation is illustrated by the following pseudocode:

set the report window message
open the window
display the report message
set the page number
print the report heading

Function Definition: print_heading

The **print_heading** function prints a report heading. Its implementation is illustrated by the following pseudocode:

print a carriage return
print the company name
print the report title
print the date
print the page number
set the number of lines

Function Definition: print_line

The **print_line** function prints a report line. Its implementation is illustrated by the following pseudocode:

print the report line
if (page is full) {
    do a form feed
    print a report heading
}

Function Definition: print_accounts

The **print_accounts** function is used by the **fs_func** function to print account groups. Its implementation is illustrated by the following pseudocode:

```
total = 0
for (i = 0; i < number of accounts; i + +) {
    if (account number is in the specified range) {
        format the report line for the account name and balance
        print the report line
        total + = account balance
    }
}
if (account range is Current Assets or Capital)
    print an underline
```

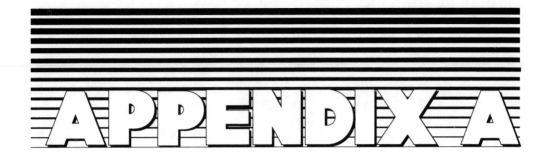

WINDOWS REFERENCE GUIDE

GLOBAL VARIABLES

As mentioned in Chapter 3, the WINDOWS toolbox defines a number of global variables in the **windows.h** header file. These global variables are used by the application programmer to change many of the WINDOWS operating environment's default settings. Thus, WINDOWS is easily customized to meet the needs of a variety of application programs.

_menu_att

Example: int _menu_att;

Description: The **_menu_att** variable is used by the WINDOWS operating environment as the default display attribute for the dialog_menu, popup, and pulldown functions. Initially, _menu_att is set in menus.c to a value of 0x70. However, the _menu_att variable can be changed to suit a particular application program's needs.

_menu_highlight

Example: int _menu_highlight;

Description: The **_menu_highlight** variable is used by the WINDOWS operating environment as the default display attribute for highlighting menu selections. Initially, _menu_highlight is set in menus.c to a value of 0x07. However, the _menu_highlight variable can be changed to suit a particular application program's needs.

_menu_hotkey

Example: int _menu_hotkey;

Description: The **_menu_hotkey** variable is used by the WINDOWS operating environment as the default display attribute for menu hotkeys. Initially, _menu_hotkey is set in menus.c to a value of 0x7f. However, the _menu_hotkey variable can be changed to suit a particular application program's needs.

_nonibm

Example: int _nonibm;

Description: The **_nonibm** variable is used by the WINDOWS operating environment to eliminate snow on an IBM CGA. When it is called,
the settext80 function determines the current display adapter's
type. If a CGA adapter is present, settext80 sets the _nonibm
variable to FALSE (0). If an MDA or EGA adapter is present,
settext80 sets the _nonibm variable to TRUE (0). If the current
display adapter is a non-IBM CGA, it is the program's responsibility to manually set the _nonibm variable to TRUE. Although
this is strictly optional, manually setting the _nonibm variable
will considerably speed up display input/output.

STANDARD DATA TYPES

In windows.h, the WINDOWS toolbox defines a number of useful data types.

boolean

Example: typedef int boolean;

Description: The **boolean** data type is used to define logical variables. To
assist in the use of the boolean data type, the following two
constants are defined in windows.h:

Constant	Value
TRUE	1
FALSE	0

MENU

Example:
```
typedef struct {
    char *string;
    int hotkey;
    void (*function)();
    void (*help)();
} MENU;
```

Description: The **MENU** structure is used to define menu items for the WINDOWS toolbox menu functions. The MENU structure is used as follows:

Data Type	Description
string	Pointer to a string, which defines the menu item.
hotkey	Position in *string* of the menu item's hotkey character.
(*function)()	Pointer to a function, which is executed if the menu item is selected.
(*help)()	Pointer to a function, which is executed if help is requested for the highlighted menu item.

MENU_HEAD

Example:
```
typedef struct {
    char *heading;
    int hotkey, number;
    MENU *mptr;
} MENU_HEAD;
```

Description: The **MENU_HEAD** structure is used to define the number of menus for the pulldown and pulldown_bar functions. The MENU_HEAD structure is used as follows:

Data Type	Description
heading	Pointer to a string, which defines the menu's heading.
hotkey	Position in *heading* of the menu's pull-down hotkey character.
number	Number of items in the pull-down menu.
mptr	Pointer to an array of MENU structures, which defines the pull-down menu.

WINDOW

Example:
```
typedef struct {
    int row1, col1, row2, col2;
    char *videoarray;
} WINDOW;
```

Description: The **WINDOW** structure is used to hold the coordinates and a pointer to a dynamically created display screen window. The WINDOW structure is used as follows:

Data Type	Description
row1	Upper left row of the window.
col1	Upper left column of the window.
row2	Lower right row of the window.
col2	Lower right column of the window.
videoarray	Pointer to a dynamically created array, which holds the previous contents of the display screen window.

171

FUNCTIONS

The WINDOWS toolbox contains numerous functions. To facilitate their use in application programs, this section describes the WINDOWS functions as follows:

Summary: Presents an exact syntactic model for each of the WINDOWS functions.

Description: Describes a function's purpose and how it is used in an application program.

Return Value: Explains any of the possible return values for a WINDOWS function.

See Also: Lists any similar or related WINDOWS functions.

Example: Illustrates how a WINDOWS function could actually be used in an application program.

clearone

Summary:
```
#include "windows.h"
void clearone(row, col, att);
int row, col;          (character position)
int att;               (character attribute)
```

Description: The **clearone** macro displays a space at the position defined by (*row, col*). Additionally, the position's attribute is set to *att*.

Return Value: No value is returned.

Example: The following program displays a message and uses the clearone macro to erase the **T** at the start of the message.

```
#include <stdio.h>
#include "windows.h"

main()
{
    save_initial_video();
    printstring(1, 1, "This is a demo of the clearone macro");
    waitkey();
    clearone(1, 1, 7);
    waitkey();
    exit(0);
}
```

clearscreen

Summary: #include "windows.h"
void clearscreen(*row1, col1, row2, col2, att*);
int *row1, col1*;   (upper left corner of the text window)
int *row2, col2*;   (lower right corner of the text window)
int *att*;   (text window attribute)

Description: The **clearscreen** macro clears an area of the display screen defined by the coordinates (*row1, col1*) and (*row2, col2*). Additionally, the cleared text window's attributes are set to *att*.

Return Value: No value is returned.

Example: The following program demonstrates how the clearscreen macro
is used to clear the display screen.

```
#include <stdio.h>
#include "windows.h"

main()
{
    settext80();
    clearscreen(1, 1, 25, 80, 7);
    printstring(1, 1, "The screen has been cleared!");
    waitkey();
    exit(0);
}
```

close_window

Summary: #include "windows.h"
WINDOW *close_window(*window*);
WINDOW *window*;   (pointer to a previously opened text
window)

Description: The **close_window** function closes a previously opened text
window.

Return Value: A NULL pointer of type WINDOW is returned by the
close_window function.

See Also: **open_window**

Example: The following program opens a text window at the coordinates
(1, 20) and (15, 50). After waiting for a key to be pressed, the
program uses the close_window function to close the text window.

```
#include <stdio.h>
#include "windows.h"

main()
{
    WINDOW *window;

    save_initial_video();
    window = open_window(1, 20, 15, 50, _DRAW, 0x70, _SINGLE_LINE, 0x70);
    waitkey();
    window = close_window(window);
    exit(0);
}
```

cursoroff, cursoron

Summary:
```
#include "windows.h"
void cursoroff(void);
void cursoron(void);
```

Description: The **cursoroff** function turns the cursor off. The **cursoron** function turns the cursor on.

Return Value: No value is returned.

Example: The following program demonstrates the cursoroff and cursoron functions by first turning the cursor off and then turning the cursor back on again.

```
#include <stdio.h>
#include "windows.h"

main()
{
    settext80();
    clearscreen(1, 1, 25, 80, 7);
    cursoroff();
    printstring(1, 1, "Press any key to continue.....");
    waitkey();
    cursoron();
    exit(0);
}
```

dialog_menu

Summary:
```
#include "windows.h"
int dialog_menu(row, col, nitems, menu, ntitles, [title, ...]);
int row, col;          (screen position to center the menu on)
int nitems;            (number of menu items)
MENU *menu;            (pointer to an array of MENU structures)
int ntitles;           (number of titles)
char *titles;          (title pointer)
```

175

Description: The **dialog_menu** function displays a dialog box menu by centering it at the position defined by (*row, col*). If any titles are specified, they are displayed above the menu items. Selection of a
menu item is accomplished by pressing its indicated hotkey.
Furthermore, the double-lined menu item can be selected by
simply pressing the Enter key. The double-lined highlighting is
moved from one menu item to the next by pressing either the
Left or Right Arrow key.

Return Value: If the menu item has a NULL function pointer, the dialog_menu
function returns the value of the item's hotkey. Otherwise, the
dialog_menu function returns a value of zero.

Example: The following program demonstrates the use of the dialog_menu
function by asking whether or not a file should be saved. If in-
structed to do so, the dialog box menu will execute the simulated
save file function.

```
#include <stdio.h>
#include "windows.h"

void save_file(void);

static MENU menu[] = {
     {"Yes", 0, save_file},
     {"No"},
     {"Cancel"} };

main()
{
     save_initial_video();
     while (dialog_menu(13, 40, 3, menu, 2, "The file hasn't been saved!",
          "Do you want me to save it?") != 'C') ;
     exit(0);
}

void save_file(void)
{
     display_error("The file has been saved");
}
```

176

display_error

Summary: #include "windows.h"
void display_error(*errmess*);
char *errmess*;   (error message pointer)

Description: The **display_error** function uses the dialog_menu function to display an error message (*errmess*) on the center of the display screen.

Return Value: No value is returned.

See Also: **dialog_menu**

Example: The following program illustrates how the display_error function is used to simulate a disk read error.

```
#include <stdio.h>
#include "windows.h"

main()
{
    save_initial_video();
    display_error("Disk Read Error");
    exit(0);
}
```

drawbox

Summary: #include "windows.h"
void far drawbox(*row1, col1, row2, col2, linetype, att*);
int *row1, col1*;   (upper left corner of the text window)
int *row2, col2*;   (lower right corner of the text window)
int *linetype*;   (line type flag)
int *att*;   (border attribute)

Description: The **drawbox** function draws a border around a text window
in which coordinates are defined by the points (*row1, col1*) and
(*row2, col2*). Additionally, the border's attributes are set to *att*.
The *linetype* parameter can be one of the following constants
(defined in windows.h):

Constant	Action
_SINGLE_LINE	Draws a single-lined border.
_DOUBLE_LINE	Draws a double-lined border.

Return Value: No value is returned.

Example: The following program demonstrates how the drawbox function is
used to draw a double-lined box in the right half of the display
screen.

```
#include <stdio.h>
#include "windows.h"

main()
{
    save_initial_video();
    drawbox(1, 41, 25, 80, _DOUBLE_LINE, 0x70);
    waitkey();
    exit(0);
}
```

draw_window

Summary:
```
#include "windows.h"
void draw_window(row1, col1, row2, col2, watt,
    bflg [,batt]);
int row1, col1;        (upper left corner of the text window)
int row2, col2;        (lower right corner of the text window)
int watt;              (text window attribute)
int bflg;              (border flag)
int batt;              (border attribute)
```

Description: The **draw_window** function draws a window at the coordinates defined by (*row1, col1*) and (*row2, col2*). The window is cleared and all attributes are set to *watt*. If a border is requested by the *bflg* parameter, it is drawn with an attribute of *batt*. The *bflg* parameter can be one of the following constants (defined in windows.h):

Constant	Action
_NO_BORDER	The window is drawn without a border.
_SINGLE_LINE	The window is drawn with a single-lined border.
_DOUBLE_LINE	The window is drawn with a double-lined border.

Return Value: No value is returned.

See Also: **open_window**

Example: The following program demonstrates how the draw_window function can be used to draw a double-lined window at the coordinates (10, 30) and (15, 50).

```
#include <stdio.h>
#include "windows.h"

main()
{
    save_initial_video();
    draw_window(10, 30, 15, 50, 0x70, _DOUBLE_LINE, 0x70);
    waitkey();
    exit(0);
}
```

error_handler

Summary: #include "windows.h"
                 void error_handler();

Description: The **error_handler** function is an MS-DOS INT 0x24 hardware
                 error handler. Once its address has been passed to MS-DOS,
                 the error_handler function will trap any hardware errors by pop-
                 ping up on the screen and displaying an appropriate error mes-
                 sage. Additionally, error_handler will ask the operator to select
                 one of three menu items: Ignore the error, Retry the operation,
                 or Abort the program.

Return Value: No value is returned.

See Also: **dialog_menu**

Example: The following program demonstrates how the error_handler
                 function traps an open disk drive door.

180

```
#include <stdio.h>
#include "windows.h"

main()
{
    FILE *stream;

    _harderr(error_handler);
    save_initial_video();
    display_error("Please open the Drive A door and press a key");
    if ((stream = fopen("a:dummy.tst", "r")) != NULL)
        fclose(stream);
    exit(0);
}
```

fillone

Summary: #include "windows.h"
void fillone(*row, col, chr, att*);
int *row, col*;   (screen position)
int *chr*;   (character)
int *att*;   (attribute)

Description: The **fillone** function sets the display screen position defined by
(*row, col*) to the specified character/attribute pair (*chr/att*).

Return Value: No value is returned.

Example: The following program demonstrates how the fillone function is
used to display a black-on-white **M** at position (4, 10)

```
#include <stdio.h>
#include "windows.h"

main()
{
    save_initial_video();
    fillone(4, 10, 'M', 0x70);
    waitkey();
    exit(0);
}
```

fillscreen

Summary: #include "windows.h"
void far fillscreen(*row1, col1, row2, col2, chr, att*);
int *row1, col1*;   (upper left corner of the text window)
int *row2, col2*;   (lower right corner of the text window)
int *chr*;   (text window character)
int *att*;   (text window attribute)

Description: The **fillscreen** function fills the text window defined by the coordinates (*row1, col1*) and (*row2, col2*) with the character/attribute pair specified by (*chr/att*).

Return Value: No value is returned.

Example: The following program demonstrates how the fillscreen function is used to fill the left half of the display screen with **R**s.

```
#include <stdio.h>
#include "windows.h"

main()
{
    save_initial_video();
    fillscreen(1, 1, 25, 50, 'R', 7);
    waitkey();
    exit(0);
}
```

getcurpos

Summary: #include "windows.h"
void getcurpos(*row, col, sline, eline*);
int **row*;   (cursor row position)
int **col*;   (cursor column position)
int **sline*;   (cursor starting line)
int **eline*;   (cursor ending line)

Description: The **getcurpos** function retrieves the cursor values by returning the cursor row position in *row*, the cursor column position in *col*, the cursor character's starting line in *sline*, and the cursor character's ending line in *eline*.

Return Value: No value is returned.

Example: Upon entry, the following program uses the getcurpos function to obtain the cursor values. After obtaining the cursor values, the display screen is cleared and the information is displayed.

```
#include <stdio.h>
#include "windows.h"

main()
{
    int row, col, sline, eline;

    settext80();
    getcurpos(&row, &col, &sline, &eline);
    clearscreen(1, 1, 25, 80, 7);
    setcurpos(1, 1);
    printf("Row: %d  Column: %d  Starting Line: %d  Ending Line: %d\n",
        row, col, sline, eline);
    waitkey();
    exit(0);
}
```

horizontal_bar

Summary: #include "windows.h"
void horizontal_bar(*window, curpos, total, att*);
WINDOW **window*; (pointer to the window's dynamic
definition structure)
int *curpos*;   (current line position)
int *total*;   (line length)
int *att*;   (scroll bar attribute)

Description: The **horizontal_bar** function displays a horizontal scroll bar at the bottom of a previously opened text window in which coordinates are defined by *window*. The scroll bar setting is derived by dividing *curpos* by *total*. Additionally, the scroll bar is displayed with an attribute of *att*.

Return Value: No value is returned.

See Also: **vertical_bar** and **open_window**

Example: The following program demonstrates how the horizontal_bar function is used to display a variety of line positions.

```
#include <stdio.h>
#include "windows.h"

main()
{
    WINDOW *window;

    save_initial_video();
    window = open_window(1, 30, 10, 70, _DRAW, 7, _SINGLE_LINE, 7);
    horizontal_bar(window, 0, 100, 0x70);
    waitkey();
    horizontal_bar(window, 50, 100, 0x70);
    waitkey();
    horizontal_bar(window, 100, 100, 0x70);
    waitkey();
    exit(0);
}
```

hotstring

Summary: #include "windows.h"
void hotstring(*row, col, hotkey, hatt, string*);
int *row, col*;   (string position)
int *hotkey*;   (hotkey position)
int *hatt*;   (hotkey attribute)
char **string*;   (string pointer)

Description: The **hotstring** function displays a string at the display screen
position defined by (*row, col*). Additionally, the string's *hotkey*
character attribute is set to *hatt*.

Return Value: No value is returned.

Example: The following program demonstrates how the hotstring function
is used to display a hotstring at the beginning of the middle display line.

```
#include <stdio.h>
#include "windows.h"

main()
{
    WINDOW *window;

    save_initial_video();
    hotstring(13, 1, 0, 0x70, "This is a hotstring demo!");
    waitkey();
    exit(0);
}
```

open_window

Summary: #include "windows.h"
WINDOW *open_window(*row1, col1, row2, col2,*
    dflg[, *watt, bflg*[, *batt*]]);
int *row1, col1*;   (upper left corner of the text window)
int *row2, col2*;   (lower right corner of the text window)
int *dflg*;   (draw window flag)
int watt;   (text window attribute)
int *blfg*;   (border flag)
int *batt*;   (border attribute)

Description: The **open_window** function dynamically opens a text window at
the coordinates defined by (*row1, col1*) and (*row2, col2*). If *dflg*
so indicates, the window is drawn by clearing the entire window
and setting the window's attributes to *watt*. Furthermore, a border will be drawn according to the *bflg*. If a border is drawn, its
attributes are set to *batt*. The *dflg* parameter can be one of the
following constants (defined in windows.h):

Constant	Action
_DRAW	Draw the window.
_NO_DRAW	Leave the window's contents intact.

The *bflg* parameter can be one of the following constants (defined
in windows.h):

Constant	Action
_NO_BORDER	The window is drawn without a border.
_SINGLE_LINE	The window is drawn with a single-lined border.
_DOUBLE_LINE	The window is drawn with a double-lined border.

Return Value: The open_window function returns a structure pointer of type WINDOW.

See Also: **close_window** and **draw_window**

Example: The following program demonstrates how the open_window function is used to dynamically open a text window at the coordinates (1, 20) and (15, 50).

```
#include <stdio.h>
#include "windows.h"

main()
{
    WINDOW *window;

    save_initial_video();
    window = open_window(1, 20, 15, 50, _DRAW, 0x70, _SINGLE_LINE, 0x70);
    waitkey();
    window = close_window(window);
    exit(0);
}
```

popup

Summary:
```
#include "windows.h"
int popup(number, menu, row, col);
int number;              (number of menu items)
MENU *menu;              (pointer to an array of MENU structures)
int row;                 (upper row for the menu)
int col;                 (column to center the menu on)
```

Description: The **popup** function displays a pop-up menu starting at *row* and centered on the column defined by *col*. Selection of a menu item is accomplished by pressing its indicated hotkey. Furthermore, the highlighted menu item can be selected by pressing the Enter key . Help, if it is available, can be requested for the highlighted menu item by pressing F1. The highlighting can be moved by pressing the Up or Down Arrow key. Pressing the Esc key will cancel the menu.

Return Value: If the selected menu item's function pointer is NULL, the popup function returns the value of the menu item's hotkey. Otherwise, the popup function calls the menu item's function and returns a value of zero.

Example: The following program uses the popup function to display a three-item pop-up menu. The program will continuously display the menu until the "Exit the Program" menu item is selected by the operator.

```c
#include <stdio.h>
#include "windows.h"

void save_file(void);
void load_file(void);
void sf_help(void);
void lf_help(void);

static MENU menu[] = {
    {"Save the File", 0, save_file, sf_help},
    {"Load the File", 0, load_file, lf_help},
    {"Exit the Program"} };

main()
{
    save_initial_video();
    while (!popup(3, menu, 3, 40));
    exit(0);
}

void save_file(void)
{
    display_error("Saving the file");
}

void load_file(void)
{
    display_error("Loading the file");
}
```

continued...

...from previous page

```
void sf_help(void)
{
    display_error("Save file help");
}

void lf_help(void)
{
    display_error("Load file help");
}
```

printcenter

Summary: #include "windows.h"
void printcenter(*row, col, string*);
int *row*;   (string row)
int *col*;   (column to center the string on)
char **string*;   (string pointer)

Description: The **printcenter** function displays *string* on the display row defined by *row* and centered on the column defined by *col*.

Return Value: No value is returned.

Example: The following program demonstrates how the **printcenter** function is used to center a string on the top line of the display screen.

```
#include <stdio.h>
#include "windows.h"

main()
{
    save_initial_video();
    printcenter(1, 40, "This message is centered on the top display line");
    waitkey();
    exit(0);
}
```

printone

Summary:
```
#include "windows.h"
void printone(row, col, chr);
int row, col;          (character position)
int chr;               (character)
```

Description: The **printone** function displays a character (*chr*) at the position defined by (*row, col*).

Return Value: No value is returned.

Example: The following program demonstrates how the printone function is used to display a **Z** at position (5, 40).

```
#include <stdio.h>
#include "windows.h"

main()
{
    save_initial_video();
    printone(5, 40, 'Z');
    waitkey();
    exit(0);
}
```

printstring

Summary: #include "windows.h"
                   void far printstring(*row, col, string*);
                   int *row, col*;   (display screen position)
                   char far *string;   (string pointer)

Description: The **printstring** function displays a string at the position defined
                   by (*row, col*).

Return Value: No value is returned.

Example: The following program demonstrates how printstring is used to
                   display a string at position (2, 10).

```
#include <stdio.h>
#include "windows.h"

main()
{
    save_initial_video();
    printstring(2, 10, "This is row 2, column 10");
    waitkey();
    exit(0);
}
```

pulldown

Summary: #include "windows.h"
int pulldown(*nmenus, menus, row, ikey, help*);
int *nmenus*;   (number of pull-down menus)
MENU_HEAD **menus*;   (pointer to an array of
                                              MENU_HEAD structures)
int *row*;   (menu bar row)
int *ikey*;   (initial key value)
void (**help*)(void);   (pointer to the overall help function)

Description: The **pulldown** function is used to implement multiple pull-down menus. The number of pull-down menus is defined by *nmenus*. The pulldown function recognizes the following control keys:

KEY	ACTION
Alt + Heading Hotkey	Pulls down the indicated menu.
Esc	Removes the current menu from the screen.
Left Arrow	Removes the current menu from the screen and pulls down the next menu to the left.
Right Arrow	Removes the current menu from the screen and pulls down the next menu to the right.
Menu Item Hotkey	Executes the selected menu item's function.
Enter	Executes the highlighted menu item's function.

F1 If a menu hasn't been pulled down, executes the overall help function defined by help. Otherwise, executes the highlighted menu item's *help* function.

Up Arrow Moves the highlight bar up to the previous menu item.

Down Arrow Moves the highlight bar down to the next menu item.

An initial key value can be sent to the pulldown function by placing the appropriate value in the *ikey* parameter. Otherwise, *ikey* must equal zero to indicate no initial key.

Return Value: If a menu item isn't selected, the pulldown function returns the value of the last key pressed. Otherwise, the pulldown function returns a value of zero.

See Also: **pulldown_bar**

Example: The following program demonstrates how the pulldown function is used to implement a series of pull-down menus for a simple general ledger program.

```
#include <stdio.h>
#include "windows.h"

void save_file(void);
void read_file(void);
void exit_prog(void);
void add_acc(void);
void del_acc(void);
void del_tra(void);
void add_tra(void);
void prt_coa(void);
void led_upd(void);
void fin_stat(void);
```

continued...

...from previous page

```
void main_help(void);
void sf_help(void);
void rf_help(void);
void aa_help(void);
void da_help(void);
void at_help(void);
void dt_help(void);
void pc_help(void);
void lu_help(void);
void fs_help(void);

static MENU file[] = {
    {"Save the File", 0, save_file, sf_help},
    {"Read the File", 0, read_file, rf_help},
    {"Exit the Program", 0, exit_prog} };

static MENU accounts[] = {
    {"Add an Account", 0, add_acc, aa_help},
    {"Delete an Account", 0, del_acc, da_help} };

static MENU transact[] = {
    {"Add a Transaction", 0, add_tra, at_help},
    {"Delete a Transaction", 0, del_tra, dt_help} };

static MENU print[] = {
    {"Print a Chart of Accounts", 8, prt_coa, pc_help},
    {"Print a Ledger Update", 15, led_upd, lu_help},
    {"Print Financial Statements", 6, fin_stat, fs_help} };

static MENU_HEAD heads[] = {
    {"File", 0, 3, file},
    {"Accounts", 0, 2, accounts},
    {"Transactions", 0, 2, transact},
    {"Print", 0, 3, print} };
```

continued...

...from previous page

```
main()
{
    save_initial_video();
    while (TRUE) {
        setcurpos(13, 1);
        printf("%3d", pulldown(4, heads, 1, 0, main_help));
    }
}

void save_file(void)
{
    display_error("Saving the File");
}

void read_file(void)
{
    display_error("Reading the File");
}

void exit_prog(void)
{
    exit(0);
}

void add_acc(void)
{
    display_error("Adding an Account");
}

void del_acc(void)
{
    display_error("Deleting an Account");
}

void add_tra(void)
{
    display_error("Adding a Transaction");
}
```

continued...

...from previous page

```
void del_tra(void)
{
    display_error("Deleting a Tranaction");
}

void prt_coa(void)
{
    display_error("Printing a Chart of Accounts");
}

void led_upd(void)
{
    display_error("Printing a Ledger Update");
}

void fin_stat(void)
{
    display_error("Printing the Financial Statements");
}

void main_help(void)
{
    display_error("Main help function");
}

void sf_help(void)
{
    display_error("Save file help function");
}

void rf_help(void)
{
    display_error("Read file help function");
}

void aa_help(void)
{
    display_error("Add account help function");
}
```

continued...

...from previous page

```
void da_help(void)
{
    display_error("Delete account help function");
}


void at_help(void)
{
    display_error("Add transaction help function");
}


void dt_help(void)
{
    display_error("Delete transaction help function");
}


void pc_help(void)
{
    display_error("Print chart of accounts help function");
}


void lu_help(void)
{
    display_error("Print ledger update help function");
}


void fs_help(void)
{
    display_error("Print financial statements help function");
}
```

pulldown_bar

Summary: #include "windows.h"
void pulldown_bar(*nmenus, menus, row*);
int *nmenus*;   (number of pull-down menus)
MENU_HEAD **menus*;   (pointer to an array of
                                                  MENU_HEAD structures)
int *row*;   (menu bar row)

Description: The **pulldown_bar** function is used to display a pull-down menu bar on the line defined by *row*.

Return Value: No value is returned.

See Also: **pulldown**

Example: The following program demonstrates how the pulldown_bar function is used to display a pull-down menu bar on the top line of the display screen.

```
#include <stdio.h>
#include "windows.h"

static MENU_HEAD heads[] = {
    {"File"},
    {"Accounts"},
    {"Transactions"},
    {"Print"} };

main()
{
    save_initial_video();
    pulldown_bar(4, heads, 1);
    waitkey();
    exit(0);
}
```

restorescreen

Summary:
```
#include "windows.h"
void far restorescreen(row1, col1, row2, col2, buffer);
int row1, col1;        (upper left corner of the text window)
int row2, col2;        (lower right corner of the text window)
char far *buffer;      (buffer pointer)
```

Description: The **restorescreen** function displays a text window, which has been previously saved in a *buffer*, at the coordinates defined by (*row1, col1*) and (*row2, col2*). Because each of the text window's characters consists of a character/attribute pair, the buffer must be ((*row2 - row1* + 1) * (*col2 - col1* + 1) * 2) bytes long.

Return Value: No value is returned.

See Also: **savescreen**

Example: The following program demonstrates how the restorescreen function is used to display a previously saved text window by saving a screen to a buffer, clearing the screen, and redisplaying the saved screen.

```
#include <stdio.h>
#include "windows.h"

static char vbuff[4000];

main()
{
    settext80();
    savescreen(1, 1, 25, 80, vbuff);
    clearscreen(1, 1, 25, 80, 7);
    waitkey();
    restorescreen(1, 1, 25, 80, vbuff);
    waitkey();
    exit(0);
}
```

save_initial_video

Summary: #include "windows.h"
void save_initial_video(void);

Description: The **save_initial_video** function is called at the start of an application program to initialize the WINDOWS operating environment, save the cursor's position and type, save a copy of the display screen, and clear the display screen. When the application program is finished executing, the save_initial_video function will automatically restore the display screen's initial contents and cursor settings.

Return Value: No value is returned.

See Also: **settext80**

Example: The following program demonstrates how the save_initial_video function saves and restores the original screen contents.

```
#include <stdio.h>
#include "windows.h"

main()
{
    save_initial_video();
    printcenter(13, 40, "This is a save_initial_video demo");
    waitkey();
    exit(0);
}
```

savescreen

Summary:
```
#include "windows.h"
void far savescreen(row1, col1, row2, col2, buffer);
int row1, col1;        (upper left corner of the text window)
int row2, col2;        (lower right corner of the text window)
char far *buffer;      (buffer pointer)
```

Description: The *savescreen* function buffers a text window at the coordinates defined by (*row1, col1*) and (*row2, col2*). Because each of the text window's characters consists of a character/attribute pair, *buffer* must be ((*row2 - row1* + 1) * (*col2 - col1* + 1) * 2) bytes long.

Return Value: No value is returned.

See Also: **restorescreen**

Example: The following program uses the **savescreen** function to duplicate the left half of the display screen onto the right half of the display screen.

```
#include <stdio.h>
#include "windows.h"

static char vbuff[2000];

main()
{
    settext80();
    savescreen(1, 1, 25, 40, vbuff);
    restorescreen(1, 41, 25, 80, vbuff);
    waitkey();
    exit(0);
}
```

scroll_window

Summary: #include "windows.h"
void scroll_window(*window, nlines, direction, att*);
WINDOW *window;   (pointer to a WINDOW structure,
which defines the text window's
coordinates)

int *nlines*;   (number of lines to be scrolled)
int *direction*;   (scroll direction)
int *att*;   (attribute for the cleared scroll
lines)

Description: The **scroll_window** function scrolls the contents of a text window,
in which coordinates are defined by *window*, for the number of
lines defined by *nlines*. If *attribute* is a non-zero value, the *nlines*
at the beginning of the scroll are cleared and their attributes are
set to the value of *att*. Otherwise, the beginning scroll lines are
left intact. The direction parameter can be one of the following
constants (defined in windows.h):

Constant	Action
_UP	Except for the text window's border, scroll the window up *nlines*.
_DOWN	Except for the text window's border, scroll the window down *nlines*.
_LEFT	Except for the text window's border, scroll the window left *nlines*.
_RIGHT	Except for the text window's border, scroll the window right *nlines*.
_UPA	Scroll the text window's entire contents up *nlines*.
_DOWNA	Scroll the text window's entire contents down *nlines*.
_LEFTA	Scroll the text window's entire contents left *nlines*.
_RIGHTA	Scroll the text window's entire contents right *nlines*.

Return Value: No value is returned.

See Also: **draw_window** and **open_window**

Example: The following program demonstrates how the scroll_window function is used to perform a variety of scrolling operations.

```
#include <stdio.h>
#include "windows.h"

main()
{
    int i, j;
    WINDOW window;

    save_initial_video();
    window.row1 = 1;
    window.col1 = 20;
    window.row2 = 10;
    window.col2 = 60;
    draw_window(1, 20, 10, 60, 0x70, _DOUBLE_LINE, 0x70);
    for (i = 2; i < 10; i++) {
        for (j = 21; j < 60; j++)
            printone(i, j, i);
    }
    waitkey();
    scroll_window(&window, 1, _UP, 0x70);
    waitkey();
    scroll_window(&window, 1, _DOWN, 0x70);
    waitkey();
    scroll_window(&window, 1, _LEFT, 0x70);
    waitkey();
    scroll_window(&window, 1, _RIGHT, 0x70);
    waitkey();
    exit(0);
}
```

setattrib

Summary: #include "windows.h"
void far setattrib(*row1, col1, row2, col2, att*);
int *row1, col1*;   (upper left corner of the text window)
int *row2, col2*;   (lower right corner of the text window)
int *att*;   (text window attribute)

Description: The **setattrib** function sets an entire text window's attributes to *att*. The text window is defined by the coordinates (*row1, col1*) and (*row2, col2*).

Return Value: No value is returned.

Example: The following program demonstrates how the setattrib function is used to set the right half of the display screen to black characters on a white background.

```
#include <stdio.h>
#include "windows.h"

main()
{
    save_initial_video();
    setattrib(1, 41, 25, 80, 0x70);
    waitkey();
    exit(0);
}
```

setcurpos

Summary: #include "windows.h"
void setcurpos(*row, col*);
int *row, col*;   (cursor position)

Description: The **setcurpos** function moves the cursor to the position defined by (*row, col*).

Return Value: No value is returned.

Example: The following program demonstrates how the setcurpos function is used to move the cursor to the right half of the display screen's center line.

```
#include <stdio.h>
#include "windows.h"

main()
{
    save_initial_video();
    setcurpos(13, 41);
    printf("Right half of the center line");
    waitkey();
    exit(0);
}
```

setcursor

Summary: #include "windows.h"
void setcursor(*sline, eline*);
int *sline*;   (cursor starting line)
int *eline*;   (cursor ending line)

Description: The **setcursor** function sets the cursor character's starting (*sline*) and ending (*eline*) lines.

Return Value: No value is returned.

Example: The following program demonstrates how the setcursor function is used to set the cursor character to a completely filled block.

```
#include <stdio.h>
#include "windows.h"

main()
{
    save_initial_video();
    setcurpos(1, 1);
    setcursor(0, 7);
    cursoron();
    waitkey();
    exit(0);
}
```

setone

Summary: #include "windows.h"
void setone(*row, col, att*);
int *row, col*;   (screen position)
int *att*;   (attribute)

Description: The **setone** function sets the attribute for the position defined by (*row, col*) to *att*.

Return Value: No value is returned.

Example: The following program demonstrates how the setone function is used to set the attribute for position (23, 2) to a black character on a white background.

```
#include <stdio.h>
#include "windows.h"

main()
{
    save_initial_video();
    setone(23, 2, 0x70);
    waitkey();
    exit(0);
}
```

settext80

Summary: #include "windows.h"
void settext80(void);

Description: The **settext80** function initializes the WINDOWS operating environment. The settext80 function should always be called before using any of the WINDOWS toolbox functions.

Return Value: No value is returned.

See Also: **save_initial_video**

Example: The following program demonstrates how the settext80 function is used to initialize the WINDOWS operating environment.

```
#include <stdio.h>
#include "windows.h"

main()
{
    settext80();
    clearscreen(1, 1, 25, 80, 7);
    setcurpos(1, 1);
    waitkey();
    exit(0);
}
```

vertical_bar

Summary: #include "windows.h"
void vertical_bar(*window, curpos, total, att*);
WINDOW **window*;   (pointer to the window's dynamic
                                              definition structure)
int *curpos*;   (current record)
int *total*;   (total number of records)
int *att*;   (scroll bar attribute)

Description: The **vertical_bar** function displays a vertical scroll bar at the right
side of a previously opened display window. The scroll bar set-
ting is derived by dividing *curpos* by *total*. Additionally, the scroll
bar is displayed with an attribute of *att*.

Return Value: No value is returned.

See Also: **horizontal_bar** and **open_window**

Example: The following program demonstrates how the vertical_bar function is used to display a variety of file positions.

```
#include <stdio.h>
#include "windows.h"

main()
{
    WINDOW *window;

    save_initial_video();
    window = open_window(1, 30, 10, 70, _DRAW, 7, _SINGLE_LINE, 7);
    vertical_bar(window, 0, 100, 0x70);
    waitkey();
    vertical_bar(window, 50, 100, 0x70);
    waitkey();
    vertical_bar(window, 100, 100, 0x70);
    waitkey();
    exit(0);
}
```

waitkey

Summary: #include "windows.h"
int waitkey(void);

Description: The **waitkey** function waits for the operator to press a key.

Return Value: The waitkey function returns the ASCII code for all nonextended-keyboard keys. Extended-keyboard keys return a value of their scan code + 256.

Example: The following program demonstrates how the waitkey function returns the values for a variety of key presses. Program execution will continue until the Esc key is pressed.

```
#include <stdio.h>
#include "windows.h"

main()
{
    int key;

    save_initial_video();
    while (TRUE) {
        if ((key = waitkey()) == 27)
            exit(0);
        printf("%d\n", key);
    }
}
```

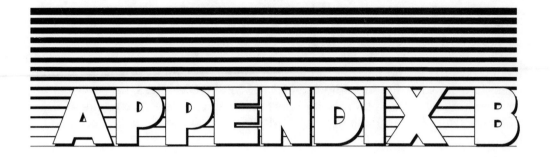

IBM PC ROM BIOS VIDEO SERVICES

As explained in Chapter 1, the IBM PC ROM BIOS video services place a wide variety of display input/output routines at a programmer's disposal. This appendix presents a detailed look at the ROM BIOS video services that are common to all IBM PCs and compatibles. Although the ROM BIOSes contained in some members of the PC family (i.e., the AT and computers with EGA adapters) offer video functions not found in the original IBM PC ROM BIOS, they will not be covered here because of their lack of portability across the entire family of IBM PCs and compatibles. Each of the ROM BIOS video functions is presented as follows:

- **Register Summary**: The register summary explains how the 8086 registers are used to pass parameters to a ROM BIOS video function and return values back to the calling program. An 8086 register model is presented for each of the ROM BIOS video functions. All of the shaded registers in the 8086 register summaries indicate registers that are used either by the calling program to pass parameters to the ROM BIOS video function or by the ROM BIOS video function to return values back to the calling program. Parameter passing is summarized in an appropriate **Call With** section. Returned values are summarized in an appropriate **Returns** section.

- **Function Description**: A description of the ROM BIOS function's purpose is presented for each of the ROM BIOS video functions. Furthermore, notes of special interest are provided.

- **Suggested Macro Definition**: A suggested assembly language macro definition is presented for each of the ROM BIOS video functions. Although the use of such a macro is strictly optional, macros can save programmers a great deal of time in developing programs that continuously use the same function calls over and over.

- **Programming Example**: A program fragment is presented for each of the ROM BIOS video functions. These examples are intended to illustrate how each of the ROM BIOS video functions are used in an application program.

SET VIDEO MODE (FUNCTION 00H)

Register Summary:

AX	AH	AL
BX	BH	BL
CX	CH	CL
DX	DH	DL

SP
BP
SI
DI

IP
FLAGS

CS
DS
SS
ES

Call With:

AH = 00H

AL = Video Mode

Returns:

Nothing

Description: ROM BIOS video function 00H sets the currently active video mode as follows:

Display Mode	Description	Adapter(s)
00H	40 × 25 black-and-white text	CGA, EGA, PCjr
01H	40 × 25 color text	CGA, EGA, PCjr
02H	80 × 25 black-and-white text	CGA, EGA, PCjr
03H	80 × 25 color text	CGA, EGA, PCjr
04H	320 × 200 4-color graphics	CGA, EGA, PCjr
05H	320 × 200 4-color (color off)	CGA, EGA, PCjr
06H	640 × 200 2-color graphics	CGA, EGA, PCjr
07H	80 × 25 black-and-white text	MDA, EGA
08H	160 × 200 16-color graphics	PCjr
09H	320 × 200 16-color graphics	PCjr
0AH	640 × 200 4-color graphics	PCjr
0DH	320 × 200 16-color graphics	EGA
0EH	640 × 200 16-color graphics	EGA
0FH	640 × 350 2-color graphics	EGA
10H	640 × 350 4/16-color graphics	EGA

Suggested Macro Definition:

```
setvidmode    macro    vidmode
              mov      ah,0
              mov      al,vidmode
              int      10h
              endm
```

Description: ROM BIOS video function 00H sets the currently active video mode as follows:

214

Display Mode	Description	Adapter(s)
00H	40 × 25 black-and-white text	CGA, EGA, PCjr
01H	40 × 25 color text	CGA, EGA, PCjr
02H	80 × 25 black-and-white text	CGA, EGA, PCjr
03H	80 × 25 color text	CGA, EGA, PCjr
04H	320 × 200 4-color graphics	CGA, EGA, PCjr
05H	320 × 200 4-color (color off)	CGA, EGA, PCjr
06H	640 × 200 2-color graphics	CGA, EGA, PCjr
07H	80 × 25 black-and-white text	MDA, EGA
08H	160 × 200 16-color graphics	PCjr
09H	320 × 200 16-color graphics	PCjr
0AH	640 × 200 4-color graphics	PCjr
0DH	320 × 200 16-color graphics	EGA
0EH	640 × 200 16-color graphics	EGA
0FH	640 × 350 2-color graphics	EGA
10H	640 × 350 4/16-color graphics	EGA

Suggested Macro Definition:

```
setvidmode      macro    vidmode
                mov      ah,0
                mov      al,vidmode
                int      10h
                endm
```

Example: The following program fragment demonstrates how ROM BIOS video function 00H is used to set the current video mode to the 80-column by 25-row color text mode.

```
    .
    .
    .
mov     ah,0        ;AH=Set video mode function code
mov     al,3        ;Set video mode to
int     10h         ; 80 x 25 color mode
    .
    .
    .
```

SET CURSOR TYPE (FUNCTION 01H)

Register Summary:

AX	AH	AL
BX	BH	BL
CX	CH	CL
DX	DH	DL

SP
BP
SI
DI

IP
FLAGS

CS
DS
SS
ES

Call With:

AH = 01H

CH = Starting cursor line

CL = Ending cursor line

Returns:

Nothing

Description: ROM BIOS function 01H sets the starting and ending lines for the blinking cursor character. The default values used by most application programs are as follows:

Cursor Type	Starting Line	Ending Line
Mode 07H	11	12
Modes 00H - 03H	6	7
Turn cursor off	32	0

Suggested Macro Definition:

```
setcurtype      macro    sline,eline
                mov      ah,1
                mov      ch,sline
                mov      cl,eline
                int      10h
                endm
```

Example: The following program fragment demonstrates how ROM BIOS video function 01H is used to turn the cursor off.

```
  .
  .
  .
mov     ah,1          ;AH=Set cursor type function
mov     cx,2000h      ;CX=Turn off cursor values
int     10H           ;Turn off the cursor
  .
  .
  .
```

SET CURSOR POSITION (FUNCTION 02H)

Register Summary:

AX	AH	AL
BX	BH	BL
CX	CH	CL
DX	DH	DL

SP
BP
SI
DI

IP
FLAGS

CS
DS
SS
ES

Call With:

AH = 02H

BH = Page number

DH = Cursor row

DL = Cursor column

Returns:

Nothing

Description: ROM BIOS video function 02H sets the current cursor position. In graphics modes, the page number passed in BH must be zero. The upper left corner of the screen is 0,0. The lower right corner of the screen is 24,79 in 80-column modes and 24,39 in 40-column modes.

Suggested Macro Definition:

```
setcurpos       macro      page,row,column
                mov        ah,2
                mov        bh,page
                mov        dh,row
                mov        dl,column
                endm
```

Example: The following program fragment demonstrates how ROM BIOS video function 02H is used to home the cursor.

```
        .
        .
        .
mov        ah,2        ;AH=Set cursor position function code
mov        bh,0        ;BH=Page 0
xor        dx,dx       ;Set cursor to upper left hand corner
int        10h         ;Position the cursor
        .
        .
        .
```

READ CURSOR VALUES (FUNCTION 03H)

Register Summary:

AX | AH | AL

BX | BH | BL

CX | CH | CL

DX | DH | DL

SP

BP

SI

DI

IP

FLAGS

CS

DS

SS

ES

Call With:

AH = 03H

BH = Page number

Returns:

CH = Cursor starting line

CL = Cursor ending line

DH = Cursor row position

DL = Cursor column position

Description: ROM BIOS video function 03H retrieves the cursor character's starting line, the cursor character's ending line, the cursor row position, and the cursor column position. In graphics modes, the page number passed in BH must be zero.

Suggested Macro Definition:

```
readcurval    macro    page
              mov      ah,3
              mov      bh,page
              endm
```

Example: The following program fragment demonstrates how ROM BIOS video function 03H is used to retrieve the page zero cursor values.

```
.
.
.
mov    ah,3     ;AH=Read cursor values function code
mov    bh,0     ;BH=Page 0
int    10h      ;Go get the values
.
.
.
```

READ LIGHT PEN VALUES (FUNCTION 04H)

Register Summary:

AX | AH | AL |

BX | BH | BL |

CX | CH | CL |

DX | DH | DL |

SP

BP

SI

DI

IP

FLAGS

CS

DS

SS

ES

Call With:

AH = 04H

Returns:

AH =   0   if light pen isn't triggered
        1   if light pen is triggered

CH = Pixel row

BX = Pixel column

DH = Character row

DL = Character column

Description: ROM BIOS video function 04H returns the light pen's trigger status, pixel position, and character position.

Suggested Macro Definition:

```
readpen      macro
             mov     ah,4
             int     10h
             int     10h
             endm
```

Example: The following program fragment demonstrates how ROM BIOS video function 04H is used to retrieve the light pen values. Note that the following code fragment will perform a continuous loop until the light pen is triggered.

```
              .
              .
              .
loop:         mov     ah,4        ;AH=Read light pen function code
              int     10h         ;Get the light pen values
              test    ah,1        ;Loop till the
              jz      loop        ; pen is triggered
              .
              .
              .
```

SELECT DISPLAY PAGE (FUNCTION 05H)

Register Summary:

AX	AH	AL
BX	BH	BL
CX	CH	CL
DX	DH	DL

SP
BP
SI
DI

IP
FLAGS

CS
DS
SS
ES

Call With:

AH = 05H

AL = Page number

Returns:

Nothing

Description: ROM BIOS video function 05H selects the currently active display page. The maximum allowable page number varies according to the video mode and the display adapter as follows:

Mode(s)	Adapter	Allowable Page Numbers
00H and 01H	CGA	0 to 7
02H and 03H	CGA	0 to 3
02H, 03H, and 0DH	EGA	0 to 7
0EH	EGA	0 to 3
0FH and 10H	EGA	0 to 1

Suggested Macro Definition:

```
seldisppag    macro    page
              mov      ah,5
              mov      al,page
              int      10h
              endm
```

Example: The following program fragment demonstrates how ROM BIOS video function 05H is used to select display page 1.

```
      .
      .
      .
mov      ah,5        ;AH=Select page function code
mov      al,1        ;Select
int      10h         ; page 1
      .
      .
      .
```

225

SCROLL WINDOW UP (FUNCTION 06H)

Register Summary:

AX	AH	AL
BX	BH	BL
CX	CH	CL
DX	DH	DL

SP
BP
SI
DI

IP
FLAGS

CS
DS
SS
ES

Call With:

AH = 06H

AL = Number of scroll lines

BH = Attribute for the cleared area

CH = Upper left row

CL = Upper left column

DH = Lower right row

DL = Lower right column

Returns:

Nothing

Description: ROM BIOS video function 06H scrolls a display screen window's contents upward. If the number of lines passed in AL is equal to zero, the entire window will be cleared. Otherwise, only the specified number of lines in AL will be scrolled and cleared.

Suggested Macro Definition:

```
windowup        macro     row1,col1,row2,col2,lines,att
                mov       ah,6
                mov       al,lines
                mov       bh,att
                mov       ch,row1
                mov       cl,col1
                mov       dh,row2
                mov       dl,col2
                int       10h
                endm
```

Example: The following program fragment demonstrates how ROM BIOS video function 06H is used to clear the left half of the display screen.

```
.
.
.
mov       ah,6          ;AH=Scroll window up function code
mov       al,0          ;AL=Clear the whole window
mov       bh,7          ;BH=Normal attribute
mov       ch,0          ;CH=Upper left row
mov       cl,0          ;CL=Upper left column
mov       dh,24         ;DH=Lower right row
mov       dl,39         ;DL=Lower right column
int       10h           ;Clear the screen
.
.
.
```

SCROLL WINDOW DOWN (FUNCTION 07H)

Register Summary:

AX — AH | AL

BX — BH | BL

CX — CH | CL

DX — DH | DL

SP

BP

SI

DI

IP

FLAGS

CS

DS

SS

ES

Call With:

AH = 07H

AL = Number of scroll lines

BH = Attribute for the cleared area

CH = Upper left row

CL = Upper left column

DH = Lower right row

DL = Lower right column

Returns:

Nothing

Description: ROM BIOS video function 07H scrolls a display screen window's contents downward. If the number of lines passed in AL is equal to zero, the window will be completely cleared. Otherwise, only the number of lines specified in AL will be scrolled and cleared.

Suggested Macro Definition:

```
windowdown    macro    row1,col1,row2,col2,lines,att
              mov      ah,7
              mov      al,lines
              mov      bh,att
              mov      ch,row1
              mov      cl,col1
              mov      dh,row2
              mov      dl,col2
              int      10h
              endm
```

Example: The following program fragment demonstrates how ROM BIOS video function 07H is used to clear the right half of the display screen's top ten lines.

```
       .
       .
       .
mov    ah,7        ;AH=Scroll window down function code
mov    al,0        ;AL=Clear the whole window
mov    bh,7        ;BH=Normal attribute
mov    ch,0        ;CH=Upper left row
mov    cl,40       ;CL=Upper left column
mov    dh,9        ;DH=Lower right row
mov    dl,79       ;DL=Lower right column
int    10h         ;Clear the window
       .
       .
       .
```

READ CHARACTER/ATTRIBUTE PAIR (FUNCTION 08H)

Register Summary:

AX	AH	AL
BX	BH	BL
CX	CH	CL
DX	DH	DL

SP
BP
SI
DI

IP
FLAGS

CS
DS
SS
ES

Call with:

AH = 08H

BH = Page number

Returns:

AH = Attribute

AL = ASCII code

Description: ROM BIOS video function 08H retrieves the character/attribute pair located at the current cursor position. While in graphics modes, the page number passed in BH must be zero.

Suggested Macro Definition:

```
readpair        macro       page
                mov         ah,8
                mov         bh,page
                int         10h
                endm
```

Example: The following program fragment demonstrates how ROM BIOS video function 08H is used to read the character/attribute pair in the upper left corner of the display screen.

```
        .
        .
        .
mov     ah,2            ;AH=Set cursor function code
mov     bh,0            ;BH=Page 0
mov     dh,0            ;DH=Cursor row position
mov     dl,0            ;DL=Cursor column position
int     10h             ;Home the cursor
mov     ah,8            ;AH=Read pair function code
mov     bh,0            ;BH=Page 0
int     10h             ;Get the char/att pair
        .
        .
        .
```

WRITE CHARACTER/ATTRIBUTE PAIR (FUNCTION 09H)

Register Summary:

AX	AH	AL
BX	BH	BL
CX	CH	CL
DX	DH	DL

SP
BP
SI
DI

IP
FLAGS

CS
DS
SS
ES

Call With:

AH = 09H

AL = ASCII code

BH = Page number

BL = Attribute

CX = Number of characters

Returns:

Nothing

Description: ROM BIOS video function 09H displays a specified number of character/attribute pairs, beginning at the current cursor position. The cursor position is not updated by ROM BIOS video function 09H. In graphics modes, the page number passed in BH must equal zero.

Suggested Macro Definition:

```
writepair      macro      page,char,att,number
               mov        ah,9
               mov        al,char
               mov        bh,page
               mov        bl,att
               mov        cx,number
               int        10h
               endm
```

Example: The following program fragment demonstrates how ROM BIOS video function 09H is used to completely fill the bottom line of the display screen with an underline character.

```
        .
        .
        .
mov     ah,2        ;AH=Set cursor function code
mov     bh,0        ;BH=Page 0
mov     dh,24       ;DH=Cursor row position
mov     dl,0        ;DL=Cursor column position
int     10h         ;Move the cursor
mov     ah,9        ;AH=Write pair function code
mov     al,'_'      ;AL=Underline character
mov     bh,0        ;BH=Page 0
mov     bl,7        ;BL=Normal attribute
mov     cx,80       ;CX=Line length
int     10h         ;Display the line
        .
        .
        .
```

WRITE CHARACTERS (FUNCTION 0AH)

Register Summary:

AX	AH	AL
BX	BH	BL
CX	CH	CL
DX	DH	DL

SP
BP
SI
DI

IP
FLAGS

CS
DS
SS
ES

Call With:

AH = 0AH

AL = ASCII code

BH = Page number

BL = Color (Graphics only)

CX = Number of characters

Returns:

Nothing

Description: ROM BIOS video function 0AH writes a specified number of characters, beginning at the current cursor position. The cursor position is not updated by ROM BIOS video function 0AH. In graphics modes, the page number passed in BH must be zero.

Suggested Macro Definition:

```
writechar      macro       page,char,number,color
               mov         ah,0ah
               mov         al,char
               mov         bh,page
               ifnb        <color>
               mov         bl,color
               endif
               mov         cx,number
               int         10h
               endm
```

Example: The following program fragment demonstrates how ROM BIOS video function 0AH is used to display 40 * (asterisk) characters, starting at the upper left corner of the display screen.

```
    .
    .
    .
mov     ah,2        ;AH=Set cursor function code
mov     bh,0        ;BH=Page 0
mov     dh,0        ;DH=Cursor row position
mov     dl,0        ;DL=Cursor column position
int     10h         ;Home the cursor
mov     ah,0ah      ;AH=Write characters function code
mov     al,'*'      ;AL=Asterisk character
mov     bh,0        ;BH=Page 0
mov     cx,40       ;CX=Number of characters
int     10h         ;Display the characters
    .
    .
    .
```

SET COLOR PALETTE (FUNCTION 0BH)

Register Summary:

AX	AH	AL
BX	BH	BL
CX	CH	CL
DX	DH	DL

SP
BP
SI
DI

IP
FLAGS

CS
DS
SS
ES

Call With:

AH = 0BH

BH = Function code

BL = Color or Palette code

Returns:

Nothing

Description: ROM BIOS video function 0BH selects either a color palette or the background and border colors. If the function code in BH is equal to zero, ROM BIOS video function 0BH sets the background and border colors. While in graphics modes, the background and the border colors will be set to the color passed in BL. While in text modes, only the border color will be set to the color passed in BL. If the function code in BH is equal to one, the new color palette code is passed in BL as follows:

Palette	Pixel Value	Color
0	0	Current Background Color
	1	Green
	2	Red
	3	Brown
1	0	Current Background Color
	1	Cyan
	2	Magenta
	3	White

Suggested Macro Definition:

```
setpalette    macro    func,color
              mov      ah,0bh
              mov      bh,func
              mov      bl,color
              endm
```

Example: The following program fragment demonstrates how ROM BIOS video function 0BH is used to set a display screen's background to white.

```
    .
    .
    .
mov     ah,0bh          ;AH=Set palette function
mov     bh,0            ;BH=Set border color function
mov     bl,7            ;BL=White color value
int     10h             ;Set border to white
    .
    .
    .
```

WRITE GRAPHICS PIXEL (FUNCTION OCH)

Register Summary:

AX | AH | AL
BX | BH | BL
CX | CH | CL
DX | DH | DL

SP
BP
SI
DI

IP
FLAGS

CS
DS
SS
ES

Call With:

AH = 0CH

AL = Color value

CX = Pixel column

DX = Pixel row

Returns:

Nothing

Description: ROM BIOS video function 0CH sets a graphics pixel to the color passed in AL. For video modes 04H and 05H, the legitimate range for color values is 0 to 3. Video mode 06H allows only color values 0 and 1. Whenever bit 7 of the color value is set, the color value is **xored** with the pixel's current color value.

Suggested Macro Definition:

```
writepixel    macro     pixelx,pixely,color
              mov       ah,0ch
              mov       al,color
              mov       cx,pixelx
              mov       dx,pixely
              endm
```

Example: The following program fragment demonstrates how ROM BIOS video function 0CH is used to draw a graphics line across the center of the display screen.

```
        .
        .
        .
        mov     cx,0        ;CX=Starting x-coordinate
        mov     dx,120      ;DX=Y-coordinate
loop:   mov     ah,0ch      ;AH=Write pixel function code
        mov     al,1        ;AL=Color value
        int     10h         ;Turn on the pixel
        inc     cx          ;Bump the x-coordinate
        cmp     cx,640      ;Loop
        jb      loop        ; till done
        .
        .
        .
```

240

READ GRAPHICS PIXEL (FUNCTION 0DH)

Register Summary:

AX	AH	AL
BX	BH	BL
CX	CH	CL
DX	DH	DL

SP
BP
SI
DI

IP
FLAGS

CS
DS
SS
ES

Call With:

AH = 0DH

CX = Pixel column

DX = Pixel row

Returns:

AL = Color value

241

Description: ROM BIOS video function 0DH retrieves the color value for a specified graphics pixel. The range of the retrieved color value depends on the current video mode.

Suggested Macro Definition:

```
readpixel    macro    pixelx,pixely
             mov      ah,0dh
             mov      cx,pixelx
             mov      dx,pixely
             int      10h
             endm
```

Example: The following program fragment demonstrates how ROM BIOS video function 0DH is used to retrieve the color value of pixel 0,25.

```
    .
    .
    .
mov      ah,0dH        ;AH=Read pixel function code
mov      cx,0          ;CX=Pixel x-coordinate
mov      dx,25         ;DX=Pixel y-coordinate
int      10h           ;Retrieve the color value
    .
    .
    .
```

WRITE CHARACTER IN TELETYPE MODE (FUNCTION 0EH)

Register Summary:

AX	AH	AL

BX	BH	BL

CX	CH	CL

DX	DH	DL

SP
BP
SI
DI

IP
FLAGS

CS
DS
SS
ES

Call With:

AH = 0EH

AL = ASCII code

BH = Page number

BL = Color value for graphics modes

Returns:

Nothing

243

Description: ROM BIOS video function 0EH displays a character by using a teletype mode. The ASCII codes for bell, backspace, carriage return, and linefeed are all recognized by the teletype mode. All other ASCII codes display their corresponding characters.

Suggested Macro Definition:

```
writetty        macro       char,page,color
                mov         ah,0eh
                mov         al,char
                mov         bh,page
                ifnb        <color>
                mov         bl,color
                endif
                int         10h
                endm
```

Example: The following program fragment demonstrates how ROM BIOS video function 0EH is used to perform a carriage return.

```
        .
        .
        .
mov     ah,0eh          ;AH=Write teletype function code
mov     al,13           ;AL=Carriage return
mov     bh,0            ;BH=Page number
int     10h             ;Do a carriage return
        .
        .
        .
```

GET VIDEO MODE (FUNCTION 0FH)

Register Summary:

AX	AH	AL
BX	BH	BL
CX	CH	CL
DX	DH	DL

SP	
BP	
SI	
DI	

IP
FLAGS

CS
DS
SS
ES

Call With:

AH = 0FH

Returns:

AH = Line length

AL = Video mode

BH = Page number

Description: ROM BIOS video function 0FH retrieves the number of columns per display line, the currently active page number, and the current video mode as follows:

Display Mode	Description	Adapter(s)
00H	40 × 25 black-and-white text	CGA, EGA, PCjr
01H	40 × 25 color text	CGA, EGA, PCjr
02H	80 × 25 black-and-white text	CGA, EGA, PCjr
03H	80 × 25 color text	CGA, EGA, PCjr
04H	320 × 200 4-color graphics	CGA, EGA, PCjr
05H	320 × 200 4-color (color off)	CGA, EGA, PCjr
06H	640 × 200 2-color graphics	CGA, EGA, PCjr
07H	80 × 25 black-and-white text	MDA, EGA
08H	160 × 200 16-color graphics	PCjr
09H	320 × 200 16-color graphics	PCjr
0AH	640 × 200 4-color graphics	PCjr
0DH	320 × 200 16-color graphics	EGA
0EH	640 × 200 16-color graphics	EGA
0FH	640 × 350 2-color graphics	EGA
10H	640 × 350 4/16-color graphics	EGA

Suggested Macro Definition

```
getvidmode    macro
              mov     ah,0fh
              int     10h
              endm
```

Example: The following program fragment demonstrates how ROM BIOS video function 0FH is used to retrieve the current video mode, the current display page, and the number of columns per line.

```
        .
        .
        .
mov     ah,0fh          ;AH=Get video mode function code
int     10h             ;Get the video mode
        .
        .
        .
```

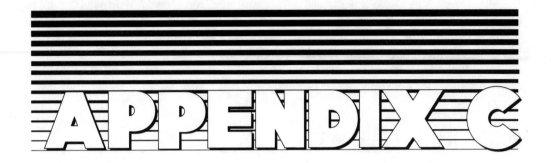

APPENDIX C

COMPILING THE WINDOWS TOOLBOX

Because the WINDOWS toolbox was originally developed using Microsoft QuickC, the portability of the programs in this book depends a great deal upon a specific C compiler's conformity to Microsoft C. Although conformity with Microsoft C may seem to limit portability, most C compilers for the IBM PC offer a great deal of compatibility with Microsoft C. Accordingly, the WINDOWS toolbox can be successfully ported to a variety of C compilers.

PORTABILITY PROBLEMS

Whereas most portability problems can be easily handled with conditional compilation statements, some portability problems just don't have a 100% solution; therefore, most of the WINDOWS toolbox programs will generate warning statements during the compilation process. Indeed, even Microsoft QuickC generates warnings for a few programs. Unfortunately, some portability problems just can't be solved. These unsolvable problems are usually the result of either inadequate run-time libraries or semantic differences in the run-time library routines. The following is a summary of the portability problems that are inherent in the WINDOWS toolbox:

PROGRAM	DESCRIPTION
All Programs	**High C:** Unfortunately, the WINDOWS toolbox can't be successfully ported to the High C compiler without a great deal of modification because High C does not conform with Microsoft C, and its run-time library is inadequate. **Objective C:** Because Objective C is an object-oriented superset translator, the WINDOWS toolbox can't be directly ported to Objective C. However, Objective C translates programs into Microsoft C. Therefore, Objective C should be able to support the WINDOWS toolbox by compiling the programs with Microsoft C.
video.asm	**DeSmet DC88:** Because DeSmet DC88 only supports the small memory model, a special DeSmet DC88 version of video.asm — video.dc — must be used for the low-level assembly language input/output functions.

PROGRAM	DESCRIPTION
	Eco-C88: Because Eco-C88 doesn't support mixed memory models, a special Eco-C88 version of video.asm — video.ec — must be used for the low-level assembly language input/output functions.
	Lattice C: Because Lattice C doesn't properly handle mixed memory models, a special Lattice C version of video.asm — video.lc — must be used for the low-level assembly language input/output functions.
	WATCOM C: Because WATCOM C uses a unique parameter-passing convention, a special WATCOM C version of video.asm, video.wc, must be used for the low-level assembly language input/output functions.
	Zortech C++: Because Zortech C++ doesn't support mixed memory models, a special Zortech C++ version of video.asm, video.zc, must be used for the low-level assembly language input/output functions.
windows.h	**Lattice C**: Because Lattice C generates a warning for the re-definition of **far**, any program that includes windows.h will generate a warning message. Accordingly, all of the WINDOWS toolbox programs will generate at least one warning message.
window.c	**Eco-C88**: Generates warning messages.
	Lattice C: Generates warning messages.
	Microsoft QuickC: Generates warning messages.
dialog.c	**Eco-C88**: Generates warning messages.
	Lattice C: Generates warning messages.
	Microsoft QuickC: Generates warning messages.

PROGRAM	DESCRIPTION
pulldown.c	**Eco-C88**: Generates warning messages.
	Lattice C: Generates warning messages.
	Zortech C+ +: Generates warning messages.
error.c	**Turbo C**: Generates warning messages.
ledger.c	**Eco-C88**: Because of numerous syntactic and semantic differences, ledger.c will not correctly compile without numerous modifications.
	Lattice C: Unfortunately, Lattice C runs out of memory.
	Microsoft C: Generates warning messages.
	Microsoft QuickC: Generates warning messages.
	Power C: Because of semantic differences in the run-time library routines, ledger.c will not execute properly.
	Turbo C: Generates warning messages.
	Zortech C+ +: Because of semantic differences in the run-time library routines, ledger.c will not execute properly.

COMPILING WINDOWS WITH C86Plus 1.20d

Batch File Listing: cccomp.bat

Listing C.1, **cccomp.bat**, is a batch file for compiling the WINDOWS toolbox, windows.lib. In addition to constructing the WINDOWS toolbox, cccomp.bat compiles and links SIMPLE LEDGER.

Listing C.1: cccomp.bat

```
rem
rem      cccomp.bat
rem      Compile WINDOWS with C86PLUS 1.20D
rem
masm /mx /dC86PLUS video,;
cc -DC86PLUS -c windio.c window.c menus.c popup.c dialog.c pulldown.c error.c
rem
rem      Build WINDOWS library - windows.lib
rem
lib windows.lib +video+windio+window+menus+popup+dialog+pulldown+error;
rem
rem      Compile and Link SIMPLE LEDGER
rem
cc -DC86PLUS -c ledger.c
cc ledger.obj windows.lib
rem
rem      Remove the Unwanted OBJ Files
rem
del video.obj
del windio.obj
del window.obj
del menus.obj
del popup.obj
del dialog.obj
del pulldown.obj
del error.obj
del ledger.obj
```

COMPILING WINDOWS WITH DeSmet DC88 3.1c

Batch File Listing: dccomp.bat

Listing C.2, **dccomp.bat**, is a batch file for compiling the WINDOWS toolbox, windows.s. In addition to constructing the WINDOWS toolbox, dccomp.bat compiles and links SIMPLE LEDGER.

Listing C.2: dccomp.bat

```
rem
rem      dccomp.bat
rem      Compile WINDOWS with DeSmet DC88 3.1c
rem
asm88 video.dc
c88 windio.c nDC88
c88 window.c nDC88
c88 menus.c nDC88
c88 popup.c nDC88
c88 dialog.c nDC88
c88 pulldown.c nDC88
c88 error.c nDC88
rem
rem      Build WINDOWS library - windows.lib
rem
lib88 -owindows error.o pulldown.o dialog.o popup.o menus.o window.o windio.o video.o
rem
rem      Compile and Link SIMPLE LEDGER
rem
c88 ledger.c nDC88
bind ledger.o windows.s
rem
rem      Remove the Unwanted O Files
rem
del video.o
del windio.o
del window.o
```

continued...

...from previous page

```
del menus.o
del popup.o
del dialog.o
del pulldown.o
del error.o
del ledger.o
```

Source Listing: video.dc

Listing C.3, **video.dc**, is a special DeSmet DC88 version of video.asm.

Listing C.3: video.dc

```
;
; VIDEO.DC - For the WINDOWS Toolbox
;           DeSmet DC88 Version of VIDEO.ASM
;


;
; ROM BIOS Locations
;
bios_data       equ     40h
crt_mode_set    equ     65h


                dseg
                public  _nonibm_
```

continued...

...from previous page

```
_nonibm_        dw      1
displayseg      dw      0b800h

                cseg

                public  settext80_, fillscreen_,setattrib_
                public  savescreen_,restorescreen_,drawbox_
                public  printstring_,waitkey_

;
; Set to 80 x 25 text mode
;
settext80_:     mov     ah,15           ;Get the
                int     10h             ; video mode
                cmp     al,2            ;Jump
                je      settext801      ; if
                cmp     al,3            ;  it's
                je      settext801      ;   already
                cmp     al,7            ;    a 80 x 25
                je      settext801      ;     video mode
                mov     ax,3            ;Set it to
                int     10h             ; 80 x 25 color
settext801:     mov     ax,0500h        ;Set the
                int     10h             ; page to 0
                mov     ah,12h          ;Check
                mov     bl,10h          ; for
                int     10h             ;  EGA
                cmp     bl,10h          ;Jump
                jne     settext803      ; if EGA
                mov     ah,15           ;Get the
                int     10h             ; video mode
                cmp     al,7            ;Jump
                je      settext802      ; if MDA
                mov     _nonibm_,0      ;Flag IBM CGA
                jmp     settext803      ;Jump
settext802:     mov     displayseg,0b000h ;Set the display segment address
settext803:     ret                     ;Return
```

continued...

...from previous page

```
;
; Fill text window
;
fillscreen_:    push    bp              ;Save BP registers
                mov     bp,sp           ;Point it to the stack
                sub     sp,4            ;Reserve local space
                push    di              ;Save DI
                mov     ax,[bp+4]       ;Figure
                mov     bx,[bp+6]       ; the
                call    fig_vid_off     ;  video offset
                mov     di,ax           ;DI=Video offset
                mov     es,displayseg   ;ES=Video segment
                mov     ax,[bp+8]       ;Figure
                sub     ax,[bp+4]       ; the number
                inc     ax              ;  of rows
                mov     [bp-2],ax       ;Save it
                mov     ax,[bp+10]      ;Figure
                sub     ax,[bp+6]       ; the number
                inc     ax              ;  of columns
                mov     [bp-4],ax       ;Save it
                cld                     ;Flag increment
                mov     al,[bp+12]      ;AL=Display character
                mov     ah,[bp+14]      ;AH=Display attribute
                call    disable_cga     ;Disable the CGA if necessary
fillscreen1:    push    di              ;Save the video offset
                mov     cx,[bp-4]       ;CX=Number of columns
        rep     stosw                   ;Display the row
                pop     di              ;Restore the video offset
                add     di,160          ;Point it to the next row
                dec     word [bp-2]     ;Loop
                jnz     fillscreen1     ; till done
                call    enable_cga      ;Enable the CGA if necessary
                pop     di              ;Restore DI
                mov     sp,bp           ;Reset the stack pointer
                pop     bp              ;Restore BP
                ret                     ;Return
```

continued...

...from previous page

```
;
; Set attributes
;
setattrib_:     push    bp                      ;Save BP
                mov     bp,sp                   ;Point it to the stack
                sub     sp,4                    ;Save space for local data
                push    di                      ;Save DI
                mov     ax,[bp+4]               ;Figure
                mov     bx,[bp+6]               ; the
                call    fig_vid_off             ;  video offset
                mov     di,ax                   ;DI=Video offset
                inc     di                      ;Bump it to the first attribute
                mov     es,displayseg           ;ES=Video segment
                mov     ax,[bp+8]               ;Figure
                sub     ax,[bp+4]               ; the number
                inc     ax                      ;  of rows
                mov     [bp-2],ax               ;Save it
                mov     ax,[bp+10]              ;Figure
                sub     ax,[bp+6]               ; the number
                inc     ax                      ;  columns
                mov     [bp-4],ax               ;Save it
                cld                             ;Flag increment
                mov     al,[bp+12]              ;AL=Display attribute
                call    disable_cga             ;Disable the CGA if necessary
setattrib1:     push    di                      ;Save the video offset
                mov     cx,[bp-4]               ;CX=Number of columns
setattrib2:     stosb                           ;Set the attribute byte
                inc     di                      ;Bump the video pointer
                loop    setattrib2              ;Loop till done
                pop     di                      ;Restore the video offset
                add     di,160                  ;Point it to the next row
                dec     word [bp-2]             ;Loop
                jnz     setattrib1              ; till done
                call    enable_cga              ;Enable the CGA if necessary
                pop     di                      ;Restore DI
                mov     sp,bp                   ;Reset the stack pointer
                pop     bp                      ;Restore BP
                ret                             ;Return
```

continued...

...from previous page

```
;
; Save screen
;
savescreen_:   push    bp              ;Save BP
               mov     bp,sp           ;Point it to the stack
               sub     sp,4            ;Make room for local data
               push    di              ;Save the
               push    si              ; registers
               mov     ax,[bp+4]       ;Figure
               mov     bx,[bp+6]       ; the
               call    fig_vid_off     ;  video offset
               mov     si,ax           ;SI=Video offset
               mov     ax,[bp+8]       ;Figure
               sub     ax,[bp+4]       ; the number
               inc     ax              ;  of rows
               mov     [bp-2],ax       ;Save it
               mov     ax,[bp+10]      ;Figure
               sub     ax,[bp+6]       ; the number
               inc     ax              ;  of columns
               mov     [bp-4],ax       ;Save it
               cld                     ;Flag increment
               call    disable_cga     ;Disable the CGA if necessary
               push    ds              ;Save DS
               push    ds              ;Point ES
               pop     es              ; the data segment
               mov     di,[bp+12]      ;DI=Array pointer
               mov     ds,displayseg   ;DS:SI=Video pointer
savescreen1:   push    si              ;Save the video offset
               mov     cx,[bp-4]       ;CX=Number of columns
        rep    movsw                   ;Save the row
               pop     si              ;Restore the video offset
               add     si,160          ;Point it to the next row
               dec     word [bp-2]     ;Loop
               jnz     savescreen1     ; till done
               pop     ds              ;Restore DS
               call    enable_cga      ;Enable the CGA if necessary
               pop     si              ;Restore
               pop     di              ; the registers
               mov     sp,bp           ;Reset the stack pointer
               pop     bp              ;Restore BP
               ret                     ;Return
```

continued...

...from previous page

```
;
; Restore screen
;
restorescreen_: push    bp              ;Save BP
                mov     bp,sp           ;Point it to the stack
                sub     sp,4            ;Make room for local data
                push    di              ;Save the
                push    si              ; registers
                mov     ax,[bp+4]       ;Figure
                mov     bx,[bp+6]       ; the
                call    fig_vid_off     ;  video offset
                mov     di,ax           ;DI=Video offset
                mov     es,displayseg   ;ES=Video segment
                mov     ax,[bp+8]       ;Figure
                sub     ax,[bp+4]       ; the number
                inc     ax              ;  of rows
                mov     [bp-2],ax       ;Save it
                mov     ax,[bp+10]      ;Figure
                sub     ax,[bp+6]       ; the number
                inc     ax              ;  of columns
                mov     [bp-4],ax       ;Save it
                cld                     ;Flag increment
                call    disable_cga     ;Disable the CGA if necessary
                mov     si,[bp+12]      ;DS:SI=Array pointer
restorescreen1: push    di              ;Save the video offset
                mov     cx,[bp-4]       ;CX=Number of columns
          rep   movsw                   ;Save the row
                pop     di              ;Restore the video offset
                add     di,160          ;Point it to the next row
                dec     word [bp-2]     ;Loop
                jnz     restorescreen1  ; till done
                call    enable_cga      ;Enable the CGA if necessary
                pop     si              ;Restore
                pop     di              ; the registers
                mov     sp,bp           ;Reset the stack pointer
                pop     bp              ;Restore BP
                ret                     ;Return
```

continued...

...from previous page

```
;
; Draw box
;
drawbox_:       push    bp              ;Save BP
                mov     bp,sp           ;Point it to the stack
                sub     sp,4            ;Save space for local data
                push    di              ;Save DI
                mov     ax,[bp+4]       ;Figure
                mov     bx,[bp+6]       ; the
                call    fig_vid_off     ;  video offset
                mov     di,ax           ;DI=Video offset
                mov     es,displayseg   ;ES=Video segment
                mov     ax,[bp+8]       ;Figure
                sub     ax,[bp+4]       ; the number
                dec     ax              ;  of rows - 2
                mov     [bp-2],ax       ;Save it
                mov     ax,[bp+10]      ;Figure
                sub     ax,[bp+6]       ; the number
                dec     ax              ;  of columns - 2
                mov     [bp-4],ax       ;Save it
                cld                     ;Flag increment
                mov     ah,[bp+14]      ;AH=Display attribute
                call    disable_cga     ;Disable the CGA if necessary
                push    di              ;Save the video offset
                mov     al,201          ;AL=Double line character
                cmp     word [bp+12],0  ;Jump if
                je      drawbox1        ; double line
                mov     al,218          ;AL=Single line character
drawbox1:       stosw                   ;Save the character/attribute pair
                mov     al,205          ;AL=Double line character
                cmp     word [bp+12],0  ;Jump if
                je      drawbox2        ; double line
                mov     al,196          ;AL=Single line character
drawbox2:       mov     cx,[bp-4]       ;CX=Line length
        rep     stosw                   ;Display the line
                mov     al,187          ;AL=Double line character
                cmp     word [bp+12],0  ;Jump if
                je      drawbox3        ; double line
                mov     al,191          ;AL=Single line character
```

continued...

...from previous page

```
drawbox3:    stosw                       ;Save the character/attribute pair
             pop     di                  ;Restore the video pointer
             add     di,160              ;Point it to the next row
drawbox4:    push    di                  ;Save the video pointer
             mov     al,186              ;AL=Double line character
             cmp     word [bp+12],0      ;Jump if
             je      drawbox5            ; double line
             mov     al,179              ;AL=Single line character
drawbox5:    stosw                       ;Save the character/attribute pair
             add     di,[bp-4]           ;Point to
             add     di,[bp-4]           ; the right side
             stosw                       ;Save the character/attribute pair
             pop     di                  ;Restore the video pointer
             add     di,160              ;Point it to the next row
             dec     word [bp-2]         ;Loop till the
             jnz     drawbox4            ; sides are complete
             mov     al,200              ;AL=Double line character
             cmp     word [bp+12],0      ;Jump if
             je      drawbox6            ; double line
             mov     al,192              ;AL=Single line character
drawbox6:    stosw                       ;Save the character/attribute pair
             mov     al,205              ;AL=Double line character
             cmp     word [bp+12],0      ;Jump if
             je      drawbox7            ; double line
             mov     al,196              ;AL=Single line character
drawbox7:    mov     cx,[bp-4]           ;CX=Line length
      rep    stosw                       ;Display the line
             mov     al,188              ;AL=Double line character
             cmp     word [bp+12],0      ;Jump if
             je      drawbox8            ; double line
             mov     al,217              ;AL=Single line character
drawbox8:    stosw                       ;Save the character/attribute pair
             call    enable_cga          ;Enable the CGA if necessary
             pop     di                  ;Restore DI
             mov     sp,bp               ;Reset the stack pointer
             pop     bp                  ;Restore BP
             ret                         ;Return
```

continued...

...from previous page

```
;
; Display string
;
printstring_:    push    bp                      ;Save BP
                 mov     bp,sp                   ;Point it to the stack
                 push    si                      ;Save
                 push    di                      ; the registers
                 mov     ax,[bp+4]               ;Figure
                 mov     bx,[bp+6]               ; the
                 call    fig_vid_off             ;  video offset
                 mov     di,ax                   ;DI=Video offset
                 mov     es,displayseg           ;ES=Video segment
                 cld                             ;Flag increment
                 mov     si,[bp+8]               ;DS:SI=String pointer
                 cmp     _nonibm_,0              ;Jump if
                 je      print_string2          ; IBM CGA
print_string1:   lodsb                           ;Get the next character
                 or      al,al                   ;Jump
                 jz      print_string6          ; if done
                 stosb                           ;Display the character
                 inc     di                      ;Bump the video pointer
                 jmp     print_string1          ;Loop till done
print_string2:   mov     dx,03dah                ;DX=Video status register
print_string3:   lodsb                           ;Get the next character
                 or      al,al                   ;Jump
                 jz      print_string6          ; if done
                 mov     ah,al                   ;Put it in AH
                 cli                             ;Disable the interrupts
print_string4:   in      al,dx                   ;Loop
                 and     al,1                    ; if in
                 jnz     print_string4          ;  horizontal retrace
print_string5:   in      al,dx                   ;Loop
                 and     al,1                    ; if not in
                 jz      print_string5          ;  horizontal retrace
                 mov     es:[di],ah              ;Display the character
                 sti                             ;Reenable the interrupts
                 inc     di                      ;Bump the
                 inc     di                      ; video pointer
                 jmp     print_string3          ;Loop till done
```

continued...

...from previous page

```
print_string6:  pop     di              ; the
                pop     si              ;   registers
                pop     bp              ;Restore BP
                ret                     ;Return


;
; Get a Key
;
waitkey_:       mov     ah,01h          ;Has a key
                int     16h             ; been pressed?
                jz      waitkey_        ;Loop if not
                mov     ah,0            ;Get
                int     16h             ; the key
                or      al,al           ;Jump if
                jz      wait_key1       ; extended key
                xor     ah,ah           ;Erase the scan code
                jmp     wait_key2       ;Jump
wait_key1:      xchg    ah,al           ;AX=Scan code
                inc     ah              ;AX=Scan code + 256
wait_key2:      ret                     ;Return


;
; Figure video offset
;
fig_vid_off:    push    dx              ;Save DX
                push    bx              ;Save the column
                dec     ax              ;Decrement the row
                mov     bx,160          ;Figure the
                mul     bx              ; row offset
                pop     bx              ;Restore the column
                dec     bx              ;Decrement it
                sal     bx,1            ;Figure the column pair offset
                add     ax,bx           ;AX=Video offset
                pop     dx              ;Restore DX
                ret                     ;Return
```

continued...

...from previous page

```
;
; Disable CGA
;
disable_cga:    cmp     _nonibm_,0      ;Jump if it
                jne     disable_cga2    ; isn't an IBM CGA
                push    ax              ;Save the
                push    dx              ; registers
                mov     dx,3dah         ;DX=Video status port
disable_cga1:   in      al,dx           ;Wait
                and     al,8            ; for
                jz      disable_cga1    ;   vertical retrace
                mov     dl,0d8h         ;DX=Video select register port
                mov     al,25h          ;Disable
                out     dx,al           ; the video
                pop     dx              ;Restore
                pop     ax              ; the registers
disable_cga2:   ret                     ;Return

;
; Enable CGA
;
enable_cga:     cmp     _nonibm_,0      ;Jump if it
                jne     enable_cga1     ; isn't an IBM CGA
                push    ax              ;Save
                push    bx              ; the
                push    dx              ;   registers
                push    ds              ;
                mov     ax,bios_data    ;Set the
                mov     ds,ax           ; data segment
                mov     bx,crt_mode_set ;BX=Video mode set value pointer
                mov     al,[bx]         ;AL=Video mode set value
                mov     dx,03d8h        ;DX=Video select register port
                out     dx,al           ;Reenable the video mode
                pop     ds              ;Restore
                pop     dx              ; the
                pop     bx              ;   registers
                pop     ax              ;
enable_cga1:    ret                     ;Return
```

COMPILING WINDOWS WITH Eco-C88 4.14

Batch File Listing: ecoccomp.bat

Listing C.4, **ecoccomp.bat**, is a batch file for compiling the WINDOWS toolbox, windows.lib.

Listing C.4: ecoccomp.bat

```
rem
rem     ecoccomp.bat
rem     Compile WINDOWS with Eco-C88 4.14
rem
masm /mx video.ec,;
cc -dECOC88 -nl windio.c window.c menus.c popup.c dialog.c pulldown.c error.c
rem
rem     Build WINDOWS library - windows.lib
rem
lib windows.lib +video+windio+window+menus+popup+dialog+pulldown+error;
rem
rem     Remove the Unwanted OBJ Files
rem
del video.obj
del windio.obj
del window.obj
del menus.obj
del popup.obj
del dialog.obj
del pulldown.obj
del error.obj
```

Source Listing: video.ec

Listing C.5, **video.ec**, is a special Eco-C88 version of video.asm.

Listing C.5: video.ec

```
;
; VIDEO.EC - For the WINDOWS Toolbox
;           Eco-C88 Version of VIDEO.ASM
;


;
; Set BIGCODE and BIGDATA as follows:
;
; Memory Model  BIGCODE BIGDATA
;
; Small         0       0
; Medium        1       0
; Compact       0       1
; Large         1       1

BIGCODE         equ     0
BIGDATA         equ     0

                include pro.h

                ifdef   cpu286
                .286
                endif


;
; ROM BIOS Locations
;
bios_data       equ     40h
crt_mode_set    equ     65h
```

continued...

...from previous page

```
$d$dataseg        segment word public 'data2'

                  public    __nonibm

__nonibm          dw        1
displayseg        dw        0b800h

$d$dataseg        ends


                  if        bigcode
$c$_video         segment word public 'code'
                  assume    cs:$c$_video
                  else
$b$prog           segment word public 'code'
                  assume    cs:$b$prog
                  endif

                  public    _settext80,_fillscreen,_setattrib
                  public    _savescreen,_restorescreen,_drawbox
                  public    _printstring,_waitkey

;
; Set to 80 x 25 text mode
;
                  if        bigcode
_settext80        proc      far
                  else
_settext80        proc      near
                  endif
                  mov       ah,15          ;Get the
                  int       10h            ; video mode
                  cmp       al,2           ;Jump
                  je        settext801     ; if
                  cmp       al,3           ;   it's
                  je        settext801     ;    already
                  cmp       al,7           ;     a 80 x 25
                  je        settext801     ;      video mode
                  mov       ax,3           ;Set it to
                  int       10h            ; 80 x 25 color
```

continued...

...from previous page

```
settext801:     mov     ax,0500h        ;Set the
                int     10h             ; page to 0
                mov     ah,12h          ;Check
                mov     bl,10h          ; for
                int     10h             ;  EGA
                cmp     bl,10h          ;Jump
                jne     settext803      ; if EGA
                mov     ah,15           ;Get the
                int     10h             ; video mode
                cmp     al,7            ;Jump
                je      settext802      ; if MDA
                mov     __nonibm,0      ;Flag IBM CGA
                jmp     short settext803 ;Jump
settext802:     mov     displayseg,0b000h ;Set the display segment address
settext803:     ret                     ;Return
_settext80      endp


;
; Fill text window
;
                if      bigcode
_fillscreen     proc    far
row1            equ     <6[bp]>
col1           equ     <8[bp]>
row2           equ     <10[bp]>
col2           equ     <12[bp]>
char           equ     <14[bp]>
att            equ     <16[bp]>
                else
_fillscreen     proc    near
row1           equ     <4[bp]>
col1           equ     <6[bp]>
row2           equ     <8[bp]>
col2           equ     <10[bp]>
char           equ     <12[bp]>
att            equ     <14[bp]>
                endif
```

continued...

269

...from previous page

```
rows            equ     <-2[bp]>
cols            equ     <-4[bp]>
                ifdef   cpu286
                enter   4,0             ;Set up the stack frame
                else
                push    bp              ;Save BP registers
                mov     bp,sp           ;Point it to the stack
                sub     sp,4            ;Reserve local space
                endif
                push    di              ;Save
                push    es              ; the registers
                mov     ax,row1         ;Figure
                mov     bx,col1         ; the
                call    fig_vid_off     ;   video offset
                mov     di,ax           ;DI=Video offset
                mov     es,displayseg   ;ES=Video segment
                mov     ax,row2         ;Figure
                sub     ax,row1         ; the number
                inc     ax              ;   of rows
                mov     rows,ax         ;Save it
                mov     ax,col2         ;Figure
                sub     ax,col1         ; the number
                inc     ax              ;   of columns
                mov     cols,ax         ;Save it
                cld                     ;Flag increment
                mov     al,byte ptr char ;AL=Display character
                mov     ah,byte ptr att ;AH=Display attribute
                call    disable_cga     ;Disable the CGA if necessary
fillscreen1:    push    di              ;Save the video offset
                mov     cx,cols         ;CX=Number of columns
        rep     stosw                   ;Display the row
                pop     di              ;Restore the video offset
                add     di,160          ;Point it to the next row
                dec     word ptr rows   ;Loop
                jnz     fillscreen1     ; till done
                call    enable_cga      ;Enable the CGA if necessary
                pop     es              ;Restore
                pop     di              ; the registers
                ifdef   cpu286
```

continued...

...from previous page

```
          leave                    ;Restore the stack
          else
          mov     sp,bp            ;Reset the stack pointer
          pop     bp               ;Restore BP
          endif
          ret                      ;Return
_fillscreen   endp

;
; Set attributes
;
          if      bigcode
_setattrib    proc    far
row1      equ     <6[bp]>
col1      equ     <8[bp]>
row2      equ     <10[bp]>
col2      equ     <12[bp]>
att       equ     <14[bp]>
          else
_setattrib    proc    near
row1      equ     <4[bp]>
col1      equ     <6[bp]>
row2      equ     <8[bp]>
col2      equ     <10[bp]>
att       equ     <12[bp]>
          endif
rows      equ     <-2[bp]>
cols      equ     <-4[bp]>
          ifdef   cpu286
          enter   4,0              ;Set up the stack frame
          else
          push    bp               ;Save BP
          mov     bp,sp            ;Point it to the stack
          sub     sp,4             ;Save space for local data
          endif
          push    di               ;Save
          push    es               ; the registers
          mov     ax,row1          ;Figure
          mov     bx,col1          ; the
```

continued...

...from previous page

```
                call    fig_vid_off       ;  video offset
                mov     di,ax             ;DI=Video offset
                inc     di                ;Bump it to the first attribute
                mov     es,displayseg     ;ES=Video segment
                mov     ax,row2           ;Figure
                sub     ax,row1           ;  the number
                inc     ax                ;   of rows
                mov     rows,ax           ;Save it
                mov     ax,col2           ;Figure
                sub     ax,col1           ;  the number
                inc     ax                ;   columns
                mov     cols,ax           ;Save it
                cld                       ;Flag increment
                mov     al,byte ptr att   ;AL=Display attribute
                call    disable_cga       ;Disable the CGA if necessary
setattrib1:     push    di                ;Save the video offset
                mov     cx,cols           ;CX=Number of columns
setattrib2:     stosb                     ;Set the attribute byte
                inc     di                ;Bump the video pointer
                loop    setattrib2        ;Loop till done
                pop     di                ;Restore the video offset
                add     di,160            ;Point it to the next row
                dec     word ptr rows     ;Loop
                jnz     setattrib1        ;  till done
                call    enable_cga        ;Enable the CGA if necessary
                pop     es                ;Restore
                pop     di                ;  the registers
                ifdef   cpu286
                leave                     ;Restore the stack
                else
                mov     sp,bp             ;Reset the stack pointer
                pop     bp                ;Restore BP
                endif
                ret                       ;Return
_setattrib      endp

;
; Save screen
;
```

continued...

...from previous page

```
                if      bigcode
_savescreen     proc    far
row1            equ     <6[bp]>
col1            equ     <8[bp]>
row2            equ     <10[bp]>
col2            equ     <12[bp]>
array           equ     <14[bp]>
                else
_savescreen     proc    near
row1            equ     <4[bp]>
col1            equ     <6[bp]>
row2            equ     <8[bp]>
col2            equ     <10[bp]>
array           equ     <12[bp]>
                endif
rows            equ     <-2[bp]>
cols            equ     <-4[bp]>
                ifdef   cpu286
                enter   4,0             ;Set up the stack frame
                else
                push    bp              ;Save BP
                mov     bp,sp           ;Point it to the stack
                sub     sp,4            ;Make room for local data
                endif
                push    di              ;Save
                push    si              ; the
                push    es              ;  registers
                mov     ax,row1         ;Figure
                mov     bx,col1         ; the
                call    fig_vid_off     ;  video offset
                mov     si,ax           ;SI=Video offset
                mov     ax,row2         ;Figure
                sub     ax,row1         ; the number
                inc     ax              ;  of rows
                mov     rows,ax         ;Save it
                mov     ax,col2         ;Figure
                sub     ax,col1         ; the number
                inc     ax              ;  of columns
```

continued...

...from previous page

```
                mov     cols,ax           ;Save it
                cld                       ;Flag increment
                call    disable_cga       ;Disable the CGA if necessary
                push    ds                ;Save DS
                if      bigdata
                les     di,array          ;ES:DI=Array Pointer
                else
                push    ds                ;Point ES
                pop     es                ; to the data segment
                mov     di,array          ;ES:DI=Array pointer
                endif
                mov     ds,displayseg     ;DS:SI=Video pointer
savescreen1:    push    si                ;Save the video offset
                mov     cx,cols           ;CX=Number of columns
        rep     movsw                     ;Save the row
                pop     si                ;Restore the video offset
                add     si,160            ;Point it to the next row
                dec     word ptr rows     ;Loop
                jnz     savescreen1       ; till done
                pop     ds                ;Restore DS
                call    enable_cga        ;Enable the CGA if necessary
                pop     es                ;Restore
                pop     si                ; the
                pop     di                ;  registers
                ifdef   cpu286
                leave                     ;Restore the stack
                else
                mov     sp,bp             ;Reset the stack pointer
                pop     bp                ;Restore BP
                endif
                ret                       ;Return
_savescreen     endp

;
; Restore screen
;
                if      bigcode
```

continued...

274

...from previous page

```
_restorescreen   proc    far
row1             equ     <6[bp]>
col1             equ     <8[bp]>
row2             equ     <10[bp]>
col2             equ     <12[bp]>
array            equ     <14[bp]>
                 else
_restorescreen   proc    near
row1             equ     <4[bp]>
col1             equ     <6[bp]>
row2             equ     <8[bp]>
col2             equ     <10[bp]>
array            equ     <12[bp]>
                 endif
rows             equ     <-2[bp]>
cols             equ     <-4[bp]>
                 ifdef   cpu286
                 enter   4,0              ;Set up the stack frame
                 else
                 push    bp               ;Save BP
                 mov     bp,sp            ;Point it to the stack
                 sub     sp,4             ;Make room for local data
                 endif
                 push    di               ;Save
                 push    si               ; the
                 push    es               ;  registers
                 mov     ax,row1          ;Figure
                 mov     bx,col1          ; the
                 call    fig_vid_off      ;  video offset
                 mov     di,ax            ;DI=Video offset
                 mov     es,displayseg    ;ES=Video segment
                 mov     ax,row2          ;Figure
                 sub     ax,row1          ; the number
                 inc     ax               ;  of rows
                 mov     rows,ax          ;Save it
                 mov     ax,col2          ;Figure
                 sub     ax,col1          ; the number
                 inc     ax               ;  of columns
```

continued...

...from previous page

```
                mov     cols,ax         ;Save it
                cld                     ;Flag increment
                call    disable_cga     ;Disable the CGA if necessary
                if      bigdata
                push    ds              ;Save DS
                lds     si,array        ;DS:SI=Array pointer
                else
                mov     si,array        ;DS:SI=Array pointer
                endif
restorescreen1: push    di              ;Save the video offset
                mov     cx,cols         ;CX=Number of columns
        rep     movsw                   ;Save the row
                pop     di              ;Restore the video offset
                add     di,160          ;Point it to the next row
                dec     word ptr rows   ;Loop
                jnz     restorescreen1  ; till done
                if      bigdata
                pop     ds              ;Restore DS
                endif
                call    enable_cga      ;Enable the CGA if necessary
                pop     es              ;Restore
                pop     si              ; the
                pop     di              ;  registers
                ifdef   cpu286
                leave                   ;Restore the stack
                else
                mov     sp,bp           ;Reset the stack pointer
                pop     bp              ;Restore BP
                endif
                ret                     ;Return
_restorescreen  endp


;
; Draw box
;
                if      bigcode
_drawbox        proc    far
row1            equ     <6[bp]>
col1           equ     <8[bp]>
row2           equ     <10[bp]>
```

continued...

...from previous page

```
col2        equ     <12[bp]>
flag        equ     <14[bp]>
att         equ     <16[bp]>
            else
_drawbox    proc    near
row1        equ     <4[bp]>
col1        equ     <6[bp]>
row2        equ     <8[bp]>
col2        equ     <10[bp]>
flag        equ     <12[bp]>
att         equ     <14[bp]>
            endif
rows        equ     <-2[bp]>
cols        equ     <-4[bp]>
            ifdef   cpu286
            enter   4,0             ;Set up the stack
            else
            push    bp              ;Save BP
            mov     bp,sp           ;Point it to the stack
            sub     sp,4            ;Save space for local data
            endif
            push    di              ;Save
            push    es              ; the registers
            mov     ax,row1         ;Figure
            mov     bx,col1         ; the
            call    fig_vid_off     ;  video offset
            mov     di,ax           ;DI=Video offset
            mov     es,displayseg   ;ES=Video segment
            mov     ax,row2         ;Figure
            sub     ax,row1         ; the number
            dec     ax              ;  of rows - 2
            mov     rows,ax         ;Save it
            mov     ax,col2         ;Figure
            sub     ax,col1         ; the number
            dec     ax              ;  of columns - 2
            mov     cols,ax         ;Save it
            cld                     ;Flag increment
            mov     ah,att          ;AH=Display attribute
            call    disable_cga     ;Disable the CGA if necessary
```

continued...

...from previous page

```
                push    di                      ;Save the video offset
                mov     al,201                  ;AL=Double line character
                cmp     word ptr flag,0 ;Jump if
                je      drawbox1                ; double line
                mov     al,218                  ;AL=Single line character
drawbox1:       stosw                           ;Save the character/attribute pair
                mov     al,205                  ;AL=Double line character
                cmp     word ptr flag,0 ;Jump if
                je      drawbox2                ; double line
                mov     al,196                  ;AL=Single line character
drawbox2:       mov     cx,cols                 ;CX=Line length
        rep     stosw                           ;Display the line
                mov     al,187                  ;AL=Double line character
                cmp     word ptr flag,0 ;Jump if
                je      drawbox3                ; double line
                mov     al,191                  ;AL=Single line character
drawbox3:       stosw                           ;Save the character/attribute pair
                pop     di                      ;Restore the video pointer
                add     di,160                  ;Point it to the next row
drawbox4:       push    di                      ;Save the video pointer
                mov     al,186                  ;AL=Double line character
                cmp     word ptr flag,0 ;Jump if
                je      drawbox5                ; double line
                mov     al,179                  ;AL=Single line character
drawbox5:       stosw                           ;Save the character/attribute pair
                add     di,cols                 ;Point to
                add     di,cols                 ; the right side
                stosw                           ;Save the character/attribute pair
                pop     di                      ;Restore the video pointer
                add     di,160                  ;Point it to the next row
                dec     word ptr rows           ;Loop till the
                jnz     drawbox4                ; sides are complete
                mov     al,200                  ;AL=Double line character
                cmp     word ptr flag,0 ;Jump if
                je      drawbox6                ; double line
                mov     al,192                  ;AL=Single line character
drawbox6:       stosw                           ;Save the character/attribute pair
                mov     al,205                  ;AL=Double line character
```

continued...

...from previous page

```
              cmp     word ptr flag,0 ;Jump if
              je      drawbox7        ; double line
              mov     al,196          ;AL=Single line character
drawbox7:     mov     cx,cols         ;CX=Line length
       rep    stosw                   ;Display the line
              mov     al,188          ;AL=Double line character
              cmp     word ptr flag,0 ;Jump if
              je      drawbox8        ; double line
              mov     al,217          ;AL=Single line character
drawbox8:     stosw                   ;Save the character/attribute pair
              call    enable_cga      ;Enable the CGA if necessary
              pop     es              ;Restore
              pop     di              ; the registers
              ifdef   cpu286
              leave                   ;Restore the stack
              else
              mov     sp,bp           ;Reset the stack pointer
              pop     bp              ;Restore BP
              endif
              ret                     ;Return
_drawbox      endp


;
; Display string
;
              if      bigcode
_printstring  proc    far
row           equ     <6[bp]>
col           equ     <8[bp]>
string        equ     <10[bp]>
              else
_printstring  proc    near
row           equ     <4[bp]>
col           equ     <6[bp]>
string        equ     <8[bp]>
              endif
              ifdef   cpu286
              enter   0,0             ;Set up the stack frame
```

continued...

...from previous page

```
                else
                push    bp                      ;Save BP
                mov     bp,sp                   ;Point it to the stack
                endif
                push    si                      ;Save
                push    di                      ; the
                push    es                      ;  registers
                mov     ax,row                  ;Figure
                mov     bx,col                  ; the
                call    fig_vid_off             ;  video offset
                mov     di,ax                   ;DI=Video offset
                mov     es,displayseg           ;ES=Video segment
                cld                             ;Flag increment
                cmp     word ptr __nonibm,0 ;IBM CGA?
                if      bigdata
                push    ds                      ;Save DS
                lds     si,string               ;DS:SI=String pointer
                else
                mov     si,string               ;DS:SI=String pointer
                endif
                je      print_string2           ;Jump if IBM CGA
print_string1:  lodsb                           ;Get the next character
                or      al,al                   ;Jump
                jz      print_string6           ; if done
                stosb                           ;Display the character
                inc     di                      ;Bump the video pointer
                jmp     print_string1           ;Loop till done
print_string2:  mov     dx,03dah                ;DX=Video status register
print_string3:  lodsb                           ;Get the next character
                or      al,al                   ;Jump
                jz      print_string6           ; if done
                mov     ah,al                   ;Put it in AH
                cli                             ;Disable the interrupts
print_string4:  in      al,dx                   ;Loop
                and     al,1                    ; if in
                jnz     print_string4           ;  horizontal retrace
print_string5:  in      al,dx                   ;Loop
                and     al,1                    ; if not in
                jz      print_string5           ;  horizontal retrace
```

continued...

...from previous page

```
                mov     es:[di],ah      ;Display the character
                sti                     ;Reenable the interrupts
                inc     di              ;Bump the
                inc     di              ; video pointer
                jmp     print_string3   ;Loop till done
print_string6: if       bigdata
                pop     ds              ;Restore DS
                endif
                pop     es              ;Restore
                pop     di              ; the
                pop     si              ;  registers
                ifdef   cpu286
                leave                   ;Restore the stack
                else
                pop     bp              ;Restore BP
                endif
                ret                     ;Return
_printstring   endp


;
; Get a Key
;
                if      bigcode
_waitkey       proc    far
                else
_waitkey       proc    near
                endif
                mov     ah,01h          ;Has a key
                int     16h             ; been pressed?
                jz      _waitkey        ;Loop if not
                mov     ah,0            ;Get
                int     16h             ; the key
                or      al,al           ;Jump if
                jz      wait_key1       ; extended key
                xor     ah,ah           ;Erase the scan code
                jmp     short wait_key2 ;Jump
wait_key1:     xchg    ah,al           ;AX=Scan code
                inc     ah              ;AX=Scan code + 256
wait_key2:     ret                     ;Return
_waitkey       endp
```

continued...

...from previous page

```
;
; Figure video offset
;
fig_vid_off     proc    near
                push    dx              ;Save DX
                push    bx              ;Save the column
                dec     ax              ;Decrement the row
                mov     bx,160          ;Figure the
                mul     bx              ; row offset
                pop     bx              ;Restore the column
                dec     bx              ;Decrement it
                sal     bx,1            ;Figure the column pair offset
                add     ax,bx           ;AX=Video offset
                pop     dx              ;Restore DX
                ret                     ;Return
fig_vid_off     endp


;
; Disable CGA
;
disable_cga     proc    near
                cmp     __nonibm,0      ;Jump if it
                jne     disable_cga2    ; isn't an IBM CGA
                push    ax              ;Save the
                push    dx              ; registers
                mov     dx,3dah         ;DX=Video status port
disable_cga1:   in      al,dx           ;Wait
                and     al,8            ; for
                jz      disable_cga1    ;   vertical retrace
                mov     dl,0d8h         ;DX=Video select register port
                mov     al,25h          ;Disable
                out     dx,al           ; the video
                pop     dx              ;Restore
                pop     ax              ; the registers
disable_cga2:   ret                     ;Return
disable_cga     endp
```

continued...

...from previous page

```
;
; Enable CGA
;
enable_cga      proc    near
                cmp     __nonibm,0      ;Jump if it
                jne     enable_cga1     ; isn't an IBM CGA
                push    ax              ;Save
                push    bx              ; the
                push    dx              ;  registers
                push    ds              ;
                mov     ax,bios_data    ;Set the
                mov     ds,ax           ; data segment
                mov     bx,crt_mode_set ;BX=Video mode set value pointer
                mov     al,[bx]         ;AL=Video mode set value
                mov     dx,03d8h        ;DX=Video select register port
                out     dx,al           ;Reenable the video mode
                pop     ds              ;Restore
                pop     dx              ; the
                pop     bx              ;  registers
                pop     ax              ;
enable_cga1:    ret                     ;Return
enable_cga      endp

                if      bigcode
$c$_video       ends
                else
$b$prog         ends
                endif

                end
```

COMPILING WINDOWS WITH LATTICE C 3.3

Batch File Listing: lccomp.bat

Listing C.6, **lccomp.bat**, is a batch file for compiling the WINDOWS toolbox, windows.lib.

Listing C.6: lccomp.bat

```
rem
rem     lccomp.bat
rem     Compile WINDOWS with Lattice C 3.3
rem
masm /mx video.lc,,;
lc -dLATTICEC -n -mp windio.c window.c menus.c popup.c dialog.c pulldown.c error.c
rem
rem     Build WINDOWS library - windows.lib
rem
lib windows.lib +video+windio+window+menus+popup+dialog+pulldown+error;
rem
rem     Remove the Unwanted OBJ Files
rem
del video.obj
del windio.obj
del window.obj
del menus.obj
del popup.obj
del dialog.obj
del pulldown.obj
del error.obj
```

Source Listing: video.lc

Listing C.7, **video.lc**, is a special Lattice C version of video.asm.

Listing C.7: video.lc

```
;
; VIDEO.LC - For the WINDOWS Toolbox
;           Lattice C Version of VIDEO.ASM
;


;
; Set LPROG and LDATA as follows:
;
;Memory Model   LPROG   LDATA
;     S           0       0
;     P           1       0
;     D           0       1
;     L           1       1
;     H           1       1

lprog           equ     1
ldata           equ     0

                ifdef   cpu286
                .286
                endif


;
; ROM BIOS Locations
;
bios_data       equ     40h
crt_mode_set    equ     65h
```

continued...

...from previous page

```
DGROUP          group   DATA
DATA            segment word public 'DATA'
                assume  ds:DGROUP

                public  _nonibm

_nonibm         dw      1
displayseg      dw      0b800h

DATA            ends



                if      lprog
VIDEO_TEXT      segment para public 'CODE'
                assume  cs:VIDEO_TEXT
                else
_TEXT           segment para public 'CODE'
                assume  cs:_TEXT
                endif

                public  settext80,fillscreen,setattrib
                public  savescreen,restorescreen,drawbox
                public  printstring,waitkey

;
; Set to 80 x 25 text mode
;
                if      lprog
settext80       proc    far
                else
settext80       proc    near
                endif
                mov     ah,15       ;Get the
                int     10h         ; video mode
                cmp     al,2        ;Jump
                je      settext801  ; if
                cmp     al,3        ;   it's
                je      settext801  ;     already
```

continued...

...from previous page

```
                cmp     al,7            ;    a 80 x 25
                je      settext801      ;      video mode
                mov     ax,3            ;Set it to
                int     10h             ; 80 x 25 color
settext801:     mov     ax,0500h        ;Set the
                int     10h             ; page to 0
                mov     ah,12h          ;Check
                mov     bl,10h          ; for
                int     10h             ;   EGA
                cmp     bl,10h          ;Jump
                jne     settext803      ; if EGA
                mov     ah,15           ;Get the
                int     10h             ; video mode
                cmp     al,7            ;Jump
                je      settext802      ; if MDA
                mov     _nonibm,0       ;Flag IBM CGA
                jmp     short settext803 ;Jump
settext802:     mov     displayseg,0b000h ;Set the display segment address
settext803:     ret                     ;Return
settext80       endp


;
; Fill text window
;
                if      lprog
fillscreen      proc    far
row1            equ     <6[bp]>
col1            equ     <8[bp]>
row2            equ     <10[bp]>
col2            equ     <12[bp]>
char            equ     <14[bp]>
att             equ     <16[bp]>
                else
fillscreen      proc    near
row1            equ     <4[bp]>
col1            equ     <6[bp]>
row2            equ     <8[bp]>
col2            equ     <10[bp]>
char            equ     <12[bp]>
att             equ     <14[bp]>
                endif
```

continued...

...from previous page

```
rows            equ      <-2[bp]>
cols            equ      <-4[bp]>
                ifdef    cpu286
                enter    4,0              ;Set up the stack frame
                else
                push     bp               ;Save BP registers
                mov      bp,sp            ;Point it to the stack
                sub      sp,4             ;Reserve local space
                endif
                push     di               ;Save the
                push     es               ; registers
                mov      ax,row1          ;Figure
                mov      bx,col1          ; the
                call     fig_vid_off      ;  video offset
                mov      di,ax            ;DI=Video offset
                mov      es,displayseg    ;ES=Video segment
                mov      ax,row2          ;Figure
                sub      ax,row1          ; the number
                inc      ax               ;  of rows
                mov      rows,ax          ;Save it
                mov      ax,col2          ;Figure
                sub      ax,col1          ; the number
                inc      ax               ;  of columns
                mov      cols,ax          ;Save it
                cld                       ;Flag increment
                mov      al,byte ptr char ;AL=Display character
                mov      ah,byte ptr att  ;AH=Display attribute
                call     disable_cga      ;Disable the CGA if necessary
fillscreen1:    push     di               ;Save the video offset
                mov      cx,cols          ;CX=Number of columns
        rep     stosw                     ;Display the row
                pop      di               ;Restore the video offset
                add      di,160           ;Point it to the next row
                dec      word ptr rows    ;Loop
                jnz      fillscreen1      ; till done
                call     enable_cga       ;Enable the CGA if necessary
                pop      es               ;Restore
                pop      di               ; the registers
                ifdef    cpu286
```

continued...

...from previous page

```
            leave                   ;Restore the stack
            else
            mov     sp,bp           ;Reset the stack pointer
            pop     bp              ;Restore BP
            endif
            ret                     ;Return
fillscreen  endp

;
; Set attributes
;
            if      lprog
setattrib   proc    far
row1        equ     <6[bp]>
col1        equ     <8[bp]>
row2        equ     <10[bp]>
col2        equ     <12[bp]>
att         equ     <14[bp]>
            else
setattrib   proc    near
row1        equ     <4[bp]>
col1        equ     <6[bp]>
row2        equ     <8[bp]>
col2        equ     <10[bp]>
att         equ     <12[bp]>
            endif
rows        equ     <-2[bp]>
cols        equ     <-4[bp]>
            ifdef   cpu286
            enter   4,0             ;Set up the stack frame
            else
            push    bp              ;Save BP
            mov     bp,sp           ;Point it to the stack
            sub     sp,4            ;Save space for local data
            endif
            push    di              ;Save the
            push    es              ; registers
            mov     ax,row1         ;Figure
            mov     bx,col1         ; the
```

continued...

...from previous page

```
                call    fig_vid_off     ;  video offset
                mov     di,ax           ;DI=Video offset
                inc     di              ;Bump it to the first attribute
                mov     es,displayseg   ;ES=Video segment
                mov     ax,row2         ;Figure
                sub     ax,row1         ; the number
                inc     ax              ;  of rows
                mov     rows,ax         ;Save it
                mov     ax,col2         ;Figure
                sub     ax,col1         ; the number
                inc     ax              ;  columns
                mov     cols,ax         ;Save it
                cld                     ;Flag increment
                mov     al,byte ptr att ;AL=Display attribute
                call    disable_cga     ;Disable the CGA if necessary
setattrib1:     push    di              ;Save the video offset
                mov     cx,cols         ;CX=Number of columns
setattrib2:     stosb                   ;Set the attribute byte
                inc     di              ;Bump the video pointer
                loop    setattrib2      ;Loop till done
                pop     di              ;Restore the video offset
                add     di,160          ;Point it to the next row
                dec     word ptr rows   ;Loop
                jnz     setattrib1      ; till done
                call    enable_cga      ;Enable the CGA if necessary
                pop     es              ;Restore
                pop     di              ; the registers
                ifdef   cpu286
                leave                   ;Restore the stack
                else
                mov     sp,bp           ;Reset the stack pointer
                pop     bp              ;Restore BP
                endif
                ret                     ;Return
setattrib       endp

;
; Save screen
;
```

continued...

...from previous page

```
            if      lprog
savescreen  proc    far
row1        equ     <6[bp]>
col1        equ     <8[bp]>
row2        equ     <10[bp]>
col2        equ     <12[bp]>
array       equ     <14[bp]>
            else
savescreen  proc    near
row1        equ     <4[bp]>
col1        equ     <6[bp]>
row2        equ     <8[bp]>
col2        equ     <10[bp]>
array       equ     <12[bp]>
            endif
rows        equ     <-2[bp]>
cols        equ     <-4[bp]>
            ifdef   cpu286
            enter   4,0             ;Set up the stack frame
            else
            push    bp              ;Save BP
            mov     bp,sp           ;Point it to the stack
            sub     sp,4            ;Make room for local data
            endif
            push    di              ;Save
            push    si              ; the
            push    es              ;  registers
            mov     ax,row1         ;Figure
            mov     bx,col1         ; the
            call    fig_vid_off     ;  video offset
            mov     si,ax           ;SI=Video offset
            mov     ax,row2         ;Figure
            sub     ax,row1         ; the number
            inc     ax              ;  of rows
            mov     rows,ax         ;Save it
            mov     ax,col2         ;Figure
            sub     ax,col1         ; the number
            inc     ax              ;  of columns
```

continued...

...from previous page

```
                mov     cols,ax         ;Save it
                cld                     ;Flag increment
                call    disable_cga     ;Disable the CGA if necessary
                push    ds              ;Save DS
                if      ldata
                les     di,array        ;ES:DI=Array pointer
                else
                push    ds              ;Point ES
                pop     es              ;  to DS
                mov     di,array        ;ES:DI=Array pointer
                endif
                mov     ds,displayseg   ;DS:SI=Video pointer
savescreen1:    push    si              ;Save the video offset
                mov     cx,cols         ;CX=Number of columns
        rep     movsw                   ;Save the row
                pop     si              ;Restore the video offset
                add     si,160          ;Point it to the next row
                dec     word ptr rows   ;Loop
                jnz     savescreen1     ; till done
                pop     ds              ;Restore DS
                call    enable_cga      ;Enable the CGA if necessary
                pop     es              ;Restore
                pop     si              ; the
                pop     di              ;  registers
                ifdef   cpu286
                leave                   ;Restore the stack
                else
                mov     sp,bp           ;Reset the stack pointer
                pop     bp              ;Restore BP
                endif
                ret                     ;Return
savescreen      endp

;
; Restore screen
;
```

continued...

...from previous page

```
                if      lprog
restorescreen   proc    far
row1            equ     <6[bp]>
col1            equ     <8[bp]>
row2            equ     <10[bp]>
col2            equ     <12[bp]>
array           equ     <14[bp]>
                else
restorescreen   proc    near
row1            equ     <4[bp]>
col1            equ     <6[bp]>
row2            equ     <8[bp]>
col2            equ     <10[bp]>
array           equ     <12[bp]>
                endif
rows            equ     <-2[bp]>
cols            equ     <-4[bp]>
                ifdef   cpu286
                enter   4,0             ;Set up the stack frame
                else
                push    bp              ;Save BP
                mov     bp,sp           ;Point it to the stack
                sub     sp,4            ;Make room for local data
                endif
                push    di              ;Save
                push    si              ; the
                push    es              ;  registers
                mov     ax,row1         ;Figure
                mov     bx,col1         ; the
                call    fig_vid_off     ;  video offset
                mov     di,ax           ;DI=Video offset
                mov     es,displayseg   ;ES=Video segment
                mov     ax,row2         ;Figure
                sub     ax,row1         ; the number
                inc     ax              ;  of rows
                mov     rows,ax         ;Save it
                mov     ax,col2         ;Figure
                sub     ax,col1         ; the number
                inc     ax              ;  of columns
```

continued...

...from previous page

```
              mov      cols,ax          ;Save it
              cld                       ;Flag increment
              call     disable_cga      ;Disable the CGA if necessary
              if       ldata
              push     ds               ;Save DS
              lds      si,array         ;DS:SI=Array pointer
              else
              mov      si,array         ;DS:SI=Array pointer
              endif
restorescreen1: push   di               ;Save the video offset
              mov      cx,cols          ;CX=Number of columns
       rep    movsw                     ;Save the row
              pop      di               ;Restore the video offset
              add      di,160           ;Point it to the next row
              dec      word ptr rows    ;Loop
              jnz      restorescreen1   ; till done
              if       ldata
              pop      ds               ;Restore DS
              endif
              call     enable_cga       ;Enable the CGA if necessary
              pop      es               ;Restore
              pop      si               ; the
              pop      di               ;   registers
              ifdef    cpu286
              leave                     ;Restore the stack
              else
              mov      sp,bp            ;Reset the stack pointer
              pop      bp               ;Restore BP
              endif
              ret                       ;Return
restorescreen endp

;
; Draw box
;
              if       lprog
drawbox       proc     far
row1          equ      <6[bp]>
col1          equ      <8[bp]>
row2          equ      <10[bp]>
```

continued...

...from previous page

```
col2        equ     <12[bp]>
flag        equ     <14[bp]>
att         equ     <16[bp]>
            else
drawbox     proc    near
row1        equ     <4[bp]>
col1        equ     <6[bp]>
row2        equ     <8[bp]>
col2        equ     <10[bp]>
flag        equ     <12[bp]>
att         equ     <14[bp]>
            endif
rows        equ     <-2[bp]>
cols        equ     <-4[bp]>
            ifdef   cpu286
            enter   4,0             ;Set up the stack
            else
            push    bp              ;Save BP
            mov     bp,sp           ;Point it to the stack
            sub     sp,4            ;Save space for local data
            endif
            push    di              ;Save the
            push    es              ;  registers
            mov     ax,row1         ;Figure
            mov     bx,col1         ; the
            call    fig_vid_off     ;  video offset
            mov     di,ax           ;DI=Video offset
            mov     es,displayseg   ;ES=Video segment
            mov     ax,row2         ;Figure
            sub     ax,row1         ; the number
            dec     ax              ;  of rows - 2
            mov     rows,ax         ;Save it
            mov     ax,col2         ;Figure
            sub     ax,col1         ; the number
            dec     ax              ;  of columns - 2
            mov     cols,ax         ;Save it
            cld                     ;Flag increment
            mov     ah,att          ;AH=Display attribute
            call    disable_cga     ;Disable the CGA if necessary
```

continued...

...from previous page

```
                push    di              ;Save the video offset
                mov     al,201          ;AL=Double line character
                cmp     word ptr flag,0 ;Jump if
                je      drawbox1        ; double line
                mov     al,218          ;AL=Single line character
drawbox1:       stosw                   ;Save the character/attribute pair
                mov     al,205          ;AL=Double line character
                cmp     word ptr flag,0 ;Jump if
                je      drawbox2        ; double line
                mov     al,196          ;AL=Single line character
drawbox2:       mov     cx,cols         ;CX=Line length
        rep     stosw                   ;Display the line
                mov     al,187          ;AL=Double line character
                cmp     word ptr flag,0 ;Jump if
                je      drawbox3        ; double line
                mov     al,191          ;AL=Single line character
drawbox3:       stosw                   ;Save the character/attribute pair
                pop     di              ;Restore the video pointer
                add     di,160          ;Point it to the next row
drawbox4:       push    di              ;Save the video pointer
                mov     al,186          ;AL=Double line character
                cmp     word ptr flag,0 ;Jump if
                je      drawbox5        ; double line
                mov     al,179          ;AL=Single line character
drawbox5:       stosw                   ;Save the character/attribute pair
                add     di,cols         ;Point to
                add     di,cols         ; the right side
                stosw                   ;Save the character/attribute pair
                pop     di              ;Restore the video pointer
                add     di,160          ;Point it to the next row
                dec     word ptr rows   ;Loop till the
                jnz     drawbox4        ; sides are complete
                mov     al,200          ;AL=Double line character
                cmp     word ptr flag,0 ;Jump if
                je      drawbox6        ; double line
                mov     al,192          ;AL=Single line character
drawbox6:       stosw                   ;Save the character/attribute pair
                mov     al,205          ;AL=Double line character
                cmp     word ptr flag,0 ;Jump if
```

continued...

...from previous page

```
                je      drawbox7        ; double line
                mov     al,196          ;AL=Single line character
drawbox7:       mov     cx,cols         ;CX=Line length
        rep     stosw                   ;Display the line
                mov     al,188          ;AL=Double line character
                cmp     word ptr flag,0 ;Jump if
                je      drawbox8        ; double line
                mov     al,217          ;AL=Single line character
drawbox8:       stosw                   ;Save the character/attribute pair
                call    enable_cga      ;Enable the CGA if necessary
                pop     es              ;Restore
                pop     di              ; the registers
                ifdef   cpu286
                leave                   ;Restore the stack
                else
                mov     sp,bp           ;Reset the stack pointer
                pop     bp              ;Restore BP
                endif
                ret                     ;Return
drawbox         endp

;
; Display string
;
                if      lprog
printstring     proc    far
row             equ     <6[bp]>
col             equ     <8[bp]>
string          equ     <10[bp]>
                else
printstring     proc    far
row             equ     <4[bp]>
col             equ     <6[bp]>
string          equ     <8[bp]>
                endif
                ifdef   cpu286
                enter   0,0             ;Set up the stack frame
                else
```

continued...

...from previous page

```
              push    bp              ;Save BP
              mov     bp,sp           ;Point it to the stack
              endif
              push    si              ;Save
              push    di              ; the
              push    es              ;  registers
              mov     ax,row          ;Figure
              mov     bx,col          ; the
              call    fig_vid_off     ;  video offset
              mov     di,ax           ;DI=Video offset
              mov     es,displayseg   ;ES=Video segment
              cld                     ;Flag increment
              cmp     word ptr _nonibm,0 ;IBM CGA?
              if      ldata
              push    ds              ;Save DS
              lds     si,string       ;DS:SI=String pointer
              else
              mov     si,string       ;DS:SI=String pointer
              endif
              je      print_string2   ;Jump if IBM CGA
print_string1: lodsb                  ;Get the next character
              or      al,al           ;Jump
              jz      print_string6   ; if done
              stosb                   ;Display the character
              inc     di              ;Bump the video pointer
              jmp     print_string1   ;Loop till done
print_string2: mov    dx,03dah        ;DX=Video status register
print_string3: lodsb                  ;Get the next character
              or      al,al           ;Jump
              jz      print_string6   ; if done
              mov     ah,al           ;Put it in AH
              cli                     ;Disable the interrupts
print_string4: in     al,dx           ;Loop
              and     al,1            ; if in
              jnz     print_string4   ;  horizontal retrace
print_string5: in     al,dx           ;Loop
              and     al,1            ; if not in
              jz      print_string5   ;  horizontal retrace
              mov     es:[di],ah      ;Display the character
```

continued...

...from previous page

```
                sti                         ;Reenable the interrupts
                inc     di                  ;Bump the
                inc     di                  ; video pointer
                jmp     print_string3       ;Loop till done
print_string6:  if      ldata
                pop     ds                  ;Restore
                endif
                pop     es                  ; the
                pop     di                  ;  registers
                pop     si                  ;
                ifdef   cpu286
                leave                       ;Restore the stack
                else
                pop     bp                  ;Restore BP
                endif
                ret                         ;Return
printstring     endp


;
; Get a Key
;
                if      lprog
waitkey         proc    far
                else
waitkey         proc    near
                endif
                mov     ah,01h              ;Has a key
                int     16h                 ; been pressed?
                jz      waitkey             ;Loop if not
                mov     ah,0                ;Get
                int     16h                 ; the key
                or      al,al               ;Jump if
                jz      wait_key1           ; extended key
                xor     ah,ah               ;Erase the scan code
                jmp     short wait_key2     ;Jump
wait_key1:      xchg    ah,al               ;AX=Scan code
                inc     ah                  ;AX=Scan code + 256
```

continued...

299

...from previous page

```
wait_key2:      ret                     ;Return
waitkey         endp


;
; Figure video offset
;
fig_vid_off     proc    near
                push    dx              ;Save DX
                push    bx              ;Save the column
                dec     ax              ;Decrement the row
                mov     bx,160          ;Figure the
                mul     bx              ; row offset
                pop     bx              ;Restore the column
                dec     bx              ;Decrement it
                sal     bx,1            ;Figure the column pair offset
                add     ax,bx           ;AX=Video offset
                pop     dx              ;Restore DX
                ret                     ;Return
fig_vid_off     endp


;
; Disable CGA
;
disable_cga     proc    near
                cmp     _nonibm,0       ;Jump if it
                jne     disable_cga2    ; isn't an IBM CGA
                push    ax              ;Save the
                push    dx              ; registers
                mov     dx,3dah         ;DX=Video status port
disable_cga1:   in      al,dx           ;Wait
                and     al,8            ; for
                jz      disable_cga1    ;  vertical retrace
                mov     dl,0d8h         ;DX=Video select register port
                mov     al,25h          ;Disable
                out     dx,al           ; the video
                pop     dx              ;Restore
                pop     ax              ; the registers
disable_cga2:   ret                     ;Return
disable_cga     endp
```

continued...

...from previous page

```
;
; Enable CGA
;
enable_cga      proc    near
                cmp     _nonibm,0       ;Jump if it
                jne     enable_cga1     ; isn't an IBM CGA
                push    ax              ;Save
                push    bx              ; the
                push    dx              ;  registers
                push    ds              ;
                mov     ax,bios_data    ;Set the
                mov     ds,ax           ; data segment
                mov     bx,crt_mode_set ;BX=Video mode set value pointer
                mov     al,[bx]         ;AL=Video mode set value
                mov     dx,03d8h        ;DX=Video select register port
                out     dx,al           ;Reenable the video mode
                pop     ds              ;Restore
                pop     dx              ; the
                pop     bx              ;  registers
                pop     ax              ;
enable_cga1:    ret                     ;Return
enable_cga      endp

                if      lprog
VIDEO_TEXT      ends
                else
_TEXT           ends
                endif

                end
```

COMPILING WINDOWS WITH MICROSOFT C 5.1

Batch File Listing: mccomp.bat

Listing C.8, **mccomp.bat**, is a batch file for compiling the WINDOWS toolbox, windows.lib. In addition to constructing the WINDOWS toolbox, mccomp.bat compiles and links SIMPLE LEDGER.

Listing C.8: mccomp.bat

```
rem
rem     mccomp.bat
rem     Compile WINDOWS with Microsoft C 5.1
rem
masm /mx /dMICROSOFTC video,;
cl /DMICROSOFTC /c windio.c window.c menus.c popup.c dialog.c pulldown.c error.c
rem
rem     Build WINDOWS library - windows.lib
rem
lib windows.lib +video+windio+window+menus+popup+dialog+pulldown+error;
rem
rem     Compile and Link SIMPLE LEDGER
rem
cl /DMICROSOFTC ledger.c /link windows
rem
rem     Remove the Unwanted OBJ Files
rem
del video.obj
del windio.obj
del window.obj
del menus.obj
del popup.obj
del dialog.obj
del pulldown.obj
del error.obj
del ledger.obj
```

COMPILING WINDOWS WITH MICROSOFT QUICKC 1.01

Batch File Listing: qccomp.bat

Listing C.9, **qccomp.bat**, is a batch file for compiling the WINDOWS toolbox. In addition to constructing the WINDOWS toolbox, qccomp.bat compiles and links SIMPLE LEDGER and also constructs a WINDOWS toolbox quick library, windows.qlb.

Listing C.9: qccomp.bat

```
rem
rem     qccomp.bat
rem     Compile WINDOWS with Microsoft QuickC 1.0
rem
masm /mx /dMICROSOFTC video,;
qcl /AM /DMICROSOFTC /c windio.c window.c menus.c popup.c dialog.c pulldown.c error.c
rem
rem     Build WINDOWS library - windows.lib
rem
lib windows.lib +video+windio+window+menus+popup+dialog+pulldown+error;
rem
rem     Build WINDOWS Quick Library - windows.qlb
rem
qlib /l windows.lib /s qcqlb.c
rem
rem     Compile and Link SIMPLE LEDGER
rem
qcl /AM /DMICROSOFTC ledger.c /link windows
rem
rem     Remove the Unwanted OBJ Files
rem
del video.obj
del windio.obj
del window.obj
del menus.obj
del popup.obj
del dialog.obj
del pulldown.obj
del error.obj
del ledger.obj
```

Source File Listing: qcqlb.c

Listing C.10, **qcqlb.c**, is used by qccomp.bat to include the _harderr and _hardresume run-time library functions in the WINDOWS toolbox quick library.

Listing C.10: qcqib.c

```
/****************************************************************************
* qcqlb.c - For the WINDOWS Toolbox
*           To Build a Quick Library With Microsoft QuickC
****************************************************************************/
_harderr();
_hardresume();
```

COMPILING WINDOWS WITH POWER C 1.1.6

Batch File Listing: pccomp.bat

Listing C.11, **pccomp.bat**, is a batch file for compiling the WINDOWS toolbox. Because Power C doesn't come with an object file librarian, the WINDOWS toolbox is compiled as a collection of separate **MIX** files.

Listing C.11: pccomp.bat

```
rem
rem      pccomp.bat
rem      Compile WINDOWS with Power C 1.1.6
rem
masm /mx /dPOWERC video,;
mix video.obj
pc /dPOWERC /c windio.c window.c menus.c popup.c dialog.c pulldown.c error.c
rem
rem      Remove the Unwanted OBJ File
rem
del video.obj
```

COMPILING WINDOWS WITH TURBO C 1.5

Batch File Listing: tccomp.bat

Listing C.12, **tccomp.bat**, is a batch file for compiling the WINDOWS toolbox, windows.lib. Besides constructing the WINDOWS toolbox, tccomp.bat compiles and links SIMPLE LEDGER.

Listing C.12: tccomp.bat

```
rem
rem     tccomp.bat
rem     Compile WINDOWS with Turbo C 1.5
rem
masm /mx /dTURBOC video,;
tcc -DTURBOC -c windio.c window.c menus.c popup.c dialog.c pulldown.c error.c
rem
rem     Build WINDOWS library - windows.lib
rem
tlib windows.lib +video+windio+window+menus+popup+dialog+pulldown+error
rem
rem     Compile and Link SIMPLE LEDGER
rem
tcc -DTURBOC ledger.c windows.lib
rem
rem     Remove the Unwanted OBJ and Temporary Files
rem
del video.obj
del windio.obj
del window.obj
del menus.obj
del popup.obj
del dialog.obj
del pulldown.obj
del error.obj
del ledger.obj
```

COMPILING WINDOWS WITH WATCOM C 6.5

Batch File Listing: wccomp.bat

Listing C.13, **wccomp.bat**, is a batch file for compiling the WINDOWS toolbox, windows.lib. Besides constructing the WINDOWS toolbox, wccomp.bat compiles and links SIMPLE LEDGER.

Listing C.13: wccomp.bat

```
rem
rem     wccomp.bat
rem     Compile WINDOWS with WATCOM C 6.5
rem
masm /mx video.wc,;
wcl windio.c window.c menus.c popup.c dialog.c pulldown.c error.c /dWATCOMC /c /d2
rem
rem     Build WINDOWS library - windows.lib
rem
wlib windows.lib +video+windio+window+menus+popup+dialog+pulldown+error
rem
rem     Compile and Link SIMPLE LEDGER
rem
wcc ledger.c /dWATCOMC /d2
wlink file ledger library windows,clibs,maths
rem
rem     Remove the Unwanted OBJ Files
rem
del video.obj
del windio.obj
del window.obj
del menus.obj
del popup.obj
del dialog.obj
del pulldown.obj
del error.obj
del ledger.obj
```

Source Listing: video.wc

Listing C.14, **video.wc**, is a special WATCOM C version of video.asm.

Listing C.14: video.wc

```
;
; VIDEO.WC - For the WINDOWS Toolbox
;           Watcom C 6.5 Version of VIDEO.ASM
;

                ifdef   cpu286
                .286
                endif


;
; ROM BIOS Locations
;
bios_data       equ     40h
crt_mode_set    equ     65h


DGROUP          group   _DATA
_DATA           segment word public 'DATA'
                assume  ds:DGROUP

                public  __nonibm

__nonibm        dw      1
displayseg      dw      0b800h

_DATA           ends


VIDEO_TEXT      segment para public 'CODE'
                assume  cs:VIDEO_TEXT

                public  settext80_,fillscreen_,setattrib_
                public  savescreen_,restorescreen_,drawbox_
                public  printstring_,waitkey_
```

continued...

...from previous page

```
;
; Set to 80 x 25 text mode
;
settext80_      proc    far
                mov     ah,15           ;Get the
                int     10h             ; video mode
                cmp     al,2            ;Jump
                je      settext801      ; if
                cmp     al,3            ;  it's
                je      settext801      ;   already
                cmp     al,7            ;    a 80 x 25
                je      settext801      ;     video mode
                mov     ax,3            ;Set it to
                int     10h             ; 80 x 25 color
settext801:     mov     ax,0500h        ;Set the
                int     10h             ; page to 0
                mov     ah,12h          ;Check
                mov     bl,10h          ; for
                int     10h             ;  EGA
                cmp     bl,10h          ;Jump
                jne     settext803      ; if EGA
                mov     ah,15           ;Get the
                int     10h             ; video mode
                cmp     al,7            ;Jump
                je      settext802      ; if MDA
                mov     __nonibm,0      ;Flag IBM CGA
                jmp     short settext803 ;Jump
settext802:     mov     displayseg,0b000h ;Set the display segment address
settext803:     ret                     ;Return
settext80_      endp

;
; Fill text window
;
fillscreen_     proc    far
char            equ     <6[bp]>
att             equ     <8[bp]>
rows           equ     <-2[bp]>
```

continued...

...from previous page

```
cols            equ     <-4[bp]>
                ifdef   cpu286
                enter   4,0             ;Set up the stack frame
                else
                push    bp              ;Save BP registers
                mov     bp,sp           ;Point it to the stack
                sub     sp,4            ;Reserve local space
                endif
                push    di              ;Save DI
                sub     bx,ax           ;Figure the
                inc     bx              ;  number of rows
                mov     rows,bx         ;Save it
                sub     cx,dx           ;Figure the
                inc     cx              ;  number of columns
                mov     cols,cx         ;Save it
                call    fig_vid_off     ;Figure the video offset
                mov     di,ax           ;DI=Video offset
                mov     es,displayseg   ;ES=Video segment
                cld                     ;Flag increment
                mov     al,byte ptr char ;AL=Display character
                mov     ah,byte ptr att ;AH=Display attribute
                call    disable_cga     ;Disable the CGA if necessary
fillscreen1:    push    di              ;Save the video offset
                mov     cx,cols         ;CX=Number of columns
        rep     stosw                   ;Display the row
                pop     di              ;Restore the video offset
                add     di,160          ;Point it to the next row
                dec     word ptr rows   ;Loop
                jnz     fillscreen1     ; till done
                call    enable_cga      ;Enable the CGA if necessary
                pop     di              ;Restore DI
                ifdef   cpu286
                leave                   ;Restore the stack
                else
                mov     sp,bp           ;Reset the stack pointer
                pop     bp              ;Restore BP
                endif
                ret                     ;Return
fillscreen      endp
```

continued...

...from previous page

```
;
; Set attributes
;
setattrib_       proc    far
att              equ     <6[bp]>
rows             equ     <-2[bp]>
cols             equ     <-4[bp]>
                 ifdef   cpu286
                 enter   4,0             ;Set up the stack frame
                 else
                 push    bp              ;Save BP
                 mov     bp,sp           ;Point it to the stack
                 sub     sp,4            ;Save space for local data
                 endif
                 push    di              ;Save DI
                 sub     bx,ax           ;Figure the
                 inc     bx              ; number of rows
                 mov     rows,bx         ;Save it
                 sub     cx,dx           ;Figure the
                 inc     cx              ; number columns
                 mov     cols,cx         ;Save it
                 call    fig_vid_off     ;Figure the video offset
                 mov     di,ax           ;DI=Video offset
                 inc     di              ;Bump it to the first attribute
                 mov     es,displayseg   ;ES=Video segment
                 cld                     ;Flag increment
                 mov     al,byte ptr att ;AL=Display attribute
                 call    disable_cga     ;Disable the CGA if necessary
setattrib1:      push    di              ;Save the video offset
                 mov     cx,cols         ;CX=Number of columns
setattrib2:      stosb                   ;Set the attribute byte
                 inc     di              ;Bump the video pointer
                 loop    setattrib2      ;Loop till done
                 pop     di              ;Restore the video offset
                 add     di,160          ;Point it to the next row
                 dec     word ptr rows   ;Loop
                 jnz     setattrib1      ; till done
                 call    enable_cga      ;Enable the CGA if necessary
```

continued...

...from previous page

```
                pop      di              ;Restore DI
                ifdef    cpu286
                leave                    ;Restore the stack
                else
                mov      sp,bp           ;Reset the stack pointer
                pop      bp              ;Restore BP
                endif
                ret                      ;Return
setattrib_      endp


;
; Save screen
;
savescreen_     proc     far
array           equ      <6[bp]>
rows            equ      <-2[bp]>
cols            equ      <-4[bp]>
                ifdef    cpu286
                enter    4,0             ;Set up the stack frame
                else
                push     bp              ;Save BP
                mov      bp,sp           ;Point it to the stack
                sub      sp,4            ;Make room for local data
                endif
                push     di              ;Save the
                push     si              ; registers
                sub      bx,ax           ;Figure the
                inc      bx              ; number of rows
                mov      rows,bx         ;Save it
                sub      cx,dx           ;Figure the
                inc      cx              ; number of columns
                mov      cols,cx         ;Save it
                call     fig_vid_off     ;Figure video offset
                mov      si,ax           ;SI=Video offset
                cld                      ;Flag increment
                call     disable_cga     ;Disable the CGA if necessary
                push     ds              ;Save DS
                les      di,array        ;ES:DI=Array pointer
                mov      ds,displayseg   ;DS:SI=Video pointer
```

continued...

...from previous page

```
savescreen1:    push    si              ;Save the video offset
                mov     cx,cols         ;CX=Number of columns
        rep     movsw                   ;Save the row
                pop     si              ;Restore the video offset
                add     si,160          ;Point it to the next row
                dec     word ptr rows   ;Loop
                jnz     savescreen1     ; till done
                pop     ds              ;Restore DS
                call    enable_cga      ;Enable the CGA if necessary
                pop     si              ;Restore
                pop     di              ; the registers
                ifdef   cpu286
                leave                   ;Restore the stack
                else
                mov     sp,bp           ;Reset the stack pointer
                pop     bp              ;Restore BP
                endif
                ret                     ;Return
savescreen_     endp


;
; Restore screen
;
restorescreen_  proc    far
array           equ     <6[bp]>
rows            equ     <-2[bp]>
cols            equ     <-4[bp]>
                ifdef   cpu286
                enter   4,0             ;Set up the stack frame
                else
                push    bp              ;Save BP
                mov     bp,sp           ;Point it to the stack
                sub     sp,4            ;Make room for local data
                endif
                push    di              ;Save the
                push    si              ; registers
                sub     bx,ax           ;Figure the
                inc     bx              ; number of rows
                mov     rows,bx         ;Save it
```

continued...

...from previous page

```
                sub     cx,dx           ;Figure the
                inc     cx              ; number of columns
                mov     cols,cx         ;Save it
                call    fig_vid_off     ;Figure the video offset
                mov     di,ax           ;DI=Video offset
                mov     es,displayseg   ;ES=Video segment
                cld                     ;Flag increment
                call    disable_cga     ;Disable the CGA if necessary
                push    ds              ;Save DS
                lds     si,array        ;DS:SI=Array pointer
restorescreen1: push    di              ;Save the video offset
                mov     cx,cols         ;CX=Number of columns
        rep     movsw                   ;Save the row
                pop     di              ;Restore the video offset
                add     di,160          ;Point it to the next row
                dec     word ptr rows   ;Loop
                jnz     restorescreen1  ; till done
                pop     ds              ;Restore DS
                call    enable_cga      ;Enable the CGA if necessary
                pop     si              ;Restore
                pop     di              ; the registers
                ifdef   cpu286
                leave                   ;Restore the stack
                else
                mov     sp,bp           ;Reset the stack pointe
                pop     bp              ;Restore BP
                endif
                ret                     ;Return
restorescreen_  endp

;
; Draw box
;
drawbox_        proc    far
flag            equ     <6[bp]>
att             equ     <8[bp]>
rows            equ     <-2[bp]>
```

continued...

...from previous page

```
cols          equ     <-4[bp]>
              ifdef   cpu286
              enter   4,0              ;Set up the stack
              else
              push    bp               ;Save BP
              mov     bp,sp            ;Point it to the stack
              sub     sp,4             ;Save space for local data
              endif
              push    di               ;Save DI
              sub     bx,ax            ;Figure the
              dec     bx               ; number of rows - 2
              mov     rows,bx          ;Save it
              sub     cx,dx            ;Figure the
              dec     cx               ; number of columns - 2
              mov     cols,cx          ;Save it
              call    fig_vid_off      ;Figure the video offset
              mov     di,ax            ;DI=Video offset
              mov     es,displayseg    ;ES=Video segment
              cld                      ;Flag increment
              mov     ah,att           ;AH=Display attribute
              call    disable_cga      ;Disable the CGA if necessary
              push    di               ;Save the video offset
              mov     al,201           ;AL=Double line character
              cmp     word ptr flag,0  ;Jump if
              je      drawbox1         ; double line
              mov     al,218           ;AL=Single line character
drawbox1:     stosw                    ;Save the character/attribute pair
              mov     al,205           ;AL=Double line character
              cmp     word ptr flag,0  ;Jump if
              je      drawbox2         ; double line
              mov     al,196           ;AL=Single line character
drawbox2:     mov     cx,cols          ;CX=Line length
      rep     stosw                    ;Display the line
              mov     al,187           ;AL=Double line character
              cmp     word ptr flag,0  ;Jump if
              je      drawbox3         ; double line
              mov     al,191           ;AL=Single line character
drawbox3:     stosw                    ;Save the character/attribute pair
              pop     di               ;Restore the video pointer
              add     di,160           ;Point it to the next row
```

continued...

...from previous page

```
drawbox4:      push    di                         ;Save the video pointer
               mov     al,186                     ;AL=Double line character
               cmp     word ptr flag,0 ;Jump if
               je      drawbox5                   ; double line
               mov     al,179                     ;AL=Single line character
drawbox5:      stosw                              ;Save the character/attribute pair
               add     di,cols                    ;Point to
               add     di,cols                    ; the right side
               stosw                              ;Save the character/attribute pair
               pop     di                         ;Restore the video pointer
               add     di,160                     ;Point it to the next row
               dec     word ptr rows   ;Loop till the
               jnz     drawbox4                   ; sides are complete
               mov     al,200                     ;AL=Double line character
               cmp     word ptr flag,0 ;Jump if
               je      drawbox6                   ; double line
               mov     al,192                     ;AL=Single line character
drawbox6:      stosw                              ;Save the character/attribute pair
               mov     al,205                     ;AL=Double line character
               cmp     word ptr flag,0 ;Jump if
               je      drawbox7                   ; double line
               mov     al,196                     ;AL=Single line character
drawbox7:      mov     cx,cols                    ;CX=Line length
       rep     stosw                              ;Display the line
               mov     al,188                     ;AL=Double line character
               cmp     word ptr flag,0 ;Jump if
               je      drawbox8                   ; double line
               mov     al,217                     ;AL=Single line character
drawbox8:      stosw                              ;Save the character/attribute pair
               call    enable_cga                 ;Enable the CGA if necessary
               pop     di                         ;Restore DI
               ifdef   cpu286
               leave                              ;Restore the stack
               else
               mov     sp,bp                      ;Reset the stack pointer
               pop     bp                         ;Restore BP
               endif
               ret                                ;Return
drawbox_       endp
```

continued...

...from previous page

```
;
; Display string
;
printstring_    proc    far
                ifdef   cpu286
                enter   0,0                 ;Set up the stack frame
                else
                push    bp                  ;Save BP
                mov     bp,sp               ;Point it to the stack
                endif
                push    si                  ;Save the
                push    di                  ; registers
                call    fig_vid_off         ;Figure the video offset
                mov     di,ax               ;DI=Video offset
                mov     es,displayseg       ;ES=Video segment
                cld                         ;Flag increment
                cmp     word ptr __nonibm,0 ;IBM CGA?
                push    ds                  ;Save DS
                mov     ds,cx               ;DS=String segment
                mov     si,bx               ;SI=String offset
                je      printstring2        ;Jump if IBM CGA
printstring1:   lodsb                       ;Get the next character
                or      al,al               ;Jump
                jz      printstring6        ; if done
                stosb                       ;Display the character
                inc     di                  ;Bump the video pointer
                jmp     printstring1        ;Loop till done
printstring2:   mov     dx,03dah            ;DX=Video status register
printstring3:   lodsb                       ;Get the next character
                or      al,al               ;Jump
                jz      printstring6        ; if done
                mov     ah,al               ;Put it in AH
                cli                         ;Disable the interrupts
printstring4:   in      al,dx               ;Loop
                and     al,1                ; if in
                jnz     printstring4        ;  horizontal retrace
```

continued...

...from previous page

```
printstring5:   in      al,dx           ;Loop
                and     al,1            ; if not in
                jz      printstring5    ;   horizontal retrace
                mov     es:[di],ah      ;Display the character
                sti                     ;Reenable the interrupts
                inc     di              ;Bump the
                inc     di              ; video pointer
                jmp     printstring3    ;Loop till done
printstring6:   pop     ds              ;Restore
                pop     di              ; the
                pop     si              ;   registers
                ifdef   cpu286
                leave                   ;Restore the stack
                else
                pop     bp              ;Restore BP
                endif
                ret                     ;Return
printstring_    endp


;
; Get a Key
;
waitkey_        proc    far
                mov     ah,01h          ;Has a key
                int     16h             ; been pressed?
                jz      waitkey_        ;Loop if not
                mov     ah,0            ;Get
                int     16h             ; the key
                or      al,al           ;Jump if
                jz      waitkey1        ; extended key
                xor     ah,ah           ;Erase the scan code
                jmp     short waitkey2  ;Jump
waitkey1:       xchg    ah,al           ;AX=Scan code
                inc     ah              ;AX=Scan code + 256
waitkey2:       ret                     ;Return
waitkey_        endp
```

continued...

...from previous page

```
;
; Figure video offset
;
fig_vid_off     proc    near
                push    dx              ;Save the column
                dec     ax              ;Decrement the row
                mov     dx,160          ;Figure the
                mul     dx              ; row offset
                pop     dx              ;Restore the column
                dec     dx              ;Decrement it
                sal     dx,1            ;Figure the column pair offset
                add     ax,dx           ;AX=Video offset
                ret                     ;Return
fig_vid_off     endp


;
; Disable CGA
;
disable_cga     proc    near
                cmp     __nonibm,0      ;Jump if it
                jne     disable_cga2    ; isn't an IBM CGA
                push    ax              ;Save the
                push    dx              ; registers
                mov     dx,3dah         ;DX=Video status port
disable_cga1:   in      al,dx           ;Wait
                and     al,8            ; for
                jz      disable_cga1    ;   vertical retrace
                mov     dl,0d8h         ;DX=Video select register port
                mov     al,25h          ;Disable
                out     dx,al           ; the video
                pop     dx              ;Restore
                pop     ax              ; the registers
disable_cga2:   ret                     ;Return
disable_cga     endp
```

continued...

...from previous page

```
;
; Enable CGA
;
enable_cga      proc    near
                cmp     __nonibm,0      ;Jump if it
                jne     enable_cga1     ; isn't an IBM CGA
                push    ax              ;Save
                push    bx              ; the
                push    dx              ;  registers
                push    ds              ;
                mov     ax,bios_data    ;Set the
                mov     ds,ax           ; data segment
                mov     bx,crt_mode_set ;BX=Video mode set value pointer
                mov     al,[bx]         ;AL=Video mode set value
                mov     dx,03d8h        ;DX=Video select register port
                out     dx,al           ;Reenable the video mode
                pop     ds              ;Restore
                pop     dx              ; the
                pop     bx              ;  registers
                pop     ax              ;
enable_cga1:    ret                     ;Return
enable_cga      endp

VIDEO_TEXT      ends

                end
```

COMPILING WINDOWS WITH WATCOM EXPRESS C 6.5

Batch File Listing: eccomp.bat

Listing C.15, **eccomp.bat**, is a batch file for compiling the WINDOWS toolbox, windows.lib. In addition to constructing the WINDOWS toolbox, eccomp.bat compiles and links SIMPLE LEDGER.

Listing C.15: eccomp.bat

```
rem
rem     eccomp.bat
rem     Compile WINDOWS with WATCOM Express C 6.5
rem
masm /mx /dWATCOMC video,;
wcexp windio.c /dWATCOMC /o /dl
wcexp window.c /dWATCOMC /o /dl
wcexp menus.c /dWATCOMC /o /dl
wcexp popup.c /dWATCOMC /o /dl
wcexp dialog.c /dWATCOMC /o /dl
wcexp pulldown.c /dWATCOMC /o /dl
wcexp error.c /WATCOMC /o /dl
rem
rem     Build WINDOWS library - windows.lib
rem
wlib windows.lib +video+windio+window+menus+popup+dialog+pulldown+error
rem
rem     Compile and Link SIMPLE LEDGER
rem
wcexp ledger.c /dWATCOMC /o /dl
wlink file ledger library windows,wcexpl
rem
rem     Remove the Unwanted OBJ Files
rem
del video.obj
del windio.obj
del window.obj
del menus.obj
del popup.obj
del dialog.obj
del pulldown.obj
del error.obj
del ledger.obj
```

COMPILING WINDOWS WITH ZORTECH C++

Batch File Listing: zccomp.bat

Listing C.16, **zccomp.bat**, is a batch file for compiling the WINDOWS toolbox, windows.lib.

Listing C.16: zccomp.bat

```
rem
rem     zccomp.bat
rem     Compile WINDOWS with Zortech C and C++
rem
masm /mx video.zc,;
ztc -c -dZORTECHC windio.c window.c menus.c popup.c dialog.c pulldown.c error.c
rem
rem     Build WINDOWS library - windows.lib
rem
lib windows.lib +video+windio+window+menus+popup+dialog+pulldown+error;
rem
rem Remove the Unwanted OBJ Files
rem
del video.obj
del windio.obj
del window.obj
del menus.obj
del popup.obj
del dialog.obj
del pulldown.obj
del error.obj
```

Source Listing: video.zc

Listing C.17, **video.zc**, is a special Zortech C++ version of video.asm.

Listing C.17: video.zc

```
;
; VIDEO.ZC - For the WINDOWS Toolbox
;            Zortech C++ Version of VIDEO.ASM
;


;
; Set BIGCODE and BIGDATA as follows:
;
; Memory Model  BIGCODE BIGDATA
;
; Small         0       0
; Medium        1       0
; Compact       0       1
; Large         1       1

BIGCODE         equ     0
BIGDATA         equ     0

                ifdef   cpu286
                .286
                endif


;
; ROM BIOS Locations
;
bios_data       equ     40h
crt_mode_set    equ     65h


DGROUP          group   _DATA
_DATA           segment word public 'DATA'
                assume  ds:DGROUP

                public  __nonibm
```

continued...

...from previous page

```
__nonibm         dw       1
displayseg       dw       0b800h


_DATA            ends



                 if       bigcode
VIDEO_TEXT       segment word public 'CODE'
                 assume  cs:VIDEO_TEXT
                 else
_TEXT            segment word public 'CODE'
                 assume  cs:_TEXT
                 endif

                 public  _settext80,_fillscreen,_setattrib
                 public  _savescreen,_restorescreen,_drawbox
                 public  _printstring,_waitkey

;
; Set to 80 x 25 text mode
;
                 if       bigcode
_settext80       proc     far
                 else
_settext80       proc     near
                 endif
                 mov      ah,15           ;Get the
                 int      10h             ; video mode
                 cmp      al,2            ;Jump
                 je       settext801      ; if
                 cmp      al,3            ;   it's
                 je       settext801      ;    already
                 cmp      al,7            ;     a 80 x 25
                 je       settext801      ;       video mode
                 mov      ax,3            ;Set it to
                 int      10h             ; 80 x 25 color
```

continued...

...from previous page

```
settext801:     mov     ax,0500h        ;Set the
                int     10h             ; page to 0
                mov     ah,12h          ;Check
                mov     bl,10h          ; for
                int     10h             ;   EGA
                cmp     bl,10h          ;Jump
                jne     settext803      ; if EGA
                mov     ah,15           ;Get the
                int     10h             ; video mode
                cmp     al,7            ;Jump
                je      settext802      ; if MDA
                mov     __nonibm,0      ;Flag IBM CGA
                jmp     short settext803 ;Jump
settext802:     mov     displayseg,0b000h ;Set the display segment address
settext803:     ret                     ;Return
_settext80      endp


;
; Fill text window
;
                if      bigcode
_fillscreen     proc    far
row1            equ     <6[bp]>
col1           equ     <8[bp]>
row2           equ     <10[bp]>
col2           equ     <12[bp]>
char           equ     <14[bp]>
att            equ     <16[bp]>
                else
_fillscreen     proc    near
row1           equ     <4[bp]>
col1           equ     <6[bp]>
row2           equ     <8[bp]>
col2           equ     <10[bp]>
char           equ     <12[bp]>
att            equ     <14[bp]>
                endif
```

continued...

...from previous page

```
rows            equ     <-2[bp]>
cols            equ     <-4[bp]>
                ifdef   cpu286
                enter   4,0               ;Set up the stack frame
                else
                push    bp                ;Save BP registers
                mov     bp,sp             ;Point it to the stack
                sub     sp,4              ;Reserve local space
                endif
                push    di                ;Save
                push    es                ; the registers
                mov     ax,row1           ;Figure
                mov     bx,col1           ; the
                call    fig_vid_off       ;  video offset
                mov     di,ax             ;DI=Video offset
                mov     es,displayseg     ;ES=Video segment
                mov     ax,row2           ;Figure
                sub     ax,row1           ; the number
                inc     ax                ;  of rows
                mov     rows,ax           ;Save it
                mov     ax,col2           ;Figure
                sub     ax,col1           ; the number
                inc     ax                ;  of columns
                mov     cols,ax           ;Save it
                cld                       ;Flag increment
                mov     al,byte ptr char ;AL=Display character
                mov     ah,byte ptr att ;AH=Display attribute
                call    disable_cga       ;Disable the CGA if necessary
fillscreen1:    push    di                ;Save the video offset
                mov     cx,cols           ;CX=Number of columns
        rep     stosw                     ;Display the row
                pop     di                ;Restore the video offset
                add     di,160            ;Point it to the next row
                dec     word ptr rows     ;Loop
                jnz     fillscreen1       ; till done
                call    enable_cga        ;Enable the CGA if necessary
                pop     es                ;Restore
                pop     di                ; the registers
```

continued...

...from previous page

```
                ifdef   cpu286
                leave                   ;Restore the stack
                else
                mov     sp,bp           ;Reset the stack pointer
                pop     bp              ;Restore BP
                endif
                ret                     ;Return
_fillscreen     endp

;
; Set attributes
;
                if      bigcode
_setattrib      proc    far
row1            equ     <6[bp]>
col1            equ     <8[bp]>
row2            equ     <10[bp]>
col2            equ     <12[bp]>
att             equ     <14[bp]>
                else
_setattrib      proc    near
row1            equ     <4[bp]>
col1            equ     <6[bp]>
row2            equ     <8[bp]>
col2            equ     <10[bp]>
att             equ     <12[bp]>
                endif
rows            equ     <-2[bp]>
cols            equ     <-4[bp]>
                ifdef   cpu286
                enter   4,0             ;Set up the stack frame
                else
                push    bp              ;Save BP
                mov     bp,sp           ;Point it to the stack
                sub     sp,4            ;Save space for local data
                endif
                push    di              ;Save
                push    es              ; the registers
```

continued...

...from previous page

```
                mov     ax,row1         ;Figure
                mov     bx,col1         ; the
                call    fig_vid_off     ;  video offset
                mov     di,ax           ;DI=Video offset
                inc     di              ;Bump it to the first attribute
                mov     es,displayseg   ;ES=Video segment
                mov     ax,row2         ;Figure
                sub     ax,row1         ; the number
                inc     ax              ;  of rows
                mov     rows,ax         ;Save it
                mov     ax,col2         ;Figure
                sub     ax,col1         ; the number
                inc     ax              ;  columns
                mov     cols,ax         ;Save it
                cld                     ;Flag increment
                mov     al,byte ptr att ;AL=Display attribute
                call    disable_cga     ;Disable the CGA if necessary
setattrib1:     push    di              ;Save the video offset
                mov     cx,cols         ;CX=Number of columns
setattrib2:     stosb                   ;Set the attribute byte
                inc     di              ;Bump the video pointer
                loop    setattrib2      ;Loop till done
                pop     di              ;Restore the video offset
                add     di,160          ;Point it to the next row
                dec     word ptr rows   ;Loop
                jnz     setattrib1      ; till done
                call    enable_cga      ;Enable the CGA if necessary
                pop     es              ;Restore
                pop     di              ; the registers
                ifdef   cpu286
                leave                   ;Restore the stack
                else
                mov     sp,bp           ;Reset the stack pointer
                pop     bp              ;Restore BP
                endif
                ret                     ;Return
_setattrib      endp
```

continued...

...from previous page

```
;
; Save screen
;
                if      bigcode
_savescreen     proc    far
row1            equ     <6[bp]>
col1            equ     <8[bp]>
row2            equ     <10[bp]>
col2            equ     <12[bp]>
array           equ     <14[bp]>
                else
_savescreen     proc    near
row1            equ     <4[bp]>
col1            equ     <6[bp]>
row2            equ     <8[bp]>
col2            equ     <10[bp]>
array           equ     <12[bp]>
                endif
rows            equ     <-2[bp]>
cols            equ     <-4[bp]>
                ifdef   cpu286
                enter   4,0             ;Set up the stack frame
                else
                push    bp              ;Save BP
                mov     bp,sp           ;Point it to the stack
                sub     sp,4            ;Make room for local data
                endif
                push    di              ;Save
                push    si              ; the
                push    es              ;   registers
                mov     ax,row1         ;Figure
                mov     bx,col1         ; the
                call    fig_vid_off     ;   video offset
                mov     si,ax           ;SI=Video offset
                mov     ax,row2         ;Figure
                sub     ax,row1         ; the number
                inc     ax              ;   of rows
                mov     rows,ax         ;Save it
                mov     ax,col2         ;Figure
```

continued...

328

...from previous page

```
                sub     ax,col1         ; the number
                inc     ax              ;  of columns
                mov     cols,ax         ;Save it
                cld                     ;Flag increment
                call    disable_cga     ;Disable the CGA if necessary
                push    ds              ;Save DS
                if      bigdata
                les     di,array        ;ES:DI=Array Pointer
                else
                push    ds              ;Point ES
                pop     es              ; to the data segment
                mov     di,array        ;ES:DI=Array pointer
                endif
                mov     ds,displayseg   ;DS:SI=Video pointer
savescreen1:    push    si              ;Save the video offset
                mov     cx,cols         ;CX=Number of columns
        rep     movsw                   ;Save the row
                pop     si              ;Restore the video offset
                add     si,160          ;Point it to the next row
                dec     word ptr rows   ;Loop
                jnz     savescreen1     ; till done
                pop     ds              ;Restore DS
                call    enable_cga      ;Enable the CGA if necessary
                pop     es              ;Restore
                pop     si              ; the
                pop     di              ;  registers
                ifdef   cpu286
                leave                   ;Restore the stack
                else
                mov     sp,bp           ;Reset the stack pointer
                pop     bp              ;Restore BP
                endif
                ret                     ;Return
_savescreen     endp
```

continued...

...from previous page

```
;
; Restore screen
;
                if      bigcode
_restorescreen  proc    far
row1            equ     <6[bp]>
col1            equ     <8[bp]>
row2            equ     <10[bp]>
col2            equ     <12[bp]>
array           equ     <14[bp]>
                else
_restorescreen  proc    near
row1            equ     <4[bp]>
col1            equ     <6[bp]>
row2            equ     <8[bp]>
col2            equ     <10[bp]>
array           equ     <12[bp]>
                endif
rows            equ     <-2[bp]>
cols            equ     <-4[bp]>
                ifdef   cpu286
                enter   4,0             ;Set up the stack frame
                else
                push    bp              ;Save BP
                mov     bp,sp           ;Point it to the stack
                sub     sp,4            ;Make room for local data
                endif
                push    di              ;Save
                push    si              ; the
                push    es              ;  registers
                mov     ax,row1         ;Figure
                mov     bx,col1         ; the
                call    fig_vid_off     ;  video offset
                mov     di,ax           ;DI=Video offset
                mov     es,displayseg   ;ES=Video segment
                mov     ax,row2         ;Figure
                sub     ax,row1         ; the number
                inc     ax              ;  of rows
```

continued...

...from previous page

```
                mov     rows,ax              ;Save it
                mov     ax,col2              ;Figure
                sub     ax,col1              ; the number
                inc     ax                   ;  of columns
                mov     cols,ax              ;Save it
                cld                          ;Flag increment
                call    disable_cga          ;Disable the CGA if necessary
                if      bigdata
                push    ds                   ;Save DS
                lds     si,array             ;DS:SI=Array pointer
                else
                mov     si,array             ;DS:SI=Array pointer
                endif
restorescreen1: push    di                   ;Save the video offset
                mov     cx,cols              ;CX=Number of columns
        rep     movsw                        ;Save the row
                pop     di                   ;Restore the video offset
                add     di,160               ;Point it to the next row
                dec     word ptr rows        ;Loop
                jnz     restorescreen1       ; till done
                if      bigdata
                pop     ds                   ;Restore DS
                endif
                call    enable_cga           ;Enable the CGA if necessary
                pop     es                   ;Restore
                pop     si                   ; the
                pop     di                   ;  registers
                ifdef   cpu286
                leave                        ;Restore the stack
                else
                mov     sp,bp                ;Reset the stack pointer
                pop     bp                   ;Restore BP
                endif
                ret                          ;Return
_restorescreen  endp
```

continued...

...from previous page

```
;
; Draw box
;
                if      bigcode
_drawbox        proc    far
row1            equ     <6[bp]>
col1            equ     <8[bp]>
row2            equ     <10[bp]>
col2            equ     <12[bp]>
flag            equ     <14[bp]>
att             equ     <16[bp]>
                else
_drawbox        proc    near
row1            equ     <4[bp]>
col1            equ     <6[bp]>
row2            equ     <8[bp]>
col2            equ     <10[bp]>
flag            equ     <12[bp]>
att             equ     <14[bp]>
                endif
rows            equ     <-2[bp]>
cols            equ     <-4[bp]>
                ifdef   cpu286
                enter   4,0             ;Set up the stack
                else
                push    bp              ;Save BP
                mov     bp,sp           ;Point it to the stack
                sub     sp,4            ;Save space for local data
                endif
                push    di              ;Save
                push    es              ; the registers
                mov     ax,row1         ;Figure
                mov     bx,col1         ; the
                call    fig_vid_off     ;  video offset
                mov     di,ax           ;DI=Video offset
                mov     es,displayseg   ;ES=Video segment
                mov     ax,row2         ;Figure
                sub     ax,row1         ; the number
```

continued...

...from previous page

```
                dec     ax              ;  of rows - 2
                mov     rows,ax         ;Save it
                mov     ax,col2         ;Figure
                sub     ax,col1         ;  the number
                dec     ax              ;  of columns - 2
                mov     cols,ax         ;Save it
                cld                     ;Flag increment
                mov     ah,att          ;AH=Display attribute
                call    disable_cga     ;Disable the CGA if necessary
                push    di              ;Save the video offset
                mov     al,201          ;AL=Double line character
                cmp     word ptr flag,0 ;Jump if
                je      drawbox1        ;  double line
                mov     al,218          ;AL=Single line character
drawbox1:       stosw                   ;Save the character/attribute pair
                mov     al,205          ;AL=Double line character
                cmp     word ptr flag,0 ;Jump if
                je      drawbox2        ;  double line
                mov     al,196          ;AL=Single line character
drawbox2:       mov     cx,cols         ;CX=Line length
        rep     stosw                   ;Display the line
                mov     al,187          ;AL=Double line character
                cmp     word ptr flag,0 ;Jump if
                je      drawbox3        ;  double line
                mov     al,191          ;AL=Single line character
drawbox3:       stosw                   ;Save the character/attribute pair
                pop     di              ;Restore the video pointer
                add     di,160          ;Point it to the next row
drawbox4:       push    di              ;Save the video pointer
                mov     al,186          ;AL=Double line character
                cmp     word ptr flag,0 ;Jump if
                je      drawbox5        ;  double line
                mov     al,179          ;AL=Single line character
drawbox5:       stosw                   ;Save the character/attribute pair
                add     di,cols         ;Point to
                add     di,cols         ;  the right side
                stosw                   ;Save the character/attribute pair
                pop     di              ;Restore the video pointer
                add     di,160          ;Point it to the next row
```

continued...

...from previous page

```
                    dec     word ptr rows    ;Loop till the
                    jnz     drawbox4         ; sides are complete
                    mov     al,200           ;AL=Double line character
                    cmp     word ptr flag,0  ;Jump if
                    je      drawbox6         ; double line
                    mov     al,192           ;AL=Single line character
drawbox6:           stosw                    ;Save the character/attribute pair
                    mov     al,205           ;AL=Double line character
                    cmp     word ptr flag,0  ;Jump if
                    je      drawbox7         ; double line
                    mov     al,196           ;AL=Single line character
drawbox7:           mov     cx,cols          ;CX=Line length
           rep      stosw                    ;Display the line
                    mov     al,188           ;AL=Double line character
                    cmp     word ptr flag,0  ;Jump if
                    je      drawbox8         ; double line
                    mov     al,217           ;AL=Single line character
drawbox8:           stosw                    ;Save the character/attribute pair
                    call    enable_cga       ;Enable the CGA if necessary
                    pop     es               ;Restore
                    pop     di               ; the registers
                    ifdef   cpu286
                    leave                    ;Restore the stack
                    else
                    mov     sp,bp            ;Reset the stack pointer
                    pop     bp               ;Restore BP
                    endif
                    ret                      ;Return
_drawbox            endp

;
; Display string
;
                    if      bigcode
_printstring        proc    far
row                 equ     <6[bp]>
col                 equ     <8[bp]>
string              equ     <10[bp]>
                    else
```

continued...

...from previous page

```
_printstring     proc    near
row              equ     <4[bp]>
col              equ     <6[bp]>
string           equ     <8[bp]>
                 endif
                 ifdef   cpu286
                 enter   0,0                 ;Set up the stack frame
                 else
                 push    bp                  ;Save BP
                 mov     bp,sp               ;Point it to the stack
                 endif
                 push    si                  ;Save
                 push    di                  ; the
                 push    es                  ;  registers
                 mov     ax,row              ;Figure
                 mov     bx,col              ; the
                 call    fig_vid_off         ;  video offset
                 mov     di,ax               ;DI=Video offset
                 mov     es,displayseg       ;ES=Video segment
                 cld                         ;Flag increment
                 cmp     word ptr __nonibm,0 ;IBM CGA?
                 if      bigdata
                 push    ds                  ;Save DS
                 lds     si,string           ;DS:SI=String pointer
                 else
                 mov     si,string           ;DS:SI=String pointer
                 endif
                 je      print_string2      ;Jump if IBM CGA
print_string1:   lodsb                       ;Get the next character
                 or      al,al               ;Jump
                 jz      print_string6       ; if done
                 stosb                       ;Display the character
                 inc     di                  ;Bump the video pointer
                 jmp     print_string1       ;Loop till done
print_string2:   mov     dx,03dah            ;DX=Video status register
print_string3:   lodsb                       ;Get the next character
                 or      al,al               ;Jump
                 jz      print_string6       ; if done
                 mov     ah,al               ;Put it in AH
                 cli                         ;Disable the interrupts
```

continued...

...from previous page

```
print_string4:  in      al,dx           ;Loop
                and     al,1            ; if in
                jnz     print_string4   ;  horizontal retrace
print_string5:  in      al,dx           ;Loop
                and     al,1            ; if not in
                jz      print_string5   ;  horizontal retrace
                mov     es:[di],ah      ;Display the character
                sti                     ;Reenable the interrupts
                inc     di              ;Bump the
                inc     di              ; video pointer
                jmp     print_string3   ;Loop till done
print_string6:  if      bigdata
                pop     ds              ;Restore DS
                endif
                pop     es              ;Restore
                pop     di              ; the
                pop     si              ;  registers
                ifdef   cpu286
                leave                   ;Restore the stack
                else
                pop     bp              ;Restore BP
                endif
                ret                     ;Return
_printstring    endp


;
; Get a Key
;
                if      bigcode
_waitkey        proc    far
                else
_waitkey        proc    near
                endif
                mov     ah,01h          ;Has a key
                int     16h             ; been pressed?
                jz      _waitkey        ;Loop if not
                mov     ah,0            ;Get
                int     16h             ; the key
                or      al,al           ;Jump if
```

continued...

...from previous page

```
                jz      wait_key1       ; extended key
                xor     ah,ah           ;Erase the scan code
                jmp     short wait_key2 ;Jump
wait_key1:      xchg    ah,al           ;AX=Scan code
                inc     ah              ;AX=Scan code + 256
wait_key2:      ret                     ;Return
_waitkey        endp


;
; Figure video offset
;
fig_vid_off     proc    near
                push    dx              ;Save DX
                push    bx              ;Save the column
                dec     ax              ;Decrement the row
                mov     bx,160          ;Figure the
                mul     bx              ; row offset
                pop     bx              ;Restore the column
                dec     bx              ;Decrement it
                sal     bx,1            ;Figure the column pair offset
                add     ax,bx           ;AX=Video offset
                pop     dx              ;Restore DX
                ret                     ;Return
fig_vid_off     endp


;
; Disable CGA
;
disable_cga     proc    near
                cmp     __nonibm,0      ;Jump if it
                jne     disable_cga2    ; isn't an IBM CGA
                push    ax              ;Save the
                push    dx              ; registers
                mov     dx,3dah         ;DX=Video status port
```

continued...

...from previous page

```
disable_cga1:   in      al,dx               ;Wait
                and     al,8                ; for
                jz      disable_cga1        ;  vertical retrace
                mov     dl,0d8h             ;DX=Video select register port
                mov     al,25h              ;Disable
                out     dx,al               ; the video
                pop     dx                  ;Restore
                pop     ax                  ; the registers
disable_cga2:   ret                         ;Return
disable_cga     endp


;
; Enable CGA
;
enable_cga      proc    near
                cmp     __nonibm,0          ;Jump if it
                jne     enable_cga1         ; isn't an IBM CGA
                push    ax                  ;Save
                push    bx                  ; the
                push    dx                  ;  registers
                push    ds                  ;
                mov     ax,bios_data        ;Set the
                mov     ds,ax               ; data segment
                mov     bx,crt_mode_set     ;BX=Video mode set value pointer
                mov     al,[bx]             ;AL=Video mode set value
                mov     dx,03d8h            ;DX=Video select register port
                out     dx,al               ;Reenable the video mode
                pop     ds                  ;Restore
                pop     dx                  ; the
                pop     bx                  ;  registers
                pop     ax                  ;
enable_cga1:    ret                         ;Return
enable_cga      endp

                if      bigcode
VIDEO_TEXT      ends
                else
_TEXT           ends
                endif

                end
```

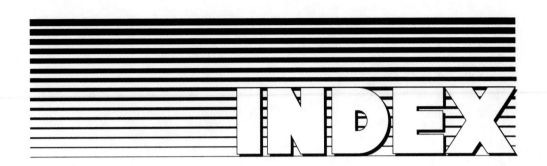

B

C

H

hardware errors, 104-106
horizontal retrace interval, 10
horizontal scroll bar, 62, 78
horizontal_bar, 78, 184
hotstring, 185

I

initcur, 59
int86, 56

L

Lattice C, 50, 76, 284-301
local variables, 19-20, 22

M

malloc, 63-64
memmove, 76
MENU, 170
MENU_HEAD, 170-171
Microsoft C, 302
Microsoft QuickC, I3, 303-304
Monochrome Display Adapter (MDA), 5, 169
monochrome display attributes, 8
MS-DOS video services, 2, 13

O

open_window, 75, 186-187

P

parameter passing, 17

popup, 84-85, 187-189
pop-up menus, 81
Power C, 109, 304
printcenter, 58, 189
printone, 58, 190
printstring, 41, 191
program portability, 250-252
pull-down menu bar, 92-93
pull-down menus, 92-94
pulldown, 100-102, 192-197
pulldown_bar, 99-100, 198

R

realloc, 63, 65-66
reset_initial_video, 78
restorescreen, 40, 67, 199
return values, 18-19
ROM BIOS video services, 3-4, 13, 218-247
   Get Video Mode (0FH), 245-247
   Read Character/Attribute Pair (08H), 230-231
   Read Cursor Values (03H), 220-221
   Read Graphics Pixel (0DH), 241-242
   Read Light Pen Values (04H), 222-223
   Scroll Window Down (07H), 228-229
   Scroll Window Up (06H), 226-227
   Select Display Page (05H), 224-225
   Set Color Palette (0BH), 236-238
   Set Cursor Position (02H), 3-4, 218-219
   Set Cursor Type (01H), 216-217
   Set Video Mode (00H), 213-215
   Write Character in Teletype Mode (0EH), 243-244
   Write Character/Attribute Pair (09H), 232-233
   Write Characters (0AH), 234-235
   Write Graphics Pixel (0CH), 239-240
run-time errors, 104

S

save_initial_video, 78, 200
savescreen, 39, 67, 201

scroll_window, 76-77, 202-203
setattrib, 39, 204
setcurpos, 57, 205
setcursor, 57, 206
setone, 58, 207
settext80, 38, 169, 208
stack frames, 17-18, 21

T

TRUE, 169
Turbo C, 305

U

user interface, defined, I2
user requirements, I3

V

V20, 21
V30, 21
variable names, 16
vertical retrace interval, 11
vertical scroll bar, 62, 77
vertical_bar, 77, 209

W

waitkey, 41, 210
Watcom C, 306-319
Watcom Express C, 320
WINDOW, 171

Z

Zortech C++, 321-338